KEYS TO
Engineering Success

Jill S. Tietjen, P. E.
UNIVERSITY OF COLORADO AT BOULDER

Kristy A. Schloss
SCHLOSS ENGINEERED EQUIPMENT

Carol Carter

Joyce Bishop

Sarah Lyman Kravits

Prentice
Hall

Upper Saddle River, New Jersey 07458

Library of Congress Cataloging-in-Publication Data

Keys to engineering success / Jill S. Tietjen ... [et al].
      p.   cm.
    Includes bibliographical references and index.
    ISBN 0-13-030482-4
      1. Engineering—Vocational guidance. I. Title: Engineering success. II. Tietjen, Jill S.

TA157.K46 2001
620'.0023—dc21

00-049198

Acquisitions Editor: Sande Johnson
Production Editor: Holcomb Hathaway
Director of Manufacturing and Production: Bruce Johnson
Managing Editor: Mary Carnis
Manufacturing Manager: Ed O'Dougherty
Art Director: Marianne Frasco
Marketing Manager: Christina Quadhamer
Marketing Assistant: Barbara Rosenberg
Editorial Assistant: Cecilia Johnson
Cover Illustration: Paul Gourhan
Composition: Aerocraft Charter Art Service

Prentice-Hall International (UK) Limited, *London*
Prentice-Hall of Australia Pty. Limited, *Sydney*
Prentice-Hall Canada Inc., *Toronto*
Prentice-Hall Hispanoamericana, S.A., *Mexico*
Prentice-Hall of India Private Limited, *New Delhi*
Prentice-Hall of Japan, Inc., *Tokyo*
Pearson Education Singapore Pte. Ltd.
Editora Prentice-Hall do Brasil, Ltda., *Rio de Janeiro*

ISBN 0-13-030482-4

Contents

CHAPTER 5 Critical and Creative Thinking 81

CHAPTER 6 Reading and Study Skills 107

CHAPTER 7   Note-Taking and Writing   131

Harnessing the Power of Words and Ideas

CHAPTER 8   Listening, Memory, and Test Taking   161

Taking In, Retaining, and Demonstrating Knowledge

CHAPTER 9   Relating to Others   187

Appreciating Your Diverse World

CHAPTER 10   Managing Career and Money   219

Preface

KEYS TO ENGINEERING SUCCESS OWNER'S MANUAL

What can you do with your engineering education and why do you have to take all that calculus, physics, and chemistry? This book provides answers to these types of questions, because the authors believe very strongly that engineering is a rewarding career, that our world would not work without the contributions of engineers that are all around us, and that the workplace needs creative, capable engineers like you!

In order to succeed in an engineering education, you will need to:

1. Take responsibility for yourself, your education and your future.
2. Learn how to study strategically.
3. Ask for help when you need it.

As your authors, we have talked to students and engineering faculty across the country. We've learned that you are concerned about your future, you want your education to serve a purpose, you are adjusting to constant life changes, and you want honest and direct guidance on how to achieve your goals. We designed the features of *Keys to Engineering Success* based on what you have told us about your needs.

THE CONTENTS OF THE PACKAGE: WHAT'S INCLUDED

We chose the topics in this book based on what you need to make the most of your engineering education experience. You need a strong sense of self and an ability to persevere in order to discover and pursue the best course of study for you. You need good study skills to absorb and retain what you learn both in and out of class. You need to set goals and manage your time, money, and relationships so that you can handle the changes that you will face in the future. *Keys to Engineering Success* can guide you in all of these areas and more.

The distinguishing characteristics and sections of this book are designed to make your life easier by helping you absorb and understand the material you read.

Lifelong learning. The ideas and strategies you learn that will help you succeed in school are the same ones that will bring you success in your career and personal life. Therefore, this book focuses on success strategies as they apply to school, work, and life, not just in the classroom.

Thinking skills. Being able to remember facts and formulas won't do you much good at school or beyond unless you can put that information to work through clear and competent thinking. This book has a chapter on creative and critical thinking that will help you understand the problem-solving and thinking skills necessary for you to succeed as an engineering student.

Skill-building exercises. Today's engineering graduates need to be effective thinkers, team players, writers, and strategic planners. The exercises at the end of the chapters will encourage you to develop these valuable career skills and to apply problem-solving processes to any topic or situation.

Diversity of voice. The workplace and our communities are becoming increasingly diverse in ethnicity, perspective, culture, lifestyle, race, choices, abilities, needs, and more. Every student, professor, course, and school is unique. One point of view can't possibly apply to everyone. Therefore, many voices will speak to you from these pages. What you read will speak to your needs, offer ideas, and treat you with respect.

User-friendly features. The following features will make your life easier in small but significant ways.

- *Perforations.* Each page of this book is perforated so you can tear out exercises to hand in, take with you somewhere, or keep in your notebook as a reference.
- *Exercises.* The exercises are together at the ends of the chapters, so if you want to hand them in you can do so without removing any of the text.
- *Definitions.* Selected words are defined in the margins of the text.
- *Long-term usefulness.* Yes, most people sell back some of the textbooks they use. If you take a good look at the material in *Keys to Engineering Success*, however, you may want to keep this book around. *Keys to Engineering Success* is a reference that you can return to over and over again as you work toward your goals in school, work, and life.

TAKE ACTION: READ

You are responsible for your education, your growth, your knowledge, and your future. The best we can do is offer some useful suggestions, strategies, ideas, and systems that can help. Ultimately, it's up to you to use whatever fits your particular self with all of its particular situations, needs, and wants, and make it your own. You've made a terrific start by choosing to pursue an engineering education—take advantage of all it has to give you.

ACKNOWLEDGMENTS

This brief edition has come about through a heroic group effort. We would like to take this opportunity to acknowledge the people who have made it happen. Many thanks to:

- Our engineering Editorial Board: Dr. Sherry Snyder, University of Colorado at Boulder; Dr. Ilene Busch-Vishniac, Dean, Whiting School of Engineering, Johns Hopkins University; Dr. George Cahen, Jr., University of Virginia; Dr. Barrett Caldwell, University of Wisconsin-Madison; Dr. John Collier, Dartmouth College; David DiLaura, University of Colorado at Boulder; Heather Doty, University of Colorado at Boulder; Dr. Ron Fannin, University of Missouri–Rolla; Dr. Victor Goldschmidt, Purdue University; Dr. John Helferty, Temple University; Dr. Peter Jenkins, P. E., Dean, College of Engineering and Applied Science, University of Colorado at Denver; Dr. Kristina Johnson, Dean, Duke University School of Engineering; Dr. Jean Malzahn Kampe, Virginia Polytechnic Institute and State University; Dr. Michael Karweit, Johns Hopkins University; Tamara Knott, Virginia Polytechnic Institute and State University; Ralph Peterson, Chairman and CEO, CH2M Hill; George Sissel, Chairman and CEO, Ball Corporation; Dr. Bevlee Watford, P. E., Virginia Polytechnic Institute and State University; Richard Weingardt, P. E., CEO and Chairman, Richard Weingardt Consultants; Dr. William Wulf, President, National Academy of Engineering.
- Our student editors, Michael Jackson and Aziza Davis.
- Student reviewers Sandi Armitage, Marisa Connell, Jennifer Moe, and Alex Toth.
- Our reviewers: Glenda Belote, Florida International University; John Bennett, Jr., University of Connecticut; Ann Bingham-Newman, California State University–LA; Mary Bixby, University of Missouri-Columbia; Barbara Blandford, Education Enhancement Center at Lawrenceville, NJ; Jerry Bouchie, St. Cloud State University; Mona Casady, SW Missouri State University; Janet Cutshall, Sussex County Community College; Valerie DeAngelis, Miami-Dade Community College; Rita Delude, NH Community Technical College; Judy Elsley, Weber State University (Ogden, UT); Sue Halter, Delgado Community College; Suzy Hampton, University of Montana; Maureen Hurley, University of Missouri-Kansas City; Karen Iversen, Heald Colleges; Kathryn Kelly, St. Cloud State University; Nancy Kosmicke, Mesa State College in Colorado; Frank T. Lyman, Jr., University of Maryland; Barnette Miller Moore, Indian River Community College in Florida; Rebecca Munro, Gonzaga University in Washington; Virginia Phares, DeVry of Atlanta; Brenda Prinzavalli, Beloit College in Wisconsin; Jacqueline Simon, Education Enhancement Center at Lawrenceville, NJ; Carolyn Smith, University of Southern Indiana; Joan Stottlemyer, Carroll College in Montana; Thomas Tyson, SUNY Stony Brook; Rose Wassman, DeAnza College; Michelle G. Wolf, Florida Southern College.

- The PRE 100 instructors at Baltimore City Community College, Liberty Campus, especially college President Dr. Jim Tschechtelin, Coordinator Jim Coleman, Rita Lenkin Hawkins, Sonia Lynch, Jack Taylor, and Peggy Winfield. Thanks also to Prentice Hall representative Alice Barr.

- The instructors at DeVry, especially Susan Chin and Carol Ozee.

- The instructors at Suffolk Community College, and Prentice Hall representative Carol Abolafia.

- Our editorial consultant Rich Bucher, professor of sociology at Baltimore City Community College.

- Dr. Frank T. Lyman, inventor of the Thinktrix system.

- Professor Barbara Soloman, developer of the Learning Styles Inventory.

- The people who contributed their stories: Dr. Ilene Busch-Vishniac, Dr. Barrett Caldwell, Sherita Ceasar, Brett Cross, Heather Doty, Katherine Osborne, Ralph Peterson, P.E., Ramon Pizarro, DeAnn Redlin, T. Meredith Ross, P. E., George Sissel, Tim Short, Tom Smith, Alexis Swoboda, P. E., The Honorable Sheila Widnall, and Corissa Young.

- Kathleen Cole, assistant and student reviewer extraordinaire, and Giuseppe Morella.

- Cynthia Leshin, author of the appendix on Internet research.

- Our editor, Sande Johnson.

- Our production team.

- The folks in our marketing department, especially Christina Quadhamer.

- The Prentice Hall representatives and management team.

- Judy Block, who contributed both editing suggestions and study skills text.

- Our families and friends.

About the Authors

Jill S. Tietjen, P. E., is a registered professional engineer whose area of expertise is electric utility power generation and transmission planning. Ms. Tietjen is the principal of Technically Speaking and previously served as the Director of the Women in Engineering Program at the University of Colorado at Boulder. She provides engineering consulting services building on her work experience with Duke Power Company and Stone & Webster Management Consultants, among others. Ms. Tietjen served as the 1991–1992 National President of the Society of Women Engineers, of which she is a Fellow. She is an electrical engineering accreditor for the Accreditation Board for Engineering and Technology. Ms. Tietjen is a contributing author to the 1995 book *She Does Math!* She has a B. S. in applied mathematics, minor in electrical engineering, and an M. B. A.

Kristy A. Schloss is the President of Schloss Engineered Equipment, an environmental equipment design and manufacturing firm. She was the 1999 National, Regional, and Colorado winner of the Exporter of the Year award from the U. S. Small Business Administration. Named a Distinguished Engineering Alumna from the University of Colorado at Boulder, Ms. Schloss has also received the Honor Award from the Colorado Engineering Council. A life member of the Society of Women Engineers, Ms. Schloss was appointed by the Secretary of Commerce to the Environmental Technologies Trade Advisory Committee and the District Export Council. Ms. Schloss writes and speaks regularly on the opportunities for and rewards of being an engineer. She has a B. S. in civil engineering.

Carol Carter is Vice President and Director of Student Programs and Faculty Development at Prentice Hall. She has written *Majoring in the Rest of Your Life: Career Secrets for College Students* and *Majoring in High School*. She has also co-authored *Graduating Into the Nineties, The Career Tool Kit, Keys to Career Success, Keys to Effective Learning,* and the first edition of *Keys to Success*. In 1992 Carol and other business people co-founded a nonprofit organization called LifeSkills, Inc., to help high school students explore their goals, their career options, and the real world through part-time employment and internships. LifeSkills is now part of the Tucson Unified School District and is featured in seventeen high schools in Tucson, Arizona.

Joyce Bishop holds a Ph.D. in psychology and has taught for more than twenty years, receiving a number of honors, including Teacher of the Year. For the past four years she has been voted "favorite teacher" by the student body and Honor Society at Golden West College, Huntington Beach, CA, where she has taught since 1986 and is a tenured professor. She is currently working with a federal grant to establish learning communities and workplace learning in her district, and has developed workshops and trained faculty in cooperative learning, active learning, multiple intelligences, workplace relevancy, learning styles, authentic assessment, team building, and the development of learning communities. She also co-authored *Keys to Effective Learning*.

Sarah Lyman Kravits comes from a family of educators and has long cultivated an interest in educational development. She co-authored *The Career Tool Kit*, *Keys to Effective Learning*, and *Keys to Success* and has served as Program Director for LifeSkills, Inc., a nonprofit organization that aims to further the career and personal development of high school students. In that capacity she helped to formulate both curricular and organizational elements of the program, working closely with instructors as well as members of the business community. Sarah holds a B. A. in English and drama from the University of Virginia, where she was a Jefferson Scholar, and an M. F. A. from Catholic University.

1

What is Engineering?

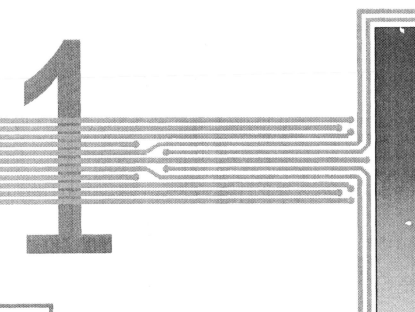

By now, you are probably deep into calculus, chemistry, and physics, wondering what in the world you have gotten yourself into and how this all relates to your goal of becoming an engineer. We know—we were there ourselves.

You are probably studying engineering because you are "good" at math or science and want to see what kind of career this field can offer you. The good news is that you are preparing yourself for almost any future that you can envision. In your engineering curriculum, regardless of the major that you choose, you are going to focus on solving problems—learning the scientific method and applying it in many areas. This is a great foundation for an engineering career, of course, but it is also good preparation for business, law, medicine, or just about any other career.

This book gives you information to help you in your engineering education, including suggestions that cover a wide variety of life skills. We hope to answer many of your questions, provide you insight into the wonderful and worthwhile world of engineering, and get you excited about your career choice.

Moreover, it is our most heartfelt hope that when you hit a crisis point—and you will, whether it be a low grade in one of your "gateway" courses (physics, calculus, chemistry, and computer science) or difficulty in understanding the concepts in one of the courses that you thought would be "easy"—you will understand and remember that we all hit our own crisis points. We hope that you will persevere and find whatever help you need—because it is there and waiting for you. Author Jill Tietjen failed her first statics test because she just couldn't visualize in three dimensions. But she persevered and found help through a tutor. She passed the class and her professor eventually hired her to do research for him.

We want this book to be positive, not discouraging like the philosophy that we call "the few, the proud, the engineer." We do not want you to have an experience that many practicing engineers remember—their dean saying on the first day of school, "Look to your left. Look to your right. Only one of you will graduate as an engineer." Engineering colleges understand the current significant demand for engineers and are now making sure that their classes include integrated applications as early as the first semester. They do this to give you an idea at the beginning of your engineering education of the excitement and value associated with engineering. You may also have selected engineering because you want to make the world a better place. We want to see you succeed in your education and in your career, and that is the underlying purpose of this book.

In this chapter, we will answer questions such as:

- What is an engineer?
- What do engineers do?
- Where can engineering take you?
- What are the types of engineers?
- What is the future demand for technically educated professionals?

WHAT IS AN ENGINEER?

Are you interested in making a contribution in the physical world? Are you good at solving problems? Do you like to understand how things work and how to make them better? Would you like to see your ideas for products become reality? If you answer yes to these questions, then odds are that you will want to become an engineer.

So, what exactly is an engineer? An engineer is someone who applies mathematics and the principles of science, especially chemistry and physics, to solve problems and meet the needs of society for products and services. Solving these problems and finding new solutions require creativity and persistence.

You may be concerned that you don't meet the stereotypical image of an engineer. Actually, most people don't even know what engineers are, so when you ask them about their stereotypical image, they often tell you about their image of a scientist. The image is often of a white male with out-of-control hair, glasses with tape holding them together over his nose, wearing a white lab coat with a pocket protector (possibly filled with leaking pens) over a plaid shirt, pants that are too short, white socks, and untied shoes. Neither author Kristy Schloss nor author Jill Tietjen conforms to that image, and neither do any of the people profiled in this book. As you will read in Chapter 9, such stereotypes mask fear of the unknown and seldom reflect the qualities and characteristics of any specific individual.

Engineers and engineering have been around for a long time, although many of the theorems that you will study during your years in college have been developed since the 1700s. The Egyptians were master engineers—witness the pyramids. The Romans built aqueducts to bring water into Rome, another significant engineering achievement. The entire city of Venice is an engineering marvel. The Great Wall of China is a good example of a man-made feature on earth that is visible from space—this too is a great engineering accomplishment. Historically, most of the major engineering accomplishments have been in the field of what is called civil engineering today—although this is changing rapidly.

WHAT DO ENGINEERS DO?

One of our engineering colleagues says that "Engineers make the world work." Engineers design and build bridges, buildings, and tunnels. They design, test, and analyze cars, pumps, and heating and air conditioning systems. They design, build, and manufacture space shuttles, airplanes, and helicopters. They design, operate, and modify power plants, gas pipelines, airports, and dams. They design computers, software, telecommunications devices, telephones (wireless and wired), fiber optics, and storage routing devices. They design the processes and equipment to manufacture VCRs, TVs, refrigerators, ovens, and toasters, as well as the appliances themselves. They create machines that cut fabrics to make our clothing, furniture, and draperies. Almost every product and process that you use in your daily life has been affected in some manner by an engineer.

You will find that engineers have had input into almost every activity that you undertake during the course of a typical day. Let's look at just a few of them.

* Engineers were involved in the design of your electric alarm clock—from its display, to its electrical connection, to the manufacturing of the battery that keeps it working when the power is off, to the sound the alarm makes, to its size, its packaging, its ability to stay in one piece when dropped on the floor, the materials of which it is constructed, and its manufacturing. Engineers were also involved in the design of all of the related equipment and process controls for the manufacturing of the alarm clock.

* Your refrigerator has been designed to be energy efficient and not to release chemicals into the atmosphere that are believed to cause depletion of the ozone layer. It turns itself on and off as dictated by its internal thermostat. If you have a frostless model, a fan turns on regularly to keep the frost from adhering to the walls. All of these features were designed, tested, and manufactured to specifications that were established by engineers.

* The streets and roads you use to get from your home to school and work were designed and built by engineers. The water you drink and bathe in was made **potable** by engineers.

Potable
Suitable for drinking.

What does an engineer have to consider in making and designing all of these products? The actual function desired for a product, the cost of the various parts and its price once it is completed, its ease or difficulty of manufacture, the impact of the product and its manufacturing on the environment, and compliance with applicable codes and laws are just a few of the important factors an engineer must consider.

What does all this mean? Let's talk about some basic examples.

The principles of **thermodynamics** describe how much energy is in steam at any combination of temperature and pressure. The combination of temperature and pressure at the inlet to a steam turbine is different from the combination of temperature and pressure at the steam turbine outlet. The difference in the energy in the steam between the inlet and outlet relates to how much work the steam turbine is able to do. Mechanical engineers use these principles to design steam turbines for use in power plants to generate electricity.

Thermodynamics
The physics that deal with the mechanical action or relations of heat.

Another basic principle in physics is that electrical energy flows over the path of least resistance. This principle has dramatic implications for the electrical engineer designing a delivery system—the transmission and distribution system—for electricity. The engineer has to know the resistance of every line between a generating plant and a delivery point, such as your house, in order to design new transmission and distribution facilities to actually get the amount of energy you need to your house. The engineer must also understand the effects of new lines on existing lines and where overloads could arise.

Gravity, the force that pulls items down to earth, is a central concept in physics. Rockets that place satellites into orbit must develop sufficient momentum and **lift** in order to overcome gravity, get off the ground, and reach the height above the earth where they are to deliver the satellite. Engineers use the principles of motion—including inertia, gravity, **momentum,** and lift—to design rockets that can take off and deliver satellites into orbit.

Weight from vehicles such as cars and buses on a bridge causes the bridge to deflect. Some **deflection** is expected, and the bridge has been designed for that load. Too much deflection, however, will cause the bridge to fall down or otherwise fail. Civil engineers use the concepts of span, distance, and weight to determine how much deflection has to be expected and accounted for in the design of a bridge.

Power plants and vehicles emit gases into the atmosphere. Some of these gases are acidic and thought to cause acid rain that damages forests and lakes. Chemical engineers use basic chemistry principles when they design equip-

> **Lift**
> An upward force that opposes the pull of gravity.

> **Momentum**
> The force that a moving body has because of its weight and motion.

> **Deflection**
> A change in shape due to an applied load.

ON ENGINEERING . . .

Herbert Hoover, *31st President of the United States*

The following was written by Herbert Hoover in August 1963.

It is a great profession. There is the fascination of watching a figment of the imagination emerge through the aid of science to a plan on paper. Then it moves to realization in stone or metal or energy. Then it brings jobs and homes to men. Then it elevates the standard of living and adds to the comforts of life. That is the engineer's high privilege.

The great liability of the engineer compared to men of other professions is that his works are out in the open where all can see them. His acts, step by step, are in hard substance. He cannot bury his mistakes in the grave like the doctors. He cannot argue them into thin air or blame the judge like the lawyers. He cannot, like architects, cover his failures with trees and vines. He cannot, like the politicians, screen his shortcomings by blaming his

opponents and hope the people will forget. The engineer simply cannot deny he did it. If his works do not work, he is damned.

On the other hand, unlike the doctor, his is not a life among the weak. Unlike the soldier, destruction is not his purpose. Unlike the lawyer, quarrels are not his daily bread. To the engineer falls the job of clothing the bare bones of science with life, comfort, and hope. No doubt as the years go by people forget which engineer did it, even if they ever knew. Or some politician puts his name on it. Or they credit it to some promoter who used other people's money. But the engineer himself looks back at the unending stream of goodness which flows from his success with satisfactions that few professions may know. And the verdict of his fellow professionals is all the accolade he wants.

Source: Herbert Hoover, *Addresses Upon the American Road* (Stanford, CA: Stanford University Press, 1995).

ment such as catalytic converters and flue gas desulfurization units (also called scrubbers) that removes the chemicals that would otherwise be released into the atmosphere during the combustion process. Sometimes this equipment converts gases into solids or liquids that in turn must be dealt with from an environmental and chemical engineering perspective.

Torque
A force that produces rotation or twisting.

Artificial hips and knees must support the weight of the body as well as stand up to the **torque** that we humans place on our joints. The joints in our bodies don't just move up and down—they must move sideways and rotate as well. Engineers design artificial joints to withstand the stresses that we place on them, enabling persons with artificial hips and knees to continue to enjoy sports such as golf, tennis, and skiing.

Algorithm
A rule or procedure for solving a problem.

Computer software controls the fuel injection in your car, the Internet, elevators, airline reservations, your microwave, your VCR, and many other systems with which you come into contact daily. Such software consists of many **algorithms** that, for example, allow you to touch "100" or "60" on your microwave and then touch "Start" to have your microwave heat the item you have placed inside for one minute.

WHERE CAN ENGINEERING TAKE YOU?

At the beginning of this chapter, we noted that an engineering education can be both the beginning of a career in engineering and the foundation for further education, whether it be in business, law, medicine, or other endeavors.

WHAT ARE THE TYPES OF ENGINEERS?

There are many different types of engineers. Here is a list of engineering fields. Your college or university may offer as a major some, but probably not all, of these. Appendix A provides greater detail on what engineers do in each of these fields.

Aerospace (or aeronautical or astronautical)	Geotechnical
Agricultural	Industrial
Architectural	Manufacturing
Biomedical	Marine or ocean
Ceramic	Materials
Chemical	Mechanical
Civil	Metallurgical
Computer	Mining
Construction	Nuclear
Electrical/electronic	Petroleum
Engineering management	Software
Engineering physics	Structural
Environmental	Surveying
Geological	Systems

Success in the Real World

The Honorable Sheila Widnall
Former Secretary of the Air Force, Professor, Massachusetts Institute of Technology

I went into engineering because I love airplanes. Coming from Seattle, I had my life planned out: I would live in Seattle, build airplanes, and climb mountains. What actually happened was far more wonderful. I had a good time studying engineering at MIT. The faculty were very supportive and encouraged me to continue on to graduate school. It was certainly no bed of roses, but on balance, I received an excellent education and the support of some quite significant mentors who have stayed with me throughout my professional career.

The courses I took in college, plus the experiences I gained in summer internships in industry, turned out to be extremely valuable. In fact I now tell students that everything they ever learn and every activity they ever volunteer for will turn out to be useful—even chemistry, not my personal favorite. Student activities provide leadership experiences, an important part of career development.

Engineering is science in service of society. Today that science is broadly defined and clearly involves the social sciences as well. Technology has brought great benefits to society; it has also brought great challenges. Well-educated engineers are in a position to mediate between society and technological developments so that the risks and rewards can be more precisely defined. Women obviously have an important role to play in this, both as citizens and as knowledgeable professionals. A career in engineering is often combined with a career in law, medicine, or business, thereby strengthening both fields.

Today's engineering education prepares students to play leadership roles in our society for the betterment of all. Most engineering curricula have been revised to emphasize project and team work, giving students a more accurate idea of the actual work environment of engineers. Everyone stresses the importance of mastery of the fundamentals. But motivation to study and apply that mastery comes from project and team work. Depending on the field, the interaction with societal values, which set the boundaries for development, are brought into the classroom.

You want to talk about fun. Well, my career is at the outer limits of fun. As Secretary of the Air Force, not only did I get to preside over the technology developments that the Air Force has underway, in air-  craft, space systems, and information, but I got to fly every aircraft that the Air Force has in its inventory that has room for two pilots. I pulled nine g's with the Thunderbirds, flew at 70,000 feet in a U-2, flew at night with sophisticated (at least I hope they were!) night-vision systems. What a blast! But these experiences were just the final chapter in a career that has been extremely rewarding. I am proud to have been an engineering educator for some 40 years. I am proud of my students, who have gone on to successful and productive careers both in the United States and abroad. And I'm proud of the fundamental research in fluid dynamics that bears my name.

Would I recommend a career in engineering to a young person? You bet I would!

Choosing a Major

How will you choose your engineering major?

First, think about where your interests lie and what types of courses you like. What is it that you would spend your time doing, if you didn't have to do all of the other things in your life? What do you look forward to doing? How do you see yourself spending your time in your job after you graduate? You will get a chance to think about many of these questions when you do Exercise 1.1 at the end of this chapter.

- Maybe you want to spend most of your time outside building roads, bridges, or buildings. If so, you probably want to look into civil or construction engineering.
- If your dream has always been associated with designing cars, then you may want to consider mechanical engineering.
- If your interests lie with computers, you have several choices, depending on your specific interest relative to computers. Do you want to make the computer itself, what is referred to as the hardware? Then you want to consider electrical or computer engineering. Does the process of logic and computer programming fascinate you? This is the software part, and you want to pursue either software or computer engineering or computer science.
- If you really want to enhance health and the human body through the design and application of equipment, then biomedical engineering could be for you.
- If chemistry fascinates you, you ought to look into chemical engineering.
- If you simply want to help clean up the environment—making clean water and clean air the order of the day for all citizens of the world— consider environmental engineering.

Either on the Web, through your university's catalog, or from the information provided by each engineering department, look at the course work required for each major and figure out what appeals to you.

What if you are undecided about which major is right for you? Start asking questions. Start with the people closest to you who have made the decision already—upperclassmen in the majors that you are considering. Ask them which classes they have taken and what they liked about those classes. Find out what their interests are and where they have worked as interns, as well as where they hope to work when they graduate.

Professors are usually willing to share their experiences with you as well. What made them decide to select a certain major? In which areas of interest do they focus their research? What attributes are typical of a person who pursues a specific major?

Don't forget that you can also ask people who are in business as practicing engineers in your fields of interest. You can find these people through the professional engineering societies. Exercise 1.3 at the end of the chapter gives you the opportunity to interview working professionals to understand how they ended up where they are, what they like about their chosen career field, and what they recommend for undergraduate students who might wish to pursue a career in their specific disciplines. Remember, today's decision is not irreversible—you can always change your major or your area of concentration.

Types of Courses for Various Engineering Majors

Almost all engineering students take courses in their freshmen year that are the same or similar across all engineering disciplines. These are often referred to as "gateway" courses—calculus, physics, and chemistry. You may also take some sort of introductory course in computer science during your freshman year. Usually, you will start to see some more specialized courses in your sophomore year, when in most universities you will have already declared your major.

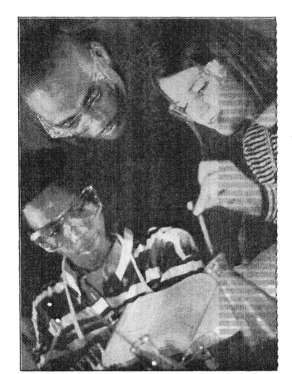

As you progress into your engineering major, you will find yourself taking increasingly specialized courses and not having much contact with students from other engineering majors. You will take required courses related to your specific discipline, technical electives within that discipline, and humanities and social sciences courses. You will probably also take some "fundamentals of engineering" courses—these relate to engineering sciences that underlie many different disciplines, such as circuits, fluids, statics, dynamics, and thermodynamics. You will probably be required to take a technical communication class (including writing and oral presentation), and we hope that discussions of engineering ethics will take place throughout your engineering educational experience.

Because engineering programs are accredited and must meet scrutiny from an accrediting body, some courses that you might choose to take may not count toward meeting the course requirements for your engineering major. ROTC courses are a good example. Although these courses may help you in your later life and be fundamental to your development, they may not count toward the hours you need for your engineering major.

What does a typical program look like over its four years? You will explore course requirements for engineering majors at your school in Exercise 1.4.

WHAT IS THE FUTURE DEMAND FOR TECHNICALLY EDUCATED PROFESSIONALS?

It is apparent that the world is becoming more technologically advanced. Thus, our society needs all of the technically educated people it can get. Almost every product—every building, appliance, automobile, gasoline pump—relies in some way on engineering and computers. Who do you think designs and builds all of these systems? Engineers do!

As a global society, we have moved from the industrial age into the information age. Our world and our industries need engineers who are technologically adept, who understand the interaction between technology and humanity, who are able to make decisions that consider a broad range of factors in addition to design parameters, and who go about their business in an ethical fashion.

⬥ ENGINEERING ETHICS ⬥

Engineers must always be aware of the ethical considerations related to doing their jobs, designing their products, and living their lives. Because engineers deal with immutable physical laws and because their efforts have a tremendous impact on humanity, they must remember that honesty and integrity must underlie all that they do. The public's health, safety, and welfare are in the hands of engineers on an ongoing basis. Engineers must remember their responsibility and uphold it. The box on the following page discusses engineering ethics in more detail.

We believe that as an individual with an engineering undergraduate degree, you will be employable and probably in relatively high demand over the course of your entire career. Whether you choose to stay in engineering; pursue a graduate engineering degree or a faculty position in engineering or any other discipline; pursue a professional degree in business, law, or medicine; or move into any other facet of the government, business, or nonprofit world, you will have the technological foundation that will serve you in good stead.

Through your engineering education, you will develop an understanding of the impact that technology has on the rest of the world. As a society, we want fast cars, wireless communication, instant Internet access, pharmaceuticals to cure any disease, and food products to satisfy our constantly changing palates and health consciousness. Engineers work to satisfy these demands of society. To do this, however, usually incurs not just economic costs, but often environmental and other types of costs as well. Engineers need to consider the human side—the ergonomic side—of their efforts to make sure the other impacts are also considered. With your engineering education, you will be one of those people who can look around you with satisfaction and say, "Yes, engineers really do make the world work."

ENDNOTES

1. C. E. Harris, Jr., et al., "Engineering Ethics: What? Why? How? and When?", *Journal of Engineering Education* 85 (1996): 93–96.

2. C. E. Harris, Jr., M. S. Pritchard, and M. J. Rabins, *Engineering Ethics: Concepts and Cases* (Belmont, CA: Wadsworth, 1995).

ENGINEERING ETHICS

Professional ethics have been defined as "special morally permissible standards of conduct that, ideally, every member of a profession wants every other member to follow, even if that means having to do the same" and which apply "to members of a group simply because they are members of that group."[1] Because engineering requires extensive, specialized training and because most engineers are autonomous in their practice (meaning their technical judgments are reviewed only by other engineers), ethical standards apply above and beyond laws and personal morals. Ethical behavior (and conversely unethical behavior) reflects on the profession as a whole. The Code of Ethics of the Accreditation Board for Engineering and Technology (ABET, the organization that accredits engineering programs) includes the following basic tenets common to the codes of ethics adopted by most of the engineering professional organizations[2]:

PRINCIPLES

Engineers uphold and advance the integrity, honor, and dignity of the engineering profession by:

1. Using their knowledge and skill for the enhancement of human welfare;
2. Being honest and impartial, and serving with fidelity the public, their employers, and clients;
3. Striving to increase the competence and prestige of the engineering profession.

CANONS

1. Engineers shall hold paramount the safety, health, and welfare of the public in the performance of their professional duties.
2. Engineers shall perform services only in their areas of competence.
3. Engineers shall issue public statements only in an objective and truthful manner.
4. Engineers shall act in professional matters for each employer or client as faithful agents or trustees, and shall avoid conflicts of interest.
5. Engineers shall build their professional reputation on the merit of their services and shall not compete unfairly with others.
6. Engineers shall act in such a manner as to uphold and enhance the honor, integrity, and dignity of the profession.
7. Engineers shall continue their professional development throughout their careers and shall provide opportunities for the professional development of those engineers under their supervision.

Name_____   Date_____

KEY INTO YOUR LIFE   *Opportunities to Apply What You Learn*

EXERCISE   1.1   Thinking About Your Major

Consider the following questions and write your responses in the spaces provided. (Note: There are no right or wrong answers to these questions—just the best answers for you.)

● How did you decide to major in engineering?

_____

_____

● What are your likes and dislikes?

_____

_____

● Do you want to work indoors or outdoors?

_____

_____

● Do you want to design things?

_____

● Do you like to build things?

_____

● Do you like computers?

_____

● Do you prefer to work in a team or by yourself?

_____

● What are your worst fears for the future?

_____

_____

● What would you most like to do for a career?

_____

_____

Engineering Through History

EXERCISE 1.2

Select a historical engineering project and examine the engineering principles underlying this significant accomplishment. Examples of such projects include: Macchu Pichu's water systems, the Pyramids of Egypt, the Great Wall of China, Bronze Age metallurgy, Roman aqueducts, Roman underwater concrete, Stonehenge, the Panama Canal, the Eiffel Tower, and the Hoover Dam. On your own paper, complete the following three tasks:

a. Describe the project.
b. Identify a significant engineering principle underlying its design.
c. Describe a project today that incorporates the same principles.

Exploring Engineering Careers

EXERCISE 1.3

Choose a field of engineering and learn about it. Locate a working professional in the field. Go interview that person. Make a presentation to the class on what this type of engineer does.

Investigating Course Requirements

EXERCISE 1.4

Look at your college catalog or on the Internet where course requirements are specified for the various engineering majors. Choose the major that corresponds to the type of engineering that you think you are interested in. Determine how many hours of each of the following categories of courses you will be required to take:

a. Basic science and mathematics courses
b. Courses specific to your major
c. Engineering courses not specific to your major
d. Humanities and social sciences electives
e. Other

Engineering Ethics

EXERCISE 1.5

Select one of the following real-life situations. Research the situation. Discuss the engineering ethics issues involved. Determine if proper attention was paid to public safety, health, and welfare.

a. The explosion of the Challenger space shuttle on January 28, 1986.
b. The collapse of the Hyatt Regency Walkways in Kansas City, Missouri, on July 17, 1981.
c. The crash of TWA Flight 800 on July 17, 1996.
d. Issues regarding side saddle fuel tanks on General Motors 1973–1987 Chevrolet and GMC pickup trucks.

Where to Get Help When You Need It

Engineering students, perhaps more so than students in any other major, seem to be reluctant to ask for help, whether it be for tutoring, where to find something on campus, how to apply for financial aid, or any other related matter. In this chapter you will learn where you might be able to find answers to some of your questions—even the ones that you are shy about or don't want to ask.

In particular, this chapter will help you answer the following questions:

* What resources are available at my school?

* What should I know about financial aid?

RESOURCES AVAILABLE AT YOUR SCHOOL

Resources
People, organizations, or services that supply help and support for different aspects of college life.

Resources help you make the most of your education. As a student, you are investing money and time. Whether you complete your studies over the course of six months or 60 years, resources can help you get where you want to go.

Like any company that makes products or provides services, your school is a business. The goal of this particular business is the successful education of all who come through its doors. Table 2.1 contains a general summary of resources, most or all of which can be found at your school. Most schools offer a student orientation, near the beginning of your first semester, that will explain resources and give other important information. Even if your school does not, you can orient yourself. The following sections describe helpful resources—people, student services, organizations, course catalogs, student handbooks, and specific engineering college resources and engineering organizations.

People

Your school has an array of people who can help you make the most of your educational experience: professors, administrative personnel, advisors and counselors, and teaching assistants. They're often busy with numerous responsibilities, but their assistance is provided as a standard part of your educational package. Take the opportunity to get to know them and to let them get to know you. Together you can explore how they can help you achieve your goals.

Professors are more than just sources of information during scheduled class time. Professors can become your mentors. Mentors are people who will help guide you as you develop yourself as an engineer. Finding a mentor involves getting to know your professors. Here are two ways you can do that:

* Become involved through research projects, work-study programs, teaching assistantships, or volunteering. Read Bob Weinstein's book. *I'll Work for Free* for other tips on finding such opportunities.
* Work hard in your classes to show the professor that you have an interest in the field. You will also be able to develop a relationship with the professor in this manner.

A mentor can do more than just help guide you while you are in school. A mentor can help you with job and graduate school recommendations through connections with other practicing engineers and universities around the country. This book uses the term professor for simplicity's sake. Professors have official titles that show their rank. From lowest to highest, these include lecturer, instructor, assistant professor, associate professor, and full professor (often just called professor).

Professors have many time-draining responsibilities outside of teaching. However, you can gain access to your professors while still respecting the demands on their time. Most professors keep office hours, and they will tell you the location and times. You are responsible for seeking out your professor during office hours. If your schedule makes this impossible, let your professor know. Perhaps you and your professor can get together at another time. If your school has an electronic mail (e-mail) system that allows you to send messages via computer, you may be able to communicate with your professor using e-mail.

Do *not* feel intimidated by your professors. They are there to educate and help you. You may miss out on valuable guidance and materials if you don't talk to your professors.

When you do go to see a professor, give careful consideration to the kind of help you are seeking. Make either a mental or, preferably, a written list of *specific* questions. If you go in with generalized complaints that you "just don't understand" the material or "this book is so bad that nobody could understand this stuff," you are going to waste your time and the professor's time. Make sure you have made a sincere effort to do the homework or read the assigned chapters before you ask for help with the material. Nothing aggravates a professor more than to have a student ask for help with homework he or she has obviously not attempted to do.[1]

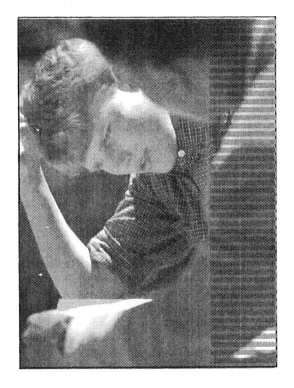

Teaching assistants (TAs) are people who help a professor with a course. You may or may not have teaching assistants in your courses. Often they are studying to be professors themselves. Sometimes they teach the smaller discussion sections that accompany a large group lecture. They can be a great resource when your professor is too swamped to talk to you.

Your school's *administrative personnel* have the responsibility of delivering to you—the student consumer—a first-rate product. That product is the sum total of your education, comprising facilities, professors, materials, and courses. Schedule a meeting with your dean, the chair of a particular department, or other school administrator if you have an issue to discuss, such as a conflict with a professor, an inability to get into a class you need, or a school regulation that causes a problem for you. Although administrators don't interact with students as often as professors do, it is their business to know how the school is serving you.

Many engineering colleges have administrative personnel as part of the dean's office, or a different related office, whose job it is to help you. Use them when you need to! Most departments have freshman as well as undergraduate advisors for the students majoring in their department in addition to a specific academic advisor assigned to each student.

Advisors and counselors can help with both the educational and personal sides of being a student. They provide information, advice, a listening ear, referrals, and other sources of help. Generally, students are assigned academic advisors with whom they meet at least once a semester. Your academic advisor will help you find out about classes, choose a schedule, and plan out the big picture of your academic life. Visit your academic advisor more than once a semester if you have questions or want to make changes.

TABLE 2.1   How resources can help you.

RESOURCE	ACADEMIC ASSISTANCE	FINANCIAL ASSISTANCE	JOB/CAREER ASSISTANCE	PERSONAL ASSISTANCE
Professors	Choosing classes, clarifying course material, completing assignments, dealing with study issues		Can tell you about their fields, may be a source of networking contacts	During office hours, are available to talk to you
Administrators	Academic problems, educational focus, problems with school services		Can be a source of valuable contacts	Can help you sort through personal problems with professors or other school employees
Academic Advisors	Choosing, changing, or dropping courses; getting over academic hurdles; selecting/changing a major		Can advise you on what job opportunities may go along with your major or academic focus	
Personal Counselors	Can help when personal problems get in the way of academic success	Services may be free or offered on a "sliding scale" depending on what you can afford		Help with all kinds of personal problems
Financial Aid Office		Information and counseling on loans, grants, scholarships, financial planning, work-study programs	Information on job opportunities within your school environment (work-study program and others)	
Academic Centers	Help with what the center specializes in (reading, writing, math)		Perhaps an opportunity to work at the center	
Organizations and Clubs	If an academic club, can broaden your knowledge or experience in an area of study; can help you balance school with other enriching activities		Can help you develop skills, build knowledge, and make new contacts that may serve you in your working life	Depending on the club focus, can be an outlet for stress, a source of personal inspiration, a source of important friendships, an opportunity to help others
Fitness Center(s)		Usually free or low cost to enrolled students		Provides opportunity to build fitness and reduce stress, may have weight room, track, fitness classes, martial arts, team sports, exercise machines, etc.

Continued.   **TABLE 2.1**

RESOURCE	ACADEMIC ASSISTANCE	FINANCIAL ASSISTANCE	JOB/CAREER ASSISTANCE	PERSONAL ASSISTANCE
Bulletin Boards	List academic events, class information, changes and additions to schedules, office hours, academic club meetings	List financial aid seminars, job opportunities, scholarship opportunities	List career forums, job sign-ups, and employment opportunities; offer a place for you to post a message if you are marketing a service	List support group meetings
Housing and Transportation Office		Can help find the most financially beneficial travel or housing plan		Can help commuters with parking, bus or train service, and permits; can help with finding on- or off-campus housing
Career Planning and Placement Office		Can help add to your income through job opportunities	Job listings, help with resumes and interviews, possible interview appointments, factual information about the workplace (job trends, salaries, etc.)	
Tutors	One-on-one help with academic subjects; assistance with specific assignments		If you decide to become a tutor, a chance to find out if teaching and working with people is for you	
Student Health Office		May provide low-cost or no-cost health care to enrolled students; may offer reduced-cost prescription plan		Wellness care (regular examinations), illness care, hospital and specialist referrals, and prescriptions
Adult Education Center	Academic help tailored to the returning adult student	May have specific financial-aid advice	May have job listings or other help with coordinating work and classes	May offer child-care assistance and opportunities to get to know other returning adults
Support Groups and Hotlines	If school-related, they offer a chance to hear how others have both stumbled and succeeded in school—and a chance to share your story			Personal help with whatever the hotline or support group specializes in; a chance to talk to someone whose job is to listen
School Publications	Academic news and course changes	News about financial aid opportunities or work-study programs	Job listings, information about the workplace and the job market	Articles and announcements about topics that may help you

Counselors, although not usually assigned, are available to you at any time, usually through student services. Don't hesitate to seek a counselor's help if you have something on your mind. The ups and downs of your personal life greatly influence the quality of your work in school. If you put some effort into working through personal problems, you will be more able to do your work well and hand it in on time. Occasionally, an illness or family difficulty may interfere with your schoolwork enough to call for special provisions for the completion of your classes. Most colleges are more than happy to assist you during challenging times.

Student Services

Your school has a variety of services aimed at helping students. Basic services offered by almost every school include the following: academic advising and personal counseling, student health/wellness, career planning and placement, tutoring, fitness/physical education, and financial aid. Depending on your school, you may also find other services: child care, housing and transportation, parking, adult education services (for adults returning to school), continuing education, disabled student services, academic centers (reading center, writing center, math center, etc.—for help with these specific subjects), various support groups, and school publications that help keep you informed of developments that affect you.

Often a school will have special services for specific populations. For example, at a school where most of the students commute, there may be a transportation office that helps students locate bus schedules and routes, find parking and sign up for permits, or track down car pools. Similarly, at a school where many students are parents, a child-care center may provide day care during class time and also refer students to outside babysitters. You will find additional details about school services in Table 2.1. They can help you earn the maximum benefit from your educational experience.

Organizations

No matter what your needs or interests are, your school probably has an organization that would interest you or can help you. Some organizations are sponsored by the school (academic clubs), some are independent but have a branch at the school (government ROTC programs), and some are student-run organizations (Latino Student Association). Some organizations focus on courses of study (American Society of Mechanical Engineers), some are primarily social (fraternities and sororities), some are artistic (Chamber Orchestra), and some are geared toward a hobby or activity (Runner's Club). Some you join in order to help others (Big Brothers or Big Sisters), and some offer help to you (Toastmasters).

When you consider adding a new activity to your life, weigh the positive effects against the negative effects. Positive effects could be new friends, fun activities, help, a break from schoolwork, stress relief, improved academic performance, increased teamwork and leadership skills, aid to others, and experience that can broaden your horizons. On the negative side there may be a heavy time commitment, dues, inconvenient location or meeting times, or too much responsibility. Explore any club carefully to see if it makes sense for you. As you make your decision, consider this: Studies have shown that students who join organizations tend to persist in their educational goals more than those who don't branch out.

To find out about organizations at your school, consult your student handbook, ask friends and professors, or check the activities office or center if your school has one. Some schools, on registration days, have an area where organizations set up tables and make themselves available to talk to interested students. Some organizations seek you out based on your academic achievements. Find out as much as you can. Ask what is expected in terms of time, responsibility, and any necessary financial commitment. Talk to students who are currently involved. Attend a meeting or two and give an organization a test run to see if you like it.

If you try out an organization, make a commitment that you will stay for the right reasons. Don't be afraid of being labeled a "dropout"; if something becomes more than you can handle, bow out gracefully. In the best of all possible worlds, your involvement in organizations will enrich your life, expand your network of acquaintances, boost your time-management skills, and help you achieve goals.

Engineering Organizations

Many opportunities are available for you to get involved in extracurricular activities on your campus. For every major, the associated professional engineering organization usually offers a student branch. Organizations that go across majors may provide additional sources of support and encouragement for you. By participating in these organizations, you will probably accomplish quite a number of objectives that could help benefit your career in the long run:

Meet new people. You will meet people different from those in your classes and will expand your network.

Learn new things. You may get involved in community service, hear a speaker who works in an area that you never considered, or find out about new and exciting job opportunities.

Learn leadership skills. Engineering organizations are the perfect place to learn and practice leadership skills.

Learn how to motivate people. You learn to persuade people, not exert authority over them, when you are in a volunteer organization. These skills are invaluable in the workplace.

Make new friends. People whom you associate with in engineering organizations often become good friends.

Work in teams. Projects that you work on through engineering organizations will enable you to further refine your teamwork skills.

Receive a scholarship or other forms of financial assistance. Certain engineering organizations offer scholarships to student members.

Below, we have listed examples of organizations that you might be able to find on your campus. Check out your college Web page or look up the national organization's Web page to find out more information.

AIAA	American Institute of Aeronautics and Astronautics
AIChE	American Institute of Chemical Engineers
AISES	American Indian Scientific and Engineering Society
ASCE	American Society of Civil Engineers
ASHRAE	American Society for Heating, Ventilating and Air Conditioning Engineers
ASME	American Society of Mechanical Engineers
IEEE	Institute of Electrical and Electronics Engineers
MAES	Mexican-American Engineering Society
NSBE	National Society of Black Engineers
SAE	Society of Automotive Engineers
SHPE	Society of Hispanic Professional Engineers
SME	Society of Manufacturing Engineers
SWE	Society of Women Engineers

College Catalogs and Student Handbooks

Navigating through your school's course offerings, the departments and resource offices, and even the layout of the campus can seem overwhelming. There are two publications that can help you find your way—the college catalog and the student handbook. Most schools provide these materials as a standard part of their enrollment information. And today, much of it is also on your university's or college's Web site.

The *college catalog* is your school's academic directory. It lists every department and course available at the school. Each course name will generally have two parts. Take "MATH100" or "PHYS101," for example. The first part is one or more letters indicating department and subject matter, and the second part is a number indicating course level (lower numbers for introductory courses and higher numbers for more advanced ones). The catalog groups courses according to subject matter and lists them from the lowest-level courses up to the most advanced, indicating the number of credits earned for each class. See Figure 2.1 for a page from the mechanical engineering course listings of the Indiana University-Purdue University Indianapolis catalog. A course book released prior to each semester will indicate details such as the professor, the days the course meets, the time of day, the location (building and room), and the maximum number of students who can take the course.

Your college catalog contains a wealth of other information. It may give general school policies such as admissions requirements, the registration process, and withdrawal procedures. It may list the departments to show the range of subjects you may study. It may outline instructional programs, detailing core requirements as well as requirements for various majors, degrees, and certificates. It may also list administrative personnel as well as faculty and staff for each department. The college catalog is an important resource in planning

FIGURE 2.1

Sample college catalog
page.

54

Mechanical Engineering (ME)

ME 196 Introduction to Computer Applications in Engineering (3 cr.) Class 3. C: MATH 163. Introduction to the engineering profession, graphs, and units. Introduction to computers, computer-aided drafting, and engineering calculations with mathematical software packages.

ME 197 Introduction to Computer Programming (3 cr.) Class 2, Recitation 1. C: MATH 163. An introduction to FORTRAN programming for engineering freshmen, with emphasis on solutions to engineering problems.

ME 200 Thermodynamics I (3 cr.) Class 3. P or C: MATH 261. First and second laws, entropy, reversible and irreversible processes, properties of pure substances. Application to engineering problems.

ME 262 Mechanical Design I (3 cr.) Class 2, Lab 2. P: ME 197, and ME 270. C: ME 274. The basic concepts of mechanical design are introduced with emphasis on use of computer-aided design techniques. Applications are chosen from the area of linkage and mechanism design. Lab involves implementation of computer techniques in solving mechanical design problems.

ME 270 Basic Mechanics I (3 cr.) Class 3. P: PHYS 152. P or C: MATH 261. Fundamental concepts of mechan... couple...

rigid bodies in three-dimensional motion. Application to projectiles, gyroscopes, machine elements, and other engineering systems.

ME 301 Thermodynamics II (3 cr.) Class 3. P: ME 200. Properties of gas mixtures, air-vapor mixtures, applications. Thermodynamics of combustion processes, equilibrium, energy conversion, power, and refrigeration systems.

ME 310 Fluid Mechanics (4 cr.) Class 3, Lab 2. P: ME 200 and ME 274. Continua, velocity fields, fluid statics, basic conservation laws for systems and control volumes, dimensional analysis. Euler and Bernoulli equations, viscous flows, boundary layers, flows in channels and around submerged bodies, and one-dimensional gas dynamics.

ME 314 Heat and Mass Transfer (4 cr.) Class 3, Lab 2. P: ME 310. Fundamental principles of heat transfer by conduction, convection, and radiation; mass transfer by diffusion and convection. Application to engineering situations.

ME 330 Modeling and Analysis of Dynamic Systems (3 cr.) Class 3. P: EE 201 and MATH 262. Introduction to dynamic engineering systems; electrical, mechanical, fluid, and thermal components; linear system response; Fourier series and Laplace transform.

ME 340 Dynamic Systems and Measurements (3 cr.) Class 2, Lab 2. P: ME 330. Modeling and formulation of differential...

Source: Purdue University Bulletin—
School of Engineering and Technology, Indiana University-Purdue University Indianapolis.

your academic career. When you have a question, consult the catalog first before you spend time and energy looking elsewhere.

Your *student handbook* looks beyond specific courses to the big picture, helping you to navigate student life. In it you will find some or all of the following, and maybe more: information on available housing (for on-campus residents) and on parking and driving (for commuters); overviews of the support offices for students, such as academic advising, counseling, career planning and placement, student health, disabled student services, child care, financial aid, and individual centers for academic subject areas such as writing or math; descriptions of special-interest clubs; and details about library and computer services. It may also list hours, locations, phone numbers and addresses for all offices, clubs, and organizations.

Your student handbook will also describe important policies such as how to add or drop a class, what the grading system means, campus rules, drug and alcohol policies, what kinds of records your school keeps, safety tips, and more. Keep your student handbook where you can find it easily, in your study area at home or someplace safe at school. The information it gives you can save you a lot of trouble when you need to find out information about a resource or service. If you call for locations and hours before you visit a particular office, you'll avoid the frustration of dropping by when the office is closed.

Making the most of your resources is one way to adjust to your new environment. Interacting with people around you is another.

Engineering College Resources

Your engineering college has a variety of resources and people ready to help you—all you have to do is ask! The faculty and staff in the college are there to provide you with the tools you need to get the best education possible. Each academic department has assigned faculty or staff advisors, and the dean's office will probably have a staff of trained counselors ready to help you. The following types of resources might be available at your school.

Tutors. Tutors may be provided under the auspices of the dean's office, or may be available through your dorm or through the engineering organizations.

Minority Engineering Programs. These programs usually aim to recruit and retain underrepresented minorities in engineering. The staff may be able to help you find tutors, mentors, sources of financial aid, and other resources.

Women in Engineering Program. These programs aim to recruit and retain women in engineering.

Dean's Office. The dean's office usually offers advising and counseling services.

Engineering Organizations. Often, the student engineering organizations have course files and test files that include copies of old tests, notebooks of old homework assignments, and other materials to help you with the coursework in your major.

WHAT YOU SHOULD KNOW ABOUT FINANCIAL AID

Seeking help from various sources of financial aid has become a way of life for much of the student population. Education is an important but often expensive investment. The cost for a year's full tuition and fees only (not including room and board) in 1998–1999 ranged from an average of $1,633 at two-year public institutions to $14,508 at four-year private institutions.[2] Many people require financial assistance in order to cover their costs of tuition and fees as well as room and board. In fact, according to the data, over 41 percent of students enrolled received some kind of aid,[3] and that number almost certainly continues to increase along with rising tuition costs.

Most sources of financial aid don't seek out recipients. Take the initiative to learn how you (or you and your parents, if they currently help to support you) can finance your education. Find the people on campus who can help you with your finances. Do some research to find out what's available, weigh the pros and cons of each option, and decide what would work best for you. Try to apply as early as you can. The types of financial aid available to you are loans, grants, and scholarships.

Success in the Real World

Sherita Ceasar

Vice President, Digital Launch Deployment, Scientific Atlanta

Engineering became an interest of mine when I went to my first college fair while I was still in high school. A man from Illinois Institute of Technology (IIT) asked me if I wanted to make a lot of money after college. My answer was YES! At that moment, my exposure to engineering started. The first engineering exposure was with a program called "Early ID Minority Engineering Program." I spent the summer of my junior year in high school in this program, learning about all the disciplines of engineering at IIT. At the end of this summer, the entire class, more than 250 high school students, was tested in their mechanical aptitude, and I placed second. I was also on the winning pre-engineering team for a rocket ship design. My team was featured on WBBM TV. To encourage minority enrollment, IIT also gave us their entrance exam. I passed this, thus sealing the path for my engineering education in mechanical engineering. This program also afforded me my first opportunity with a summer internship right out of high school at General Electric Appliance Motor Department, in DeKalb, Ill.

Engineering school was a challenge from day one. I lived in the Chicago Housing Authority (the projects), not four blocks from the college. I used to walk to school every day past the winos, and they would encourage me to make something of my life. My family didn't understand why I stayed at school so late to study. My mom and I were always arguing about cleaning the house, cooking, etc., during the first six months, until I finally got additional scholarship money to move on campus. That's when the world really opened for me. Living in the dorms, studying all through the night was the norm, especially during the mid-terms and finals. It never occurred to me until my junior year that as I entered my mechanical engineering classes I was in most cases the only woman and the only black in the room.

College was not easy for me. I had to study! I also had to work, so I took part-time employment as a technician with Illinois Institute of Technology's Research Institute, known as IITRI. This is where I had my first mentor—a senior mechanical designer. He helped me understand the application of engineering to real life. I learned so much from him and the design team about engineering, and the lessons stay with me today. Lessons like defining the problem, getting the facts, and looking for the root cause of the problem, along with making sure you can control the problem by turning it on and off. I continued to work and get promoted at IITRI throughout college, becoming a senior technician level 2 as I approached graduation. They offered me a job as an associate engineer after my graduation, and I worked for them for about a year.

Graduation was an emotional experience for me. I was not ready to leave the comfortable world of college. I applied for the Graduate Engineering Minorities scholarship (GEMS) in my senior year. To my surprise, they awarded me the scholarship! I elected to stay at IIT and work on my M. S. in mechanical engineering. Key decision factors were my boyfriend, whom I wanted as my husband, and the support of my family. I elected to stay in Chicago and at IIT, eventually graduating from IIT with a B. S. and an M. S. in mechanical engineering.

All through my life I have had a lot of support and encouragement from many family members and friends. My parents have been truly proud of my accomplishments, and I consider what I have done a blessing. I learned very early in my life to face my fears and learn from my mistakes. I am a survivor. These characteristics make me who I am today: "a committed leader who will make a difference in the world."

Student Loans

A loan is given to you by a person, bank, or other lending agency, usually to put toward a specific purchase. You, as the recipient of the loan, then must pay back the amount of the loan, plus interest, in regular payments that stretch over a particular period of time. Interest is the fee that you pay for the privilege of using money that belongs to someone else.

Making a Loan Application

What happens when you apply for a loan?

1. The loaning agency must approve you. You may be asked about what you and any other family members earn, how much savings you have, your credit history, anything you own that is of substantial value (a home or business), and your history of payment on any previous loans.

2. An interest charge will be set. Interest can range from 5 percent to over 20 percent, depending on the loan and the economy. Variable-interest loans shift charges as the economy strengthens or weakens. Fixed-rate loans have one interest rate that remains constant.

3. The loaning agency will establish a payment plan. Most loan payments are made monthly or quarterly (four times per year). The payment amount depends on the total amount of the loan, how much you can comfortably pay per month, and the length of the repayment period.

Types of Student Loans

The federal government administers or oversees most student loans. To receive aid from any federal program, you must be a citizen or eligible nonci-

tizen and be enrolled in a program of study that the government has determined is eligible. Individual states may differ in their aid programs. Check with your campus financial aid office to find out details about your state and your school in particular.

Following are the main student loan programs to which you can apply if you are eligible. Amounts vary according to individual circumstances. Contact your school or federal student aid office for further information. In most cases, the amount is limited to the cost of your education minus any other financial aid you are receiving. All the information on federal loans and grants comes from the *1998–1999 Student Guide to Financial Aid,* published by the U. S. Department of Education.[4]

Perkins Loans. Carrying a low, fixed rate of interest, these loans are available to those with exceptional financial need (need is determined by a government-determined formula that indicates how large a contribution toward your education your family should be able to make). Schools issue these loans from their own allotment of federal education funds. After you graduate, you have a "grace period" (up to nine months, depending on whether you were a part-time or full-time student) before you have to begin repaying your loan in monthly installments.

Stafford Loans. Students enrolled in school at least half-time may apply for a Stafford Loan. Exceptional need is not required. However, students who can prove exceptional need may qualify for a "subsidized" Stafford Loan, for which the government pays your interest until you begin repayment. There are two types of Stafford Loans. A Direct Stafford Loan comes from government funds, and an FFEL Stafford Loan comes from a bank or credit union participating in the FFEL (Federal Family Education Loan) program. The type available to you depends on your school's financial aid program. You begin to repay a Stafford Loan six months after you graduate, leave school, or drop below half-time enrollment.

Plus Loans. Your parents can apply for a Plus Loan if they currently claim you as a dependent and if you are enrolled at least half-time. They must also undergo a credit check in order to be eligible, although the loans are not based on income. If they do not pass the credit check, they may be able to sponsor the loan through a relative or friend who does qualify. Interest is variable; the loans are available from either the government or banks and credit unions. Your parents will have to begin repayment 60 days after they receive the last loan payment; there is no grace period.

Grants and Scholarships

Both grants and scholarships require no repayment, and therefore give your finances a terrific boost. Grants, funded by the government, are awarded to students who show financial need. Scholarships are awarded to students who show talent or ability in the area specified by the scholarship. They may be financed by government or private organizations, schools, or individuals.

Federal Grant Programs

Pell Grants. These grants are need-based. The Department of Education uses a standard formula to evaluate the financial information you report on your application, and determines your eligibility from that "score" (called an EFC, or Expected Family Contribution, number). You must also be an undergraduate student who has earned no other degrees to be eligible. The Pell Grant serves as a foundation of aid to which you may add other aid sources, and the amount of the grant varies according to the cost of your education and your EFC. Pell Grants require no repayment.

FSEOG (Federal Supplemental Educational Opportunity Grants). Administered by the financial aid administrator at participating schools, SEOG eligibility depends on need. Whereas the government guarantees that every student eligible for a Pell Grant will receive one, each school receives a limited amount of federal funds for SEOGs, and once it's gone, it's gone. Schools set their own application deadlines. Apply early. No repayment is required.

Work-Study Program. Although you work in exchange for the aid, work-study is considered a grant because a limited number of positions are available. This program is need-based and encourages community-service work or work related in some way to your course of study. You will earn at least the federal minimum wage and will be paid hourly. Jobs can be on-campus (usually for your school) or off-campus (often with a nonprofit organization or a local, state, or federal public agency). Find out who is in charge of the work-study program on your campus.

There is much more to say about these financial aid opportunities than can be touched on here. Many other important details about federal grants and loans are available in the current edition of the *Student Guide to Financial Aid.* You might find this information at your school's financial aid office, or you can request it by mail, phone, or on-line service:

Address:	Federal Student Aid Information Center
	P.O. Box 84
	Washington, D.C. 20044
Phone:	1-800-4-FED-AID (1-800-433-3243)
	TDD for the hearing-impaired: 1-800-730-8913
Internet address:	www.ed.gov/prog_info/SFA/StudentGuide

Scholarships

Scholarships are given for different kinds of abilities and talents. Some reward academic achievement. Some reward exceptional abilities in sports or the arts. Some reward citizenship or leadership. Certain scholarships are sponsored by federal agencies. If you display exceptional ability or are disabled, female, of an ethnic background classified as a minority (such as African-American or Native American), or a child of someone who draws benefits from a state agency (such as a POW or MIA), you might find scholarship opportunities geared toward you.

All kinds of organizations offer scholarships. You may receive scholarships from individual departments at your school or your school's independent scholarship funds, local organizations such as the Rotary Club, or privately operated aid foundations. Labor unions and companies may offer scholarship opportunities for children of their employees. Membership groups such as scouting organizations or the Y might offer scholarships, and religious, ethnic, and fraternal organizations such as the Knights of Columbus or the Council of Jewish Federations might be another source.

Researching Grants and Scholarships

It can take work to locate scholarships and work-study programs because many of them aren't widely advertised. Ask at your school's financial aid office. Visit your library or bookstore and look in the section on College or Financial Aid. Guides to funding sources, such as Richard Black's *The Complete Family Guide to College Financial Aid,* catalog thousands of organizations and help you find what fits you. Check out on-line scholarship search services. Use common sense and time management when applying for aid—fill out the application as neatly as possible and send it in on time or even early. In addition, be wary of scholarship scam artists who ask you to pay a fee up front for them to find aid for you.

No matter where your money comes from—financial aid, family, or paychecks from one or more jobs—you can take steps to help it stretch as far as it can go.

Chapter 10 includes sections that will help you develop a philosophy about your money and budgeting effectively. Using those skills, you can more efficiently cover your expenses, and still have some left over for savings and fun.

ENDNOTES

1. University of Colorado at Boulder *Advising Guide 1999–2000.*

2. The College Board, "Exhibit 1: Average Fixed Charges for Undergraduates, 1998–1999 (weighted)," *News from the College Board,* <www.collegeboard.org/press/cost98/html/exhib01.html> (19 June 2000).

3. U. S. Department of Education, National Center for Education Statistics, *Digest of Education Statistics 1996*, NCES 96-133, by Thomas D. Snyder. Production Manager, Charlene M. Hoffman. Program Analyst, Claire M. Geddes (Washington, D. C.: U. S. Government Printing Office, 1996), 320–321.

4. U. S. Department of Education, *The 1998–99 Student Guide to Financial Aid.*

Name   Date

CHAPTER 2 Applications

KEY INTO YOUR LIFE   *Opportunities to Apply What You Learn*

EXERCISE   2.1   Who Can Help You?

Every school is unique and offers its own particular range of opportunities. Investigate your school. Use Table 2.1 as a guide, and explore your student handbook. Make a check mark by the resources that you think will be most helpful to you.

_____ Advisors and counselors   _____ Adult education center

_____ Library/media center   _____ Support groups/hotlines

_____ Professors   _____ Career/job placement office

_____ Clubs/organizations   _____ Administration

_____ Bulletin boards   _____ Academic centers

_____ Student health center   _____ School publications

_____ Housing and transportation   _____ Tutoring

_____ Wellness/fitness centers   _____ Financial-aid office

Gather in small groups; or, if you have a small class, work as one large group together. Each member of each group should choose one or more different resources (make sure no two people within a group explore the same resource). Make sure all resources on the grid on pages 32 and 33 are accounted for. Then, each group member will investigate the resources and fill in the information on the grid, answering the questions listed across the top of the grid. The two blank spaces at the bottom are for you to use if you find resources not listed here.

After each person has completed the investigation, meet again to exchange information and fill in the information on the grid. You now have a resource guide that you can refer to any time. Write here how you will use the three resources that you feel will benefit you the most.

1. _____

_____

_____

2. _____

_____

_____

3. _____

_____

_____

Student Organizations

Identify three student organizations on your campus that look interesting to you. List them.

_____

_____

_____

a. Find out when and how often they meet.

_____

_____

_____

b. Find out what type of activities they undertake.

_____

_____

_____

c. Find out if this is a chapter of a national organization that requires a membership application and dues.

_____

_____

_____

RESOURCE	WHO PROVIDES IT?	WHERE CAN YOU FIND IT?	WHEN IS IT AVAILABLE?	HOW CAN IT HELP YOU?	HOW DO YOU ASK FOR IT?	PHONE # OR OTHER KEY DETAILS
Administrative help						
Professor advice						
Academic advising						
Personal counseling						
Financial aid						
Academic centers						
Organizations and clubs						
Bulletin boards						
Housing and transportation						
Career planning and placement						

RESOURCE	WHO PROVIDES IT?	WHERE CAN YOU FIND IT?	WHEN IS IT AVAILABLE?	HOW CAN IT HELP YOU?	HOW DO YOU ASK FOR IT?	PHONE # OR OTHER KEY DETAILS
Tutoring						
Student health						
Adult education center						
Fitness						
Support groups/ hotlines						
Disabled-student services						
English as a second language						

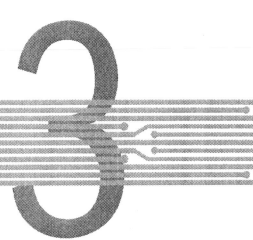

Individual Realities

Who You Are and How You Learn

Learning is not something you do just in college. Throughout your life, learning can help you keep up with the rapid pace at which the world is changing Technology, for example, is changing so fast that you cannot learn today about all of the computer operations that will be commonplace five years from now. However, you can learn how to be an effective learner in school and in the workplace so that you can keep pace with changes as they occur. In this chapter you will become aware of your learning style by completing three different learning style assessments. Each assessment will add a different dimension to the picture you are forming of yourself. You will then explore other important elements of self: your self-perception, your preferences, your habits, your abilities, and your attitudes.

In this chapter, you will explore answers to the following questions:

- Is there one best way to learn?

- How can you discover your learning styles?

- What are the benefits of knowing your learning styles?

- How do you explore who you are?

IS THERE ONE BEST WAY TO LEARN?

Your mind is the most powerful tool you will ever possess. You are accomplished at many skills and can process all kinds of information. However, when you have trouble accomplishing a particular task, you may become convinced that you can't learn how to do anything new. You may feel that those who can do what you can't have the "right" kind of ability. Not only is this perception incorrect, it can also damage your belief in yourself.

Every individual is highly developed in some abilities and underdeveloped in others. Many famously successful people were brilliant in one area but functioned poorly in other areas. Winston Churchill failed the sixth grade. Abraham Lincoln was demoted to a private in the Black Hawk War. Louis Pasteur was a poor student in chemistry. Walt Disney was fired from a job and told he had no good ideas. What some might interpret as a deficiency or disability may be simply a different method of learning.

Learning style
A particular way in which the mind receives and processes information.

There is no one "best" way to learn. Instead, there are many different **learning styles,** and different styles are suited to different situations. Your individual learning profile is made up of a combination of learning styles. Each person's profile is unique. Just like personality traits, learning styles are part of your personal characteristics. Knowing how you learn is one of the first steps in discovering who you are.

HOW CAN YOU DISCOVER YOUR LEARNING STYLES?

Your brain is so complex that one inventory cannot give you all the information you need to maximize your learning skills. You will learn about and complete three assessments: the *Learning Styles Inventory*, the *Pathways to Learning* inventory based on the Multiple Intelligences Theory, and the *Personality Spectrum*. Each of these assessments evaluates your mind's abilities in a different way, although they often have related ideas. Your results will combine to form your learning-styles profile, consisting of the styles and types that best fit the ways that you learn and interact with others. After you complete the various learning-styles inventories, you will read about strategies that can help you make the most of particular styles and types, both in school and beyond. Your learning-styles profile will help you to improve your understanding of yourself, how you learn, and how you may function as a learner in the workplace.

Learning Styles Inventory

One of the first instruments to measure psychological types, the Myers-Briggs Type Indicator® (MBTI), was designed by Katharine Briggs and her daughter, Isabel Briggs Myers. Later David Keirsey and Marilyn Bates combined the sixteen Myers-Briggs types into four temperaments (see http://keirsey.com for additional information). Barbara Soloman, Associate Director of the University Undesignated Student Program at North Carolina State University, has developed the following learning styles inventory based on these theories and on her work with thousands of students.[1]

"Students learn in many ways," says Professor Soloman. "Mismatches often exist between common learning styles and standard teaching styles. Therefore, students often do poorly and get discouraged. Some students doubt themselves and doubt their ability to succeed in the curriculum of their choice. Some settle for low grades and even leave school. If students understand how they learn most effectively, they can tailor their studying to their own needs."

"Learning effectively" and "tailoring studying to your own needs" means choosing study techniques that help you learn. For example, if a student responds more to visual images than to words, he or she may want to construct notes in a more visual way. Or, if a student learns better when talking to people than when studying alone, he or she may want to study primarily in pairs or groups.

Engineering courses use a variety of teaching methods. For instance, in one course you may be doing a great deal of problem solving, while in another you will do hands-on work in a laboratory or in the field. A variety of teaching styles helps hold your attention and helps you learn.

> "To be what we are, and to become what we are capable of becoming, is the only end of life."
>
> ROBERT LOUIS STEVENSON

The Dimensions of Learning

This inventory has four "dimensions," within each of which are two opposing styles. At the end of the inventory, you will have two scores in each of the four dimensions. The difference between your two scores in any dimension tells you which of the two styles in that dimension is dominant for you. A few people will score right in between the two styles, indicating that they have fairly equal parts of both styles. Following are brief descriptions of the four dimensions. You will learn more about them after you complete all three assessments.

Active/Reflective. *Active* learners learn best by experiencing knowledge through their own actions. *Reflective* learners understand information best when they have had time to reflect on it on their own.

Factual/Theoretical. *Factual* learners learn best through specific facts, data, and detailed experimentation. *Theoretical* learners are more comfortable with big-picture ideas, symbols, and new concepts.

Visual/Verbal. *Visual* learners remember best what they see: diagrams, flowcharts, time lines, films, and demonstrations. *Verbal* learners gain the most learning from reading, hearing spoken words, participating in discussion, and explaining things to others.

Holistic
Relating to the wholes of complete systems rather than the analysis of parts.

Linear/Holistic. *Linear* learners find it easiest to learn material presented step by step in a logical, ordered progression. **Holistic** learners progress in fits and starts, perhaps feeling lost for a while, but eventually seeing the big picture in a clear and creative way.

Please complete this inventory by circling **a** or **b** to indicate your answer to each question. Answer every question and choose only one answer for each question. If both answers seem to apply to you, choose the answer that applies more often.

LEARNING STYLES INVENTORY

1. I study best
    a. in a study group.
    b. alone or with a partner.

2. I would rather be considered
    a. realistic.
    b. imaginative.

3. When I recall what I did yesterday, I am most likely to think in terms of
    a. pictures/images.
    b. words/verbal descriptions.

4. I usually think new material is
    a. easier at the beginning and then harder as it becomes more complicated.
    b. often confusing at the beginning but easier as I start to understand what the whole subject is about.

5. When given a new activity to learn, I would rather first
    a. try it out.
    b. think about how I'm going to do it.

6. If I were an instructor, I would rather teach a course
    a. that deals with real-life situations and what to do about them.
    b. that deals with ideas and encourages students to think about them.

7. I prefer to receive new information in the form of
    a. pictures, diagrams, graphs, or maps.
    b. written directions or verbal information.

8. I learn
    a. at a fairly regular pace. If I study hard I'll "get it" and then move on.
    b. in fits and starts. I might be totally confused and then suddenly it all "clicks."

9. I understand something better after
    a. I attempt to do it myself.
    b. I give myself time to think about how it works.

10. I find it easier
    a. to learn facts.
    b. to learn ideas/concepts.

11. In a book with lots of pictures and charts, I am likely to
    a. look over the pictures and charts carefully.
    b. focus on the written text.

12. It's easier for me to memorize facts from
    a. a list.
    b. a whole story/essay with the facts embedded in it.

13. I will more easily remember
    a. something I have done myself.
    b. something I have thought or read about.

14. I am usually
    a. aware of my surroundings. I remember people and places and usually recall where I put things.
    b. unaware of my surroundings. I forget people and places. I frequently misplace things.

15. I like instructors
    a. who put a lot of diagrams on the board.
    b. who spend a lot of time explaining.

16. Once I understand
    a. all the parts, I understand the whole thing.
    b. the whole thing, I see how the parts fit.

17. When I am learning something new, I would rather
    a. talk about it.
    b. think about it.

18. I am good at
    a. being careful about the details of my work.
    b. having creative ideas about how to do my work.

19. I remember best
    a. what I see.
    b. what I hear.

20. When I solve problems that involve some math, I usually
    a. work my way to the solutions one step at a time.
    b. see the solutions but then have to struggle to figure out the steps to get to them.

21. In a lecture class, I would prefer occasional in-class
    a. discussions or group problem-solving sessions.
    b. pauses that give opportunities to think or write about ideas presented in the lecture.

22. On a multiple-choice test, I am more likely to
    a. run out of time.
    b. lose points because of not reading carefully or making careless errors.

23. When I get directions to a new place, I prefer
    a. a map.
    b. written instructions.

24. When I'm thinking about something I've read,
    a. I remember the incidents and try to put them together to figure out the themes.
    b. I just know what the themes are when I finish reading and then I have to back up and find the incidents that demonstrate them.

25. When I get a new computer or VCR, I tend to
    a. plug it in and start punching buttons.
    b. read the manual and follow instructions.

26. In reading for pleasure, I prefer
    a. something that teaches me new facts or tells me how to do something.
    b. something that gives me new ideas to think about.

27. When I see a diagram or sketch in class, I am most likely to remember
    a. the picture.
    b. what the instructor said about it.

28. It is more important to me that an instructor
    a. lay out the material in clear, sequential steps.
    b. give me an overall picture and relate the material to other subjects.

SCORING SHEET: Use Table 3.1 to enter your scores.

1. Put 1's in the appropriate boxes in the table (e.g., if you answered *a* to Question 3, put a 1 in the column headed *a* next to the number 3).

2. Total the 1's in the columns and write the totals in the indicated spaces at the base of the columns.

TABLE 3.1   Learning styles inventory scores.

	ACTIVE/REFLECTIVE			FACTUAL/THEORETICAL			VISUAL/VERBAL			LINEAR/HOLISTIC	
Q#	a	b	Q#	a	b	Q#	a	b	Q#	a	b
1	✓		2	✓	✓	3	✓		4	✓	
5		✓	6	✓		7		✓	8		✓
9	✓		10		✓	11	✓		12	✓	
13		✓	14	✓		15	✓		16		✓
17	✓		18		✓	19	✓		20	✓	
21		✓	22		✓	23	✓		24		✓
25		✓	26		✓	27		✓	28		✓
Total			Total		✓	Total		✓	Total		✓

3. For each of the four dimensions, circle your two scores on the bar scale and then fill in the bar between the scores. For example, if under "ACTV/REFL" you had 2 a and 5 b responses, you would fill in the bar between those two scores, as this sample shows:

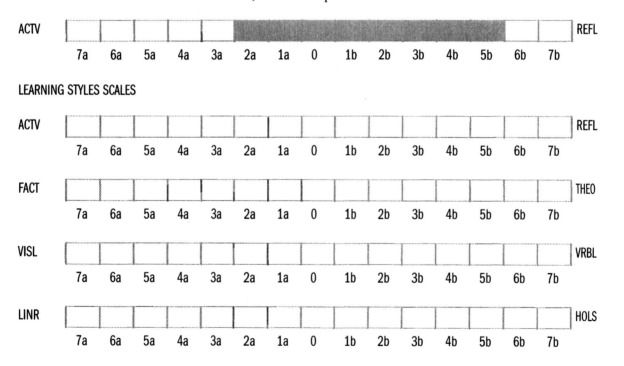

If your filled-in bar has the 0 close to its center, you are well balanced on the two dimensions of that scale. If your bar is drawn mainly to one side, you have a strong preference for that one dimension and may have difficulty learning in the other dimension.

Continue on to the next assessment. After you complete all three, the next section of the chapter will help you understand and make use of your results from each assessment.

Multiple Intelligences Theory

Howard Gardner, a Harvard University professor, has developed a theory called Multiple Intelligences. He believes there are at least eight distinct intelligences possessed by all people, and that every person has developed some intelligences more fully than others. Most people have experienced a time when they learned something very quickly and comfortably. Most have also had the opposite experience when, no matter how hard they tried, something they wanted to learn just would not sink in. According to the Multiple Intelligences Theory, when you find a task or subject easy, you are probably using a more fully developed **intelligence;** when you have more trouble, you may be using a less developed intelligence.[2]

Following are brief descriptions of the focus of each of the intelligences. Study skills that reinforce each intelligence will be described later in the chapter.

- Verbal-Linguistic Intelligence—ability to communicate through language (listening, reading, writing, speaking)
- Logical-Mathematical Intelligence—ability to understand logical reasoning and problem solving (math, science, patterns, sequences)
- Bodily-Kinesthetic Intelligence—ability to use the physical body skillfully and to take in knowledge through bodily sensation (coordination, working with hands)
- Visual-Spatial Intelligence—ability to understand spatial relationships and to perceive and create images (visual art, graphic design, charts and maps)
- Interpersonal Intelligence—ability to relate to others, noticing their moods, motivations, and feelings (social activity, cooperative learning, teamwork)
- Intrapersonal Intelligence—ability to understand one's own behavior and feelings (independence, time spent alone)
- Musical Intelligence—ability to comprehend and create meaningful sound (music, sensitivity to sound)
- Naturalistic Intelligence—ability to understand features of the environment (interest in nature, environmental balance, ecosystem, stress relief brought by natural environments)

Please complete the following assessment of your multiple intelligences, called Pathways to Learning, developed by Joyce Bishop. It will help you determine which of your intelligences are most fully developed. Don't be concerned if some of your scores are low. That is true of most people, even your professors and your authors!

Learning styles and multiple intelligences are gauges to help you understand yourself. Instead of labeling yourself narrowly using one category or another, learn as much as you can about your preferences and how you can maximize your learning. Most people are a blend of styles and preferences, with one or two being dominant. In addition, you may change preferences depending on the situation. For example, a student might find it easy to take notes in outline style when the professor lectures in an organized way. However, if another professor jumps from topic to topic, the student might choose to use the adapted Cornell note-taking system or a concept map (Chapter 7 goes into detail about note-taking styles).

Intelligence
As defined by H. Gardner, an ability to solve problems or fashion products that are useful in a particular cultural setting or community.

Kinesthetic
Coming from physical sensation caused by body movements and tensions.

PATHWAYS TO LEARNING[3]

Directions: Rate each statement as follows: rarely 1; sometimes 2; usually 3; always 4.

Write the number of your response (1–4) in the box next to the statement and total each set of six questions.

Developed by Joyce Bishop, Ph.D., and based on Howard Gardner, *Frames of Mind: The Theory of Multiple Intelligences* (New York: Basic Books, 1993).

☐ 1. I enjoy physical activities.

☐ 2. I am uncomfortable sitting still.

☐ 3. I prefer to learn through doing.

☐ 4. When sitting I move my legs or hands.

☐ 5. I enjoy working with my hands.

☐ 6. I like to pace when I'm thinking or studying.

☐   **TOTAL for Bodily/Kinesthetic**

☐ 7. I use maps easily.

☐ 8. I draw pictures/diagrams when explaining ideas.

☐ 9. I can assemble items easily from diagrams.

☐ 10. I enjoy drawing or photography.

☐ 11. I do not like to read long paragraphs.

☐ 12. I prefer a drawn map over written directions.

☐   **TOTAL for Visual/Spatial**

☐ 13. I enjoy telling stories.

☐ 14. I like to write.

☐ 15. I like to read.

☐ 16. I express myself clearly.

☐ 17. I am good at negotiating.

☐ 18. I like to discuss topics that interest me.

☐   **TOTAL for Verbal/Linguistic**

☐ 19. I like math in high school.

☐ 20. I like science.

☐ 21. I problem-solve well.

☐ 22. I question how things work.

☐ 23. I enjoy planning or designing something new.

☐ 24. I am able to fix things.

☐   **TOTAL for Logical/Mathematical**

☐ 25. I listen to music.

☐ 26. I move my fingers or feet when I hear music.

☐ 27. I have good rhythm.

☐ 28. I like to sing along with music.

☐ 29. People have said I have musical talent.

☐ 30. I like to express my ideas through music.

☐   **TOTAL for Musical**

☐ 31. I like doing a project with other people.

☐ 32. People come to me to help settle conflicts.

☐ 33. I like to spend time with friends.

☐ 34. I am good at understanding people.

☐ 35. I am good at making people feel comfortable.

☐ 36. I enjoy helping others.

☐   **TOTAL for Interpersonal**

☐ 37. I need quiet time to think.

☐ 38. I think about issues before I want to talk.

☐ 39. I am interested in self-improvement.

☐ 40. I understand my thoughts and feelings.

☐ 41. I know what I want out of life.

☐ 42. I prefer to work on projects alone.

☐   **TOTAL for Intrapersonal**

☐ 43. I enjoy nature whenever possible.

☐ 44. I think about having a career involving nature.

☐ 45. I enjoy studying plants, animals, or oceans.

☐ 46. I avoid being indoors except when I sleep.

☐ 47. As a child I played with bugs and leaves.

☐ 48. When I feel stressed, I want to be out in nature.

☐   **TOTAL for Naturalistic**

Write each of your eight intelligences in the column where it fits below. For each, choose the column that corresponds with your total in that intelligence.

SCORES OF 20-24 HIGHLY DEVELOPED		SCORES OF 14-19 MODERATELY DEVELOPED		SCORES BELOW 14 UNDERDEVELOPED	
Scores	Intelligences	Scores	Intelligences	Scores	Intelligences

Personality Spectrum

This final assessment, through its evaluation of personality types, focuses on how you relate to others. It is a system that simplifies learning styles into four personality types, developed by Joyce Bishop (1997). Her work is based on the Myers-Briggs and Keirsey theories discussed earlier in the chapter. The Personality Spectrum will give you a personality perspective on your learning styles. Please complete the following assessment.

PERSONALITY SPECTRUM

Step 1. Rank all four responses to each question from **most** like you (4) to **least** like you (1). Place a 1, 2, 3, or 4 in each box next to the responses, and use each number only once per question.

1. I like instructors who
   ☐ a. tell me exactly what is expected of me.
   ☐ b. make learning active and exciting.
   ☐ c. maintain a safe and supportive classroom.
   ☐ d. challenge me to think at higher levels.

2. I learn best when the material is
   ☐ a. well organized.
   ☐ b. something I can do hands-on.
   ☐ c. about understanding and improving the human condition.
   ☐ d. intellectually challenging.

3. A high priority in my life is to
   ☐ a. keep my commitments.
   ☐ b. experience as much of life as possible.
   ☐ c. make a difference in other's lives.
   ☐ d. understand how things work.

4. Other people think of me as
   ☐ a. dependable and loyal.
   ☐ b. dynamic and creative.
   ☐ c. caring and honest.
   ☐ d. intelligent and inventive.

5. When I experience stress, I most likely
☐ a. do something to help me feel more in control.
☐ b. do something physical and daring.
☐ c. talk with a friend.
☐ d. go off by myself and think about my situation.

6. The greatest flaw someone can have is to be
☐ a. irresponsible.
☐ b. unwilling to try new things.
☐ c. selfish and unkind to others.
☐ d. an illogical thinker.

7. My vacations could best be described as
☐ a. traditional.
☐ b. adventuresome.
☐ c. pleasing to others.
☐ d. a new learning experience.

8. One word that best describes me is
☐ a. sensible.
☐ b. spontaneous.
☐ c. giving.
☐ d. analytical.

Step 2. Add up the total points for each column.

Total for (A)	Total for (B)	Total for (C)	Total for (D)
☐	☐	☐	☐
Organizer	Adventurer	Giver	Thinker

Step 3. Plot these numbers on the brain diagram on the following page.

When you have tallied your scores, plot them on Figure 3.1 to create a visual representation of your spectrum.

Your Personality Spectrum assessment can help you maximize your functioning at school and at work. Each personality type has its own abilities that improve work and school performance, suitable learning techniques, and ways of relating in interpersonal relationships. Table 3.2 explains what suits each type.

TABLE 3.2 Personality spectrum at school and work.	PERSONALITY RELATIONSHIPS	STRENGTHS AT WORK AND SCHOOL	INTERPERSONAL
	Organizer	⚹ Can efficiently manage heavy work loads ⚹ Good organizational skills ⚹ Natural leadership qualities	⚹ Loyal ⚹ Dependable ⚹ Traditional
	Adventurer	⚹ Adaptable to most changes ⚹ Creative and skillful ⚹ Dynamic and fast-paced	⚹ Free ⚹ Exciting ⚹ Intense
	Giver	⚹ Always willing to help others ⚹ Honest and sincere ⚹ Good people skills	⚹ Giving ⚹ Romantic ⚹ Warm
	Thinker	⚹ Good analytical skills ⚹ Can develop complex designs ⚹ Is thorough and exact	⚹ Quiet ⚹ Good problem solver ⚹ Inventive

Personality spectrum—thinking preferences and learning styles.   **→ FIGURE 3.1**

Place a dot on the appropriate number line for each of your four scores and connect the dots. A new shape will be formed inside each square. Color each shape in a different color.

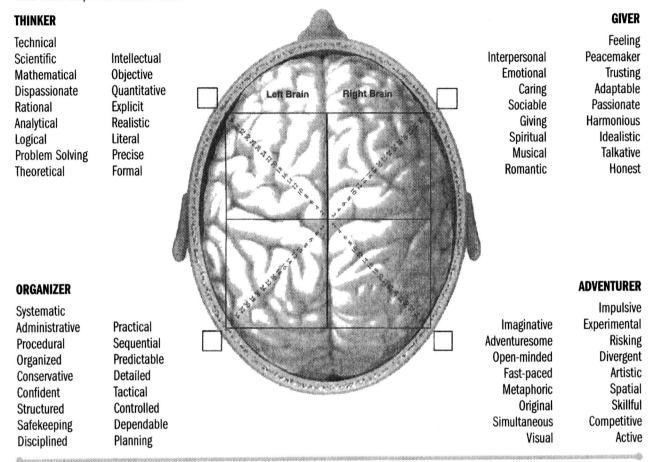

THINKER

Technical	
Scientific	Intellectual
Mathematical	Objective
Dispassionate	Quantitative
Rational	Explicit
Analytical	Realistic
Logical	Literal
Problem Solving	Precise
Theoretical	Formal

GIVER

	Feeling
Interpersonal	Peacemaker
Emotional	Trusting
Caring	Adaptable
Sociable	Passionate
Giving	Harmonious
Spiritual	Idealistic
Musical	Talkative
Romantic	Honest

ORGANIZER

Systematic	
Administrative	Practical
Procedural	Sequential
Organized	Predictable
Conservative	Detailed
Confident	Tactical
Structured	Controlled
Safekeeping	Dependable
Disciplined	Planning

ADVENTURER

	Impulsive
Imaginative	Experimental
Adventuresome	Risking
Open-minded	Divergent
Fast-paced	Artistic
Metaphoric	Spatial
Original	Skillful
Simultaneous	Competitive
Visual	Active

Source: Understanding Psychology, 3/E, by Morris, © 1996. Adapted by permission of Prentice-Hall, Inc., Upper Saddle River, NJ.

WHAT ARE THE BENEFITS OF KNOWING YOUR LEARNING STYLES ?

Determining your learning-styles profile takes work and self-exploration. For it to be worth your while, you need to understand what knowing your profile can do for you. The following sections will discuss benefits specific to study skills as well as more general benefits.

Study Benefits

Most students aim to maximize learning while minimizing frustration and time spent studying. If you know your particular learning style, you can use techniques that complement it. Such techniques take advantage of your highly developed areas while helping you through your less developed ones. For example, perhaps you perform better in smaller, discussion-based classes.

When you have the opportunity, you might choose a course section that is smaller or that is taught by a professor who prefers group discussion. You might also apply specific strategies to improve your retention in a lecture situation.

This section describes the techniques that tend to complement the strengths and shortcomings of each style. Students in Professor Soloman's program made many of these suggestions according to what worked for their own learning styles. Concepts from different assessments that benefit from similar strategies are grouped together. In Figure 3.2 you can see which styles tend to be dominant among students.

Remember that you may have characteristics from many different styles, even though some are dominant. Therefore, you may see suggestions for styles other than your dominant ones that may apply to you. What's important is that you use what works. Note the boxes next to the names of each style or type. In order to spot your best suggestions quickly, mark your most dominant styles or types by making check marks in the appropriate boxes.

Are You Active or Reflective?

Active learners ☐ include *Bodily-Kinesthetic* ☐ and *Interpersonal* ☐ learners as well as *Adventurers* ☐.   They like to apply the information to the real world, experience it in their own actions, or discuss or explain to others what they have learned.

Student-suggested strategies for active learners:

* Study in a group in which members take turns explaining topics to each other and then discussing them.
* Think of practical uses of the course material.
* Pace and recite while you learn.
* Act out material or design games.
* Use flash-cards with other people.
* Teach the material to someone else.

FIGURE 3.2

Percentages of students with particular learning styles

VISUAL	VERBAL
80%	20%

ACTIVE	REFLECTIVE
80%	20%

FACTUAL	THEORETICAL
70%	30%

LINEAR	HOLISTIC
85%	15%

Source: Barbara Soloman, North Carolina State University.

Reflective learners ☐ include *Intrapersonal* ☐ and *Logical/Mathematical* ☐ learners as well as *Thinkers* ☐. They retain and understand information better after they have taken time to think about it.

Student-suggested strategies for reflective learners:

* Study in a quiet setting.
* When you are reading, stop periodically to think about what you have read.
* Don't just memorize material; think about why it is important and what it relates to, considering the causes and effects involved.
* Write short summaries of what the material means to you.

Are You Factual or Theoretical?

Factual learners ☐ and *Organizers* ☐ prefer concrete and specific facts, data, and detailed experimentation. They like to solve problems with standard methods and are patient with details. They don't respond well to surprises and unique complications that upset normal procedure. They are good at memorizing facts.

Student-suggested strategies for factual learners:

* Ask the professor how ideas and concepts apply in practice.
* Ask for specific examples of the ideas and concepts.
* Brainstorm specific examples with classmates or by yourself.
* Think about how theories make specific connections with the real world.

Theoretical learners ☐ are often also logical/mathematical and prefer innovation and theories.   They are good at grasping new concepts and big-picture ideas. They dislike repetition and fact-based learning. They are comfortable with symbols and abstractions, often connecting them with prior knowledge and experience. Most classes are aimed at theoretical learners.

Student-suggested strategies for theoretical learners:

* If a class deals primarily with factual information, try to think of concepts, interpretations, or theories that link the facts together.
* Because you become impatient with details, you may be prone to careless mistakes on tests. Read directions and entire questions before answering, and be sure to check your work.
* Look for systems and patterns that arrange facts in a way that makes sense to you.
* Spend time analyzing the material.

Are You Visual/Spatial or Verbal/Linguistic?

Visual/Spatial learners ☐ remember best what they see: diagrams, flow-charts, time lines, films, and demonstrations. They tend to forget spoken words and ideas. Classes generally don't include much visual information. Note that although words written on paper or shown with an overhead projector are something you see, visual learners learn most easily from visual cues that don't involve words.

Student-suggested strategies for visual/spatial learners:

* Add diagrams to your notes whenever possible. Dates can be drawn on a time line; math functions can be graphed; percentages can be drawn in a pie chart.
* Organize your notes so that you can clearly see main points and supporting facts and how things are connected. You will learn more about different styles of note-taking in Chapter 7.
* Connect related facts in your notes by drawing arrows.
* Color-code your notes using different colored highlighters so that everything relating to a particular topic is the same color.

Verbal/Linguistic learners □ (often also interpersonal) remember much of what they hear and more of what they hear and then say. They benefit from discussion, prefer verbal explanation to visual demonstration, and learn effectively by explaining things to others. Because written words are processed as verbal information, verbal learners learn well through reading. The majority of classes, since they present material through the written word, lecture, or discussion, are geared to verbal learners.

Student-suggested strategies for verbal learners:

* Talk about what you learn. Work in study groups so that you have an opportunity to explain and discuss what you are learning.
* Read the textbook and highlight no more than 10 percent.
* Rewrite your notes.
* Outline chapters.
* Recite information or write scripts and debates.

Are You Linear or Holistic?

Linear learners □ find it easiest to learn material presented in a logical, ordered progression. They solve problems in a step-by-step manner. They can work with sections of material without yet fully understanding the whole picture. They tend to be stronger when looking at the parts of a whole rather than understanding the whole and then dividing it up into parts. They learn best when taking in material in a progression from easiest to more complex to most difficult. Many courses are taught in a linear fashion.

Student-suggested strategies for linear learners:

* If you have a professor who jumps around from topic to topic, spend time outside of class with the professor or a classmate who can help you fill the gaps in your notes.
* If class notes are random, rewrite the material according to whatever logic helps you understand it best.
* Outline the material.

Holistic learners □ learn in fits and starts. They may feel lost for days or weeks, unable to solve even the simplest problems or show the most basic understanding, until they suddenly "get it." They may feel discouraged when struggling with material which many other students seem to learn easily.

Once they understand, though, they tend to see the big picture to an extent that others may not often achieve. They are often highly creative.

Student-suggested strategies for the holistic learner:

- Recognize that you are not slow or stupid. Don't lose faith in yourself. You will get it!

- Before reading a chapter, preview it by reading all the subheadings, summaries, and any margin glossary terms. The chapter may also start with an outline and overview of the entire chapter.

- Instead of spending a short time on every subject every night, try setting aside evenings for specific subjects and immerse yourself in just one subject at a time.

- Try taking difficult subjects in summer school when you are handling fewer courses.

- Try to relate subjects to other things you already know. Keep asking yourself how you could apply the material.

Study Techniques for Additional Multiple Intelligences

People who score high in the *Musical/Rhythmic* ☐ intelligence have strong memories for rhymes and can be energized by music. They often have a song running through their minds and find themselves tapping a foot or their fingers when they hear music.

Student-suggested strategies for musical/rhythmic people:

- Create rhymes out of vocabulary words.
- Beat out rhythms when studying.
- Play instrumental music while studying if it does not distract you, but first determine what type of music improves your concentration the most.
- Take study breaks and listen to music.
- Write a rap about your topic.

Naturalistic learners ☐ feel energized when they are connected to nature. Their career choices and hobbies reflect their love of nature.

Student-suggested strategies for naturalistic people:

- Study outside whenever practical, but only if it is not distracting.
- Explore subject areas that reflect your love for nature. Learning is much easier when you have a passion for it.
- Relate abstract information to something concrete in nature.
- Take breaks with something you love from nature—a walk, watching your fish, or a nature video. Use nature as a reward for getting other work done.

Study Techniques for Different Personality Types

The different personality types of the Personality Spectrum combine the learning styles and multiple intelligences you have explored. Table 3.3 shows learning techniques that benefit each type.

TABLE 3.3	PERSONALITY TYPES	RELATED LEARNING STYLES	LEARNING TECHNIQUES TO USE
Types and learning techniques.	Organizer	Factual, Linear	❂ Organize material before studying. ❂ Whenever possible, select professors who have well-planned courses. ❂ Keep a daily planner and to-do list.
	Adventurer	Active, Bodily-Kinesthetic	❂ Keep study sessions moving quickly. ❂ Make learning fun and exciting. ❂ Study with other Adventurers but also with Organizers.
	Giver	Interpersonal	❂ Form study groups. ❂ Help someone else learn. ❂ Pick classes that relate to your interest in people.
	Thinker	Reflective, Intrapersonal, Logical-Mathematical, Theoretical	❂ Study alone. ❂ Allow time to think about material. ❂ Pick classes and professors who are intellectually challenging.

General Benefits

Although schools have traditionally favored verbal-linguistic students, there is no general advantage to one style over another. The only advantage is in discovering your profile through accurate and honest analysis. Following are three general benefits of knowing your learning styles.

1. You will have a better chance of avoiding problematic situations. If you don't explore what works best for you, you risk forcing yourself into career or personal situations that stifle your creativity, development, and happiness. Knowing how you learn and how you relate to the world can help you make smarter choices.

2. You will be more successful on the job. Your learning style is essentially your working style. If you know how you learn, you will be able to look for an environment that suits you best and you'll be able to work effectively on work teams. This will prepare you for successful employment.

3. You will be more able to target areas that need improvement. The more you know about your learning styles, the more you will be able to pinpoint the areas that are more difficult for you. That has two advantages. One, you can begin to work on difficult areas, step by step. Two, when a task comes up requiring a skill that is tough for you, you can either take special care with it or suggest someone else whose style may be better suited to it.

Your learning-style profile is one important part of self-knowledge. Next you will explore other important factors that help to define you.

HOW DO YOU EXPLORE WHO YOU ARE?

You are an absolutely unique individual. Although you may share individual characteristics with others, your combination of traits is one-of-a-kind. It could take a lifetime to learn everything there is to know about yourself, because you are constantly changing. However, you can start by exploring these facets of yourself: self-perception, interests, habits, abilities, and limitations.

Self-Perception

Having an accurate image of yourself is difficult. Unfortunately, many people do not have an accurate self-image. Feeling inadequate from time to time is normal, but a constantly negative **self-perception** can have destructive effects. Look at people you know who think that they are less intelligent, capable, or attractive than they really are. Observe how that shuts down their confidence and motivation. You do the same to yourself when you perceive yourself negatively.

> **Self-perception**
> How one views oneself, one's opinion of oneself.

Negative self-perception has a series of effects that lead to a "self-fulfilling prophecy," something that comes true because you have convinced yourself it will: First you believe that you are incapable of being or doing something, then you neglect to try, and finally, you most likely don't do or become what you had already decided was impossible.

For example, perhaps you think you can't pass a certain course. Since you feel you don't have a chance, you don't put as much effort into the work for that course. Sure enough, at the end of the semester, you don't pass. The worst part is that you may see your failure as proof of your incapability, instead of realizing that you didn't allow yourself to try. This chain of events can occur in many situations. When it happens in the workplace, people lose jobs. When it happens in personal life, people lose relationships.

Refine your self-image so that it reflects more of your true self. These strategies might help.

- Believe in yourself.   If you don't believe in yourself, others may have a harder time believing in you. Work to eliminate negative self-talk. Have faith in your abilities. When you set your goals, stick to them. Know that your mind and will are very powerful.

- Talk to other people whom you trust.   People who know you well often have a more realistic perception of you than you do of yourself.

- Take personal time.   Stress makes having perspective on your life more difficult. Take time out to clear your mind and think realistically about who you are and who you want to be.

- Look at all of the evidence.   Mistakes can loom large in your mind. Consider what you do well and what you have accomplished as carefully as you consider your stumbles.

"The greatest discovery of any generation is that human beings can alter their lives by altering their attitudes of mind."

ALBERT SCHWEITZER

Building a positive self-perception is a lifelong challenge. If you maintain a bright but realistic vision of yourself, it will take you far along the road toward achieving your goals.

Interests

Taking some time now to explore your interests will help you later when you select a career. You may be aware of many of your general interests already. For example, you can ask yourself:

- What areas of study do I like?
- What activities make me happy?
- What careers seem interesting to me?
- What kind of daily schedule do I like to keep (early riser, night owl)?
- What type of home and work environment do I prefer?

Interests play an important role in the workplace. Many people, however, do not take their interests seriously when choosing a career. Some make salary or stability their first priority. Some feel they have to take the first job that comes along. Some may not realize they can do better. Not considering what you are interested in may lead to an area of study or a job that leaves you unhappy, uninterested, or unfulfilled.

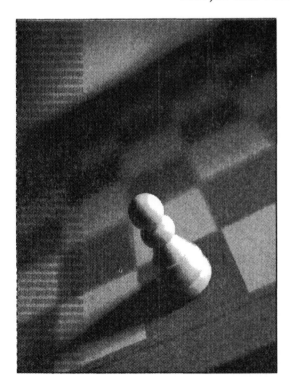

Choosing to consider your interests and happiness takes courage but brings benefits. Think about your life. You spend hours of time both attending classes and studying outside of class. You will spend at least eight hours a day, five or more days a week, up to fifty or more weeks a year as a working contributor to the world. Although your studies and work won't always make you deliriously happy, it is possible to spend your school and work time in a manner that suits you.

For instance, you may be a computer science major because everyone told you that you'd never get a job, or make money, as an artist—but art was what you really wanted to study in college. Rather than choosing one or the other, you may be able to combine them. You can continue as a computer science major and take plenty of art courses as electives. Plan on continuing your study of art as a lifelong pursuit *and* working as a computer scientist. Your various interests are not mutually exclusive; they can actually enhance each other. Creativity helps you in computer science, while computer science and engineering can help you in your other pursuits.

Here are three positive effects of focusing on your interests.

1. You will have more energy. Think about how you feel when you are looking forward to seeing a special person, participating in a favorite sports activity, or enjoying some entertainment. When you're doing

something you like, time seems to pass very quickly. You will be able to get much more done in a subject or career area that you enjoy.

2. **You will perform better.** When you were in high school, you probably got your best grades in your favorite classes and excelled in your favorite activities. That doesn't change as you get older. The more you like something, the harder you work at it—and the harder you work, the more you will improve.

3. **You will have a positive attitude.** A positive **attitude** creates a positive environment and might even make up for areas in which you lack ability or experience. Because businesses currently emphasize teamwork to such a great extent, your ability to maintain a positive attitude might mean the difference between success and failure.

> **Attitude**
> A state of mind or feeling toward something.

Habits

A preference for a particular action that you do a certain way, and often on a regular basis or at certain times, is a habit. You might have a habit of showering in the morning, eating raisins, channel surfing with the TV remote control, hitting the snooze button on your clock, talking for hours on the phone, or studying late at night. Your habits reveal a lot about you. Some habits may be considered to be good habits, and others, bad habits.

Bad habits earn that title because they can prevent you from reaching important goals. Some bad habits, such as chronic lateness, cause obvious problems. Other habits, such as renting movies three times a week, may not seem bad until you realize that you needed to spend those hours studying. People maintain bad habits because they offer immediate, enjoyable rewards, even if later effects are negative. For example, going out to eat frequently may drain your budget, but at first it seems easier than shopping for food, cooking, and washing dishes.

Good habits are those that have positive effects on your life. You often have to wait longer and work harder to see a reward for good habits, which makes them harder to maintain. If you cut out fattening foods, you wouldn't lose weight in two days. If you reduced your nights out to gain study time, your grades wouldn't improve in a week. When you strive to maintain good habits, trust that the rewards are somewhere down the road.

> "To fall into a habit is to begin to cease to be."
>
> **MIGUEL DE UNAMUNO**

Take time to evaluate your habits. Look at the positive and negative effects of each, and decide which are helpful and which harmful to you. Changing a habit can be a long process. Here are steps you can take to change a habit that has more negative effects than positive ones.

1. **Be honest about your habits.** Admitting negative or destructive habits can be hard to do. You can't change a habit until you admit that it is a habit.

2. **Recognize the habit as troublesome.** Sometimes the trouble may not seem to come directly from the habit. For example, spending every weekend skiing may seem important, but you may be overdoing it and ignoring your schoolwork.

3. Decide to change. You might realize what your bad habits are but do not yet care about their effects on your life. Until you are convinced that you will receive something positive and useful from changing, your efforts will not get you far.

4. Start today. Don't put it off until after this week, after your mid-terms, or after the semester. Each day lost is a day you haven't had the chance to benefit from a new lifestyle.

5. Change one habit at a time. Changing and breaking habits is difficult. Trying to spend more time studying, reducing TV time, increasing work hours, and saving more money all at once can bring on a fit of deprivation, sending you scurrying back to all your old habits. Easy does it.

6. Reward yourself appropriately for positive steps taken. If you earn a good grade, avoid slacking off on your studies the following week. Choose a reward that will not encourage you to stray from your target.

7. Keep it up. To have the best chance at changing a habit, be consistent for at least three weeks. Your brain needs time to become accustomed to the new habit. If you go back to the old habit during that time, you may feel like you're starting all over again.

8. Don't get too discouraged. Rarely does someone make the decision to change and do so without a setback or two. Being too hard on yourself might cause frustration that tempts you to give up and go back to the habit.

Abilities

Everyone's abilities include both strengths and limitations. And both can change. Examining both strengths and limitations is part of establishing the kind of clear vision of yourself that will help you maximize your potential.

Strengths

As you think about your preferences, your particular strengths will come to mind, because you often like best the things you can do well. Some strengths seem to be natural—things you learned to do without ever having to work too hard. Others you struggled to develop and continue to work hard to maintain. Asking yourself these questions may help you define more clearly what your abilities are:

- What have I always been able to do well?
- What have others often praised about me?
- What do I like most about myself, and why?
- What is my learning-style profile?
- What are my accomplishments—at home, at school, at work?

As with your preferences, knowing your abilities will help you find a job that makes the most of them. When your job requires you to do work you like, you are more likely to perform to the best of your ability. Keep that in mind as you explore career areas. Assessments and inventories that will help you further assess your abilities may be available at your school's career center or library. Once you know yourself, you will be more able to set appropriate goals.

Limitations

Nobody is perfect, and no one is good at everything. Everyone has limitations. However, that doesn't mean they are any easier to take. Limitations can make you feel frustrated, stressed, or angry. You may feel as though no one else has the limitations you have, or that no one else has as many.

There are three ways to deal with your limitations. The first two—ignoring them or dwelling on them—are the most common. Both are natural, but neither is wise or productive. The third way is to face them and to work to improve them while keeping the strongest focus on your abilities.

Ignoring your limitations can cause you to be unable to accomplish your goals. For example, say you are an active, holistic learner with a well-developed interpersonal intelligence. You have limitations in logical-mathematical intelligence and in linear thought. Ignoring that fact, you decide that you can make good money in computer programming, and you sign up for math and programming courses. You certainly won't fail automatically. However, if you ignore your limited ability in those courses and don't seek extra help, you may have more than a few stumbles.

Dwelling on your limitations can make you forget you have any strengths at all. This results in negative self-talk and a poor self-perception. Continuing the example, if you were to dwell on your limitations in math, you might very likely stop trying altogether.

Facing limitations and working to improve them is the best response. A healthy understanding of your limitations can help you avoid troublesome situations. In the example, you could face your limitations in math and explore other career areas that use your more well-developed abilities and intelligences. If you decided to stick with computer technology, you could study an area of the field that focuses on management and interpersonal relationships. Or you could continue to aim for a career as a programmer, taking care to seek special help in areas that give you trouble.

ENDNOTES

1. Barbara Solomon, North Carolina State University.
2. Howard Gardner, *Multiple Intelligences: The Theory in Practice* (New York: HarperCollins, 1993), 5–49.
3. Joyce Bishop, Ph.D., Psychology faculty, Golden West College, Huntington Beach, CA.

Name   Date

CHAPTER 3   Applications

KEY INTO YOUR LIFE   *Opportunities to Apply What You Learn*

EXERCISE 3.1

How Do You Learn Best?

Start by writing your scores next to each term.

LEARNING STYLES INVENTORY	PATHWAYS TO LEARNING	PERSONALITY SPECTRUM
_____ Active	_____ Bodily-Kinesthetic	_____ Organizer
_____ Reflective	_____ Visual-Spatial	_____ Adventurer
_____ Factual	_____ Verbal-Linguistic	_____ Giver
_____ Theoretical	_____ Logical-Mathematical	_____ Thinker
_____ Visual	_____ Musical	
_____ Verbal	_____ Interpersonal	
_____ Linear	_____ Intrapersonal	
_____ Holistic	_____ Naturalist	

Circle your highest preferences (largest numbers) for each assessment.

What positive experiences have you had at work and school that you can link to the strengths you circled?

_____

_____

_____

_____

What negative experiences have you had that may be related to your least developed learning styles or intelligences?

_____

_____

_____

_____

Making School More Enjoyable

List two required classes that you are not necessarily looking forward to taking. Discuss what parts of your learning-style profile may relate to your lack of enthusiasm. Name learning-styles–related study techniques that may help you get the most out of the class and enjoy it more.

CLASS	REASON FOR LACK OF ENTHUSIASM	LEARNING OR STUDY TECHNIQUES
1.		
2.		

Your Habits

You have the power to change your habits. List three habits that you want to change. Discuss the effects of each and how those effects keep you from reaching your goals.

HABIT	EFFECTS THAT PREVENT YOU FROM REACHING GOALS
1.	
2.	
3.	

Out of these three, put a star by the habit you want to change first. Write down a step you can take today toward overcoming that habit.

_____

_____

What helpful habit do you want to develop in its place? For example, if your problem habit were a failure to express yourself when you are angry, a replacement habit might be to talk calmly about situations that upset you as soon as they arise. If you have a habit of cramming for tests at the last minute, you could replace it with a regular study schedule that allows you to cover your material bit by bit over a longer period of time.

_____

_____

One way to help yourself abandon your old habit is to think about how your new habit will improve your life. List two benefits of your new habit.

1. _____

2. _____

Give yourself one month to complete your habit shift. Set a specific deadline. Keep track of your progress by indicating on a chart or calendar how well you did each day. If you avoided the old habit, write an X below the day. If you used the new one, write an N. Therefore, a day when you only avoided the old habit will have an X; a day when you did both will have both letters; a day when you did neither will be left blank. You can use the chart below or mark your own calendar. Try pairing up with another student and arranging to check up on each other's progress.

1	2	3	4	5	6	7	8	9	10	11	12	13	14	15	16
17	18	19	20	21	22	23	24	25	26	27	28	29	30	31	

Don't forget to reward yourself for your hard work. Write here what your reward will be when you feel you are on the road to a new and beneficial habit.

_____

_____

_____

_____

_____

4

Goal Setting and Time Management

Mapping Your Course

People dream of what they want out of life, but not everyone knows how to turn dreams into reality. Often dreams seem far off in time, too difficult, or even completely unreachable. You can build paths to your dreams, however, by identifying the goals you need to achieve, one by one, to arrive at your destination. When you set goals, prioritize, and manage your time effectively, you increase your ability to take those steps to achieve your long-term goals.

This chapter explains how taking specific steps toward goals can help you turn your dreams into reality. You will explore how your values relate to your goals, how to create a framework for your life's goals, how to set long-term and short-term goals, and how to set priorities. The section on time management will discuss how to translate those goals into daily, weekly, monthly, and yearly steps. Finally, you will explore the effects of procrastination.

In this chapter, you will explore answers to the following questions:

- What defines your values?

- How do you set and achieve goals?

- What are your priorities?

- How can you manage your time?

- Why is procrastination a problem?

WHAT DEFINES YOUR VALUES?

Values
Principles or qualities that one considers important, right, or good.

Your personal **values** are the beliefs that guide your choices. Examples of values include family togetherness, a good education, caring for others, working to protect the environment, and worthwhile employment. The sum total of all your values is your *value system*. You demonstrate your particular value system in the priorities you set, how you communicate with others, your family life, your educational and career choices, the material things with which you surround yourself, and your lifestyle.

Choosing and Evaluating Values

Examining the sources of your values can help you define those values, trace their origin, and question the reasons why you have adopted them. Value sources, however, aren't as important as the process of considering each value carefully to see if it makes sense to you. Some of your current values may have come from television or other media but still ring true. Some may come from what others have taught you. Some you may have constructed from your own personal experience and opinion. You make the final decision about what to value, regardless of the source.

Each individual value system is unique, even if many values come from other sources. Your value system is yours alone. Your responsibility is to make sure that your values are your own choice, and not the choice of others. Make value choices for yourself based on what feels right for you, for your life, and for those who are touched by your life.

You can be more sure of making choices that are right for you if you try to always question and evaluate your values. Before you adopt a value, ask yourself: Does it feel right? What effects might it have on my life? Am I choosing it to please someone else, or is it truly my choice? Values are a design for life, and you are the one who has to live the life you design.

Because life change and new experiences may bring a change in values, try to continue to examine values as time goes by. Periodically evaluate the effects that having each value has on your life, and see if a shift in values might suit your changing circumstances. For example, losing your sight may cause you to value your hearing intensely. The difficulty of a divorce may have a positive result: a new value of independence and individuality. After growing up in a homogeneous community, a student who meets other students from unfamiliar backgrounds may learn a new value of living in a diverse community. Your values will grow and develop as you do if you continue to think them through.

How Values Relate to Goals

Understanding your values will help you set career and personal goals, because the most ideal goals help you achieve what you value. Values of financial independence or simple living may generate goals, such as working while going to school and keeping credit card debt low, that reflect the value. If you value helping others, try to make time for volunteer work.

Goals enable you to put values into practice. When you set and pursue goals that are based on values, you demonstrate and reinforce values through taking action. The strength of those values, in turn, reinforces your goals. You will experience a much stronger drive to achieve if you build goals around what is most important to you.

HOW DO YOU SET AND ACHIEVE GOALS?

A **goal** may be something as concrete as taking Physics 2 or as abstract as working to control your temper. When you set goals and work to achieve them, you engage your intelligence, abilities, time, and energy in order to move ahead. From major life decisions to the tiniest day-to-day activities, setting goals will help you define how you want to live and what you want to achieve.

> **Goal**
> An end toward which effort is directed; an aim or intention.

Without some sort of goal or at least a sense of direction, you won't know where you are going or when you have arrived at your destination. When she was wondering about the next step at one point in her career, one of author Jill Tietjen's mentors told her about a classic interchange from Lewis Carroll's *Alice in Wonderland.*

Alice: Would you tell me, please, which way I ought to go from here?

Chesire Cat: That depends a good deal on where you want to get to.

Alice: I don't much care where . . .

Chesire Cat: Then it doesn't matter which way you go.[1]

Paul Timm, a best-selling author and teacher who is an expert in self-management, feels that focus is a key ingredient in setting and achieving goals. "Focus adds power to our actions. If somebody threw a bucket of water on you, you'd get wet, and probably get mad. But if water was shot at you through a high-pressure nozzle, you might get injured. The only difference is focus."[2] Each part of this section will explain ways to focus your energy through goal-setting. You can set and achieve goals by defining a personal mission statement, placing your goals in long-term and short-term time frames, and evaluating goals in terms of your values.

"Obstacles are what people see when they take their eyes off the goal."

NEW YORK CITY SUBWAY BULLETIN BOARD

Identifying Your "Personal Mission Statement"

Some people go through their lives without ever really thinking about what they can do or what they want to achieve. If you choose not to set goals or explore what you want out of life, you may look back on your past with a sense of emptiness. You may not know what you've done or why you did it. However, you can avoid that emptiness by periodically taking a few steps back and thinking about where you've been and where you want to be.

One helpful way to determine your general direction is to write a *personal mission statement*. Dr. Stephen Covey, author of the best-seller *The Seven Habits of Highly Effective People*, defines a mission statement as a philosophy that outlines what you want to be (character), what you want to do (contributions and achievements), and the principles by which you live. Dr. Covey compares the personal mission statement to the Constitution of the United States, a statement of principles that gives this country guidance and standards in the face of constant change.[3]

Your personal mission isn't written in stone. It should change as you move from one phase of life to the next—from single person to spouse, from parent to single parent to caregiver of an older parent. Stay flexible and reevaluate your personal mission from time to time.

Sherita Ceasar, Vice President of Digital Launch Deployment for Scientific Atlanta and a mechanical engineer profiled in this book, lives by the following words that she has hanging on the wall in her office: "I am a committed, empowering leader who will make a difference in the world."

Companies as well as nonprofit organizations need to establish standards and principles to guide their activities. Organizations have mission statements so that *every* member of that organization, from the bottom to the top, clearly understands how to direct his or her focus and what to strive for. If an organization fails to identify its mission, thousands of well-intentioned employees might focus their energies in just as many different directions, creating chaos and low productivity.

Here are mission statements from organizations that provide significant direction and focus for their employees and, in the case of nonprofit organizations, for their members and volunteers:

General Electric Rail Services: GE Rail Services is dedicated to providing customers with intelligent rail freight solutions that are based on a solid foundation of quality support.[4]

American Society of Mechanical Engineers: To promote and enhance the technical competency and professional well-being of our members, and through quality programs and activities in mechanical engineering, better enable its practitioners to contribute to the well-being of humankind.[5]

Mile High United Way: To unite and focus the community's resources to help people help themselves.[6]

Writing a mission statement is much more than an in-school exercise. It is truly for you. Thinking through your personal mission can help you begin to take charge of your life. It helps to put you in control instead of allowing circumstances and events to control you. If you frame your mission statement carefully so that it truly reflects your goals, it can be your guide in everything you do.

Placing Goals in Time

Everyone has the same 24 hours in a day, but it often doesn't feel like enough. Have you ever had a busy day flash by so quickly that it seems you accomplished nothing? Have you ever felt that way about a longer period of time, like a month or even a year? Your commitments can overwhelm you unless you decide how to use time to plan your steps toward goal achievement.

If developing a personal mission statement establishes the big picture, placing your goals within particular time frames allows you to bring individual areas of that picture into the foreground. Planning your progress step by step will help you maintain your efforts over the extended time period often needed to accomplish a goal. Goals fall into two categories: long-term and short-term.

Setting Long-Term Goals

Establish first the goals that have the largest scope, the *long-term goals* that you aim to attain over a lengthy period of time, up to a few years or more. As an engineering student, you know what long-term goals are all about. You have set yourself a goal of attending school and earning a bachelor's degree in a specific field of engineering. Becoming educated is an admirable goal that takes a good number of years to reach.

Some long-term goals are lifelong, such as a goal to continually learn more about yourself and the world around you. Others have a more definite end, such as a goal to complete a course successfully. To determine your long-term goals, think about what you want out of your professional, educational, and personal life. Here is an example of a long-term goal statement from the American Society of Mechanical Engineers:

> To foster communication and collaboration among engineers, other professions, industry, government, academia, and the general public for mutual understanding of the true role and contributions of engineers and technology to the well-being of the United States and the world community.[7]

You may establish long-term goals such as these:

- I will graduate from engineering college with the degree I most desire, having learned and understood as much as I could in a wide range of subjects.
- I will build my problem-solving skills and understanding of the opportunities available in engineering careers through work, volunteering, and internships or through relationships with professors, other professionals in my field of interest, classmates, and co-workers.

Long-term goals can change later in your life. To begin long-term goal setting, start with next year. Deciding what you want to accomplish in the next year and writing it down will help you to focus clearly on proactive actions. These goals are not like New Year's resolutions; they are based on what you really are willing to work toward and accomplish.

Your goals should reflect who you are and will require tailoring to your personality and your individual interests. Personal missions and goals are as unique as each individual. Continuing the example above, you might adopt these goals for the coming year:

- I will earn passing grades in all my classes.
- I will join two clubs and make an effort to take leadership roles in each.

Setting Short-Term Goals

When you divide your long-term goals into smaller, manageable goals that you hope to accomplish within a relatively short time, you are setting *short-term goals*. Short-term goals narrow your focus, helping you to maintain your progress toward your long-term goals. They are the steps that take you where you want to go. Say you have set the two long-term goals you just read in the previous section. To stay on track toward those goals, you may want to accomplish these short-term goals in the next six months:

- I will pass Calculus II so that I can move on to Calculus III.
- I will attend monthly meetings of the American Society of Civil Engineers (ASCE).

These same goals can be broken down into even smaller parts, such as one month.

- I will complete all of my homework for Calculus II and talk to the TA if I have any problems.
- I will get to know the current officers of ASCE.

> "Even if you're on the right track, you'll get run over if you just sit there."
>
> **WILL ROGERS**

In addition to monthly goals, you may have short-term goals that extend for a week, a day, or even a couple of hours in a given day. Take as an example the lab that you must finish by Friday (and it is now Monday morning). Your short-term goals might be the following:

- By Friday, 3 pm: Lab is complete and ready to hand in to the professor.
- By Thursday: My study group has confirmed the results and agrees upon the findings. Each person has drafted a portion of the lab and provided it to the other study group members.
- By Wednesday: The lab has been completed and the necessary data gathered.
- By Tuesday: The study group has met, agreed on responsibilities for the lab and determined when we will work in the lab to conduct our experiment.
- By tonight: I have read the lab and gotten my questions answered by the TA so that I am ready to work with my study group.

As you consider your long-term and short-term goals, notice how all of your goals are linked to one another. As Figure 4.1 shows, your long-term goals establish a context for the short-term goals. In turn, your short-term goals make the long-term goals seem clearer and more reachable. The whole system works to keep you on track.

Linking Goals With Values

If you are not sure how to start formulating your mission, look to your values to guide you. Define your mission and goals based on what is important to you.

You are probably studying engineering because you are good in math and science and want to apply those skills in a meaningful way. You value education. Your mission statement might emphasize making the world a better place through the application of technology. Your long-term goal might be to go to work for an organization that works to clean up hazardous wastes. Your short-term goal could emphasize seeking an internship to learn about the opportunities available in the industry.

You can use a classical engineering approach to looking at your future and establishing your mission and goals. In identifying your goals and expectations, weigh such factors as your desire for money, the extent of independence

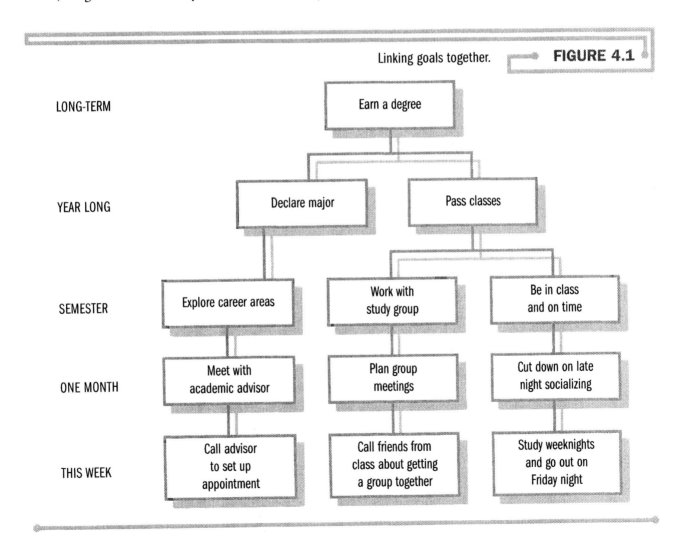

Linking goals together.   **FIGURE 4.1**

LONG-TERM
Earn a degree

YEAR LONG
Declare major | Pass classes

SEMESTER
Explore career areas | Work with study group | Be in class and on time

ONE MONTH
Meet with academic advisor | Plan group meetings | Cut down on late night socializing

THIS WEEK
Call advisor to set up appointment | Call friends from class about getting a group together | Study weeknights and go out on Friday night

that is important to you, the desired flexibility of your work schedule, and other such factors. You can even develop a matrix and apply weightings to each factor in laying out the path for your future.

Current and Personal Values Mean Appropriate Goals

When you use your values as a compass for your goals, make sure the compass is pointed in the direction of your real feelings. Watch out for the following two pitfalls that can occur.

Setting goals according to other peoples' values. Friends or family may encourage you to strive for what they think you should value, rather than what is right for you. If you follow their advice without believing in it, you may have a harder time sticking to your path. For example, someone who attends school primarily because a parent or spouse thought it was right may have less motivation and initiative than someone who made an independent decision to become a student. Look hard at what you really want, and why. Staying in tune with your own values will help you make decisions that are right for you.

Setting goals that reflect values you held in the past. What you felt yesterday may no longer apply, because life changes can alter your values. The best goals reflect what you believe today. For example, a person who has been through a near-fatal car accident may experience a dramatic increase in how he or she values time with friends and family, and a drop in how he or she values material possessions. Someone who survives a serious illness may value healthy living above all else. Keep in touch with your life's changes so your goals can reflect who you are.

Values Can Help You Identify Educational Goals

Education is a major part of your life right now. In order to define a context for your school goals, explore what you value about pursuing an education. People have many reasons for attending college. You may identify with one or more of the following possible reasons.

- I want to earn a higher salary.
- I want to build marketable skills.
- My supervisor at work says that a degree will help me move ahead in my career.
- Most of my friends are going.
- I want to be a student and learn all that I can.
- It seems like the only option for me right now.
- I am recently divorced and need to find a way to earn money.
- Everybody in my family goes to college; it's expected.
- I don't feel ready to jump into the working world yet.
- I got a scholarship.
- My friend loves his job and encouraged me to take courses in the field.

- My parent (or a spouse or partner) pushed me to go to college.
- I am studying for a specific career.
- I don't really know.

All of these answers are legitimate, even the last one. Being honest with yourself is crucial if you want to discover who you are and what life paths make sense for you. Whatever your reasons are for being in school, you are at the gateway to a journey of discovery.

It isn't easy to enroll in college, pay tuition, decide what to study, sign up for classes, gather the necessary materials, and actually get yourself to the school and into the classroom. Many people drop out at different places along the way, but somehow your reasons have been compelling enough for you to have arrived at this point. Thinking about why you value your education will help you stick with it.

Achieving goals becomes easier when you are realistic about what is possible. Setting priorities will help you make that distinction.

WHAT ARE YOUR PRIORITIES?

When you set a **priority**, you identify what's important at any given moment. *Prioritizing* helps you focus on your most important goals, even when they are difficult to achieve. If you were to pursue your goals in no particular order, you might tackle the easy ones first and leave the tough ones for later. The risk is that you might never reach for goals that are important to your success. Setting priorities helps you focus your plans on accomplishing your most important goals.

Priority
An action or intention that takes precedence in time, attention, or position.

To explore your priorities, think about your personal mission and look at your goals in the five life areas: personal, family, school/career, finances, and lifestyle. These five areas may not all be equally important to you right now. At this stage in your life, which two or three are most critical? Is one particular category more important than others? How would you prioritize your goals from most important to least important?

You are a unique individual, and your priorities are yours alone. What may be top priority to someone else may not mean that much to you, and vice versa. You can see this in Figure 4.2, which compares the priorities of two very different students. Each student's priorities are listed in order, with the first priority at the top and the lowest priority at the bottom.

First and foremost, your priorities should reflect your personal goals. In addition, they should reflect your relationships with others. For example, if you are a parent, your children's needs will probably be high on the priority list. You may decide to go back to school so you can get a better paying job. If you are in a committed relationship, you may consider the needs of your partner. You may schedule your classes so that you and your partner are home together as often as possible. Even as you consider the needs of others, though, never lose sight of your personal goals. Be true to your goals and priorities so that you can make the most of who you are.

Setting priorities moves you closer to accomplishing specific goals. It also helps you begin planning to achieve your goals within specific time frames. Being able to achieve your goals is directly linked to effective time management.

FIGURE 4.2   Two students compare priorities.

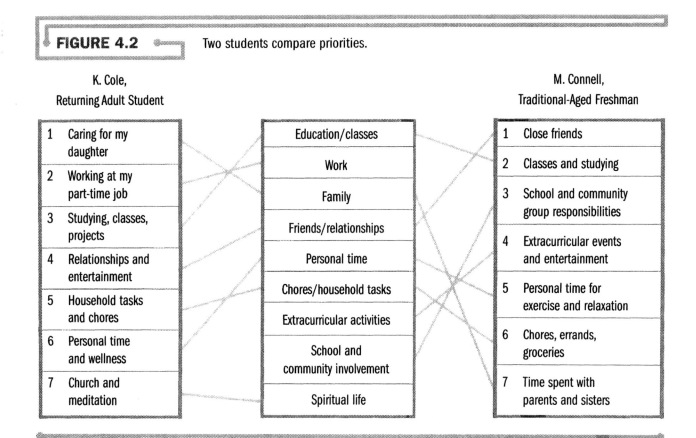

HOW CAN YOU MANAGE YOUR TIME?

Time is one of your most valuable and precious resources. Time doesn't discriminate—everyone has the same 24 hours in a day, every day. Your responsibility, and your potential for success, lie in how you use yours. You cannot manipulate or change how time passes, but you can spend it taking steps to achieve your goals. Efficient time management helps you achieve your goals in a steady, step-by-step process.

Engineering classes can be time consuming because they often include lab time or recitation time and many hours of study. As an engineering student, you can promote your own success by learning to manage your time creatively and accurately.

People have a variety of different approaches to time management. Your learning style (explained in more detail in Chapter 3) can help you identify the particular way you currently use your time. For example, factual and linear learners tend to organize activities within a framework of time. Because they stay aware of how long it takes them to do something or travel somewhere, they are usually prompt. Theoretical and holistic learners tend to miss the passing of time while they are busy thinking of something else. Because they focus on the big picture, they may neglect details such as structuring their activities within available time. They frequently lose track of time and can often be late without meaning to be.

Time management, like physical fitness, is a lifelong pursuit. No one can plan a perfect schedule or build a terrific physique and then be "done." You'll work at time management throughout your life, and it can be tiring. Your ability to manage your time will vary with your mood, your stress level, how busy you are, and other factors. You're human; don't expect perfection. Just do your best. Time management involves building a schedule and making your schedule work through lists and other strategies.

Building a Schedule

Being in control of how you manage your time is a key factor in taking responsibility for yourself and your choices. When you plan your activities with an eye toward achieving your most important goals, you are taking personal responsibility for how you live. Building a schedule helps you be responsible.

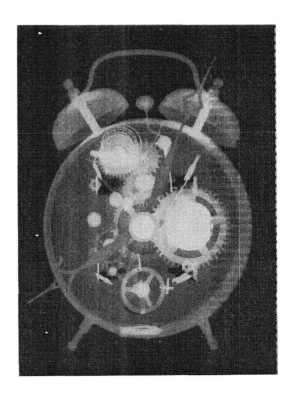

Just as a road map helps you travel from place to place, a *schedule* is a time-and-activity map that helps you get from the beginning of the day (or week, or month) to the end as smoothly as possible. A written schedule helps you gain control of your life. Schedules have two major advantages: They allocate segments of time for the fulfillment of your daily, weekly, monthly, and longer-term goals, and they serve as a concrete reminder of tasks, events, due dates, responsibilities, and deadlines. Few moments are more stressful than suddenly realizing you have forgotten to pick up a prescription, take a test, or be on duty at work. Scheduling can help you avoid events like these.

Keep a Date Book

Gather the tools of the trade: a pen or pencil and a *date book* (sometimes called a planner). Some of you already have date books and may have used them for years. Others may have had no luck with them or have never tried. Even if you don't feel you are the type of person who would use one, give it a try. A date book is indispensable for keeping track of your time. Paul Timm says, "Most time management experts agree that rule number one in a thoughtful planning process is: Use some form of a planner where you can write things down."

There are two major types of date books. The *day-at-a-glance* version devotes a page to each day. While it gives you ample space to write the day's activities, this version makes it difficult to see what's ahead. The *week-at-a-glance* book gives you a view of the week's plans, but has less room to write per day. If you write out your daily plans in detail, you might like the day-at-a-glance version. If you prefer to remind yourself of plans ahead of time, try the book that shows a week's schedule all at once. Some date books contain additional sections that allow you to note plans and goals for the year as a whole and for each month. You can also create your own sheets for yearly and monthly notations in a notepad section, if your book has one, or on plain paper that you can then insert into the book. It is also possible to do much of your schedule electronically on a personal computer using ready-made software developed for that purpose.

Another option to consider is an *electronic planner*. These are compact mini-computers that can hold a large amount of information. You can use them to schedule your days and weeks, make to-do lists, and create and store an address book. Electronic planners are powerful, convenient, and often fun. On the other hand, they certainly cost more than the paper version, and you can lose a lot of important data if something goes wrong with the computer inside. Evaluate your options and decide what you like best.

Set Weekly and Daily Goals

The most ideal time management starts with the smallest tasks and builds to bigger ones. Setting short-term goals that tie in to your long-term goals lends the following benefits:

- Increased meaning for your daily activities
- Shaping your path toward the achievement of your long-term goals
- A sense of order and progress

For college students as well as working people, the week is often the easiest unit of time to consider at one shot. Weekly goal-setting and planning allows you to keep track of day-to-day activities while giving you the larger perspective of what is coming up during the week. Take some time before each week starts to remind yourself of your long-term goals. Keeping long-term goals in mind will help you determine related short-term goals you can accomplish during the week to come.

Figure 4.3 shows parts of a daily schedule and a weekly schedule.

Link Daily and Weekly Goals With Long-Term Goals

After you evaluate what you need to accomplish in the coming year, semester, month, week, and day in order to reach your long-term goals, use your schedule to record those steps. Write down the short-term goals that will enable you to stay on track. Here is how a student might map out two different goals over a year's time.

This year:	Complete enough courses to graduate.
	Improve my physical fitness.
This semester:	Complete my calculus class with a B average or higher.
	Lose 10 pounds and exercise regularly.
This month:	Set up study-group schedule to coincide with quizzes.
	Begin walking and weight lifting.
This week:	Meet with study group; go over material for Friday's quiz.
	Go for a fitness walk three times; go to weight room twice.
Today:	Go over Chapter 3 in calculus text.
	Walk for 40 minutes.

Prioritize Goals

Prioritizing enables you to use your date book with maximum efficiency. On any given day, you will need to determine the order of completing your goals. Record your goals first, and then label them according to the order in which they

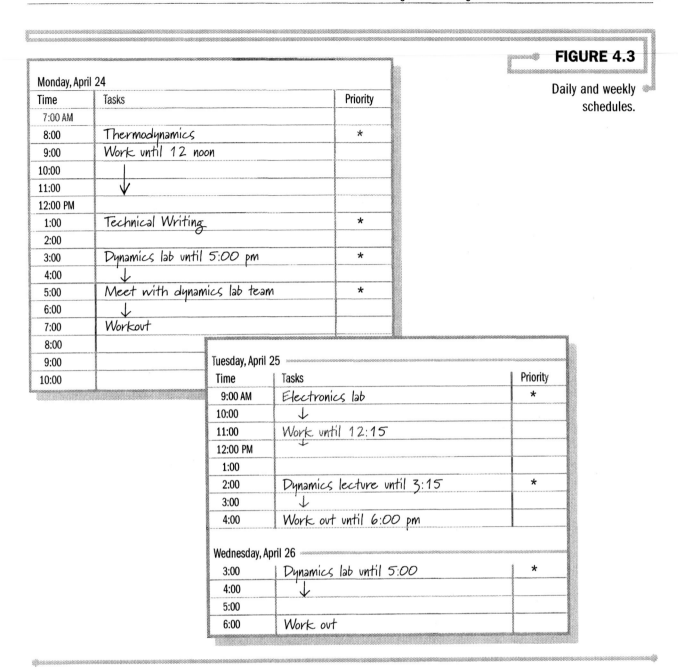

FIGURE 4.3

Daily and weekly schedules.

Monday, April 24		
Time	Tasks	Priority
7:00 AM		
8:00	Thermodynamics	*
9:00	Work until 12 noon	
10:00	↓	
11:00		
12:00 PM		
1:00	Technical Writing	*
2:00		
3:00	Dynamics lab until 5:00 pm	*
4:00	↓	
5:00	Meet with dynamics lab team	*
6:00	↓	
7:00	Workout	
8:00		
9:00		
10:00		

Tuesday, April 25		
Time	Tasks	Priority
9:00 AM	Electronics lab	*
10:00	↓	
11:00	Work until 12:15	
12:00 PM		
1:00		
2:00	Dynamics lecture until 3:15	*
3:00	↓	
4:00	Work out until 6:00 pm	

Wednesday, April 26		
3:00	Dynamics lab until 5:00	*
4:00	↓	
5:00		
6:00	Work out	

need to be completed using these categories: Priority 1, Priority 2, and Priority 3. Identify these categories using any code that makes sense to you. Some people use numbers, as above. Some use letters (A, B, C). Some write activities in different colors according to priority level. Some use symbols (*, +, -).

Priority 1 activities are the most critical or necessary to complete. They may include attending classes, taking tests, preparing labs, studying, completing homework assignments, picking up a child from day care, putting gas in the car, and paying bills.

Priority 2 activities are part of your routine. Examples include grocery shopping, working out, participating in a school organization, or cleaning. Priority 2 tasks are important but you can be more flexible in scheduling them than priority 1's.

Success in the Real World

Heather Doty

Civil Engineering Student, University of Colorado at Boulder

n high school I thought I was a busy, involved person and I liked my planner. After six years of college, I have just begun to learn what busy really is and I *love* my planner. I am pursuing three concurrent degrees: a combined BS/MS in Civil Engineering and a BA in Music. I have all the commitments of homework and research for engineering as well as the need to practice my flute on a regular basis for music. Additionally, I have held a part-time job for five years; I am active in three student societies; I help organize an annual three-day outreach program for high school students; and, believe it or not, I do have a social life.

Many of my friends cannot figure out how I do everything I do, but it all boils down to time management. I keep a detailed to-do list with different colored pens for various types of activities (i.e., homework in red, extracurricular activities in blue, work in black). This helps me to keep track of my priorities. Although homework and research are my most important commitments, I need to work to pay the rent and I need free time and outside interests to protect my sanity. My planner is in a two-page-per-week format with hourly divisions every day. I move

my to-do list along each week, and the hourly scheduling allows me to sketch out the upcoming days so I do not forget anything. Not only do I plan ahead for the things I need to do, but I set aside time for fun and relaxation as well. This allows me to fully enjoy my free time because I do not have to worry about all the things I have to do later, since these have already been scheduled. I have learned that my schoolwork usually takes me longer than I think it will, so I try to schedule twice as much time as I actually anticipate. That way, if I finish early, it is like a little bonus.

Although they are called "extracurricular," I firmly believe that my education would be incomplete without

out the student groups I participate in. I have access to guest speakers, career contacts, special services, and lots of wonderful people. I have also come to the conclusion that the more I have to do, the more efficient I am about getting it done simply because I have to think about it and plan carefully. The best advice I can give to anyone is to get involved as much as possible, but learn your limits and be able to say no when necessary.

Priority 3 activities are those you would like to do but can reschedule without much sacrifice. Examples might be a trip to the mall, a visit to a friend, a social phone call, a sports event, a movie, or a hair appointment. As much as you would like to accomplish them, you don't consider them urgent. Many people don't enter priority 3 tasks in their date books until they are sure they have time to get them done. You may want to list Priority 3 tasks separately and refer to the list when you have some extra time.

Prioritizing your activities is essential for two reasons. First, some activities are more important than others, and effective time management requires that you focus most of your energy on priority 1 items. Second, looking at all your priorities helps you plan when you can get things done. Often, it's not possible to get all your priority 1 activities done early in the day, especially if these activities involve scheduled classes or meetings. Prioritizing helps you set priority 1 items and then schedule priority 2 and 3 items around them as they fit.

"The right time is any time that one is still so lucky as to have . . . live!"

HENRY JAMES

Keep Track of Events

Your date book also enables you to schedule *events*. Rather than thinking of events as separate from goals, tie them to your long-term goals just as you would your other tasks. For example, attending a wedding in a few months contributes to your commitment to spending time with your family. Being aware of quiz dates, due dates for assignments, and meeting dates will aid your goals to achieve in school and become involved.

Note events in your date book so that you can stay aware of them ahead of time. Write them in daily, weekly, monthly, or even yearly sections, where a quick look will remind you that they are approaching. Writing them down will also help you see where they fit in the context of all your other activities. For example, if you have three big tests and a presentation all in one week, you'll want to take time in the weeks before to prepare for them all.

Following are some kinds of events worth noting in your date book:

- Due dates for homework, labs, papers, projects, presentations, and tests
- Important meetings, medical appointments, or due dates for bill payments
- Birthdays, anniversaries, social events, holidays, and other special occasions
- Benchmarks for steps toward a goal, such as due dates for sections of a project or a deadline for losing five pounds on your way to 20

Time Management Strategies

Managing time takes thought and energy. Here are some additional strategies to try.

1. Plan your schedule each week. Before each week starts, note events, goals, and priorities. Look at the map of your week to decide where to fit high-priority activities like studying and lower priority 3 items. For example, if you have a test on Thursday, you can plan study sessions on the days up until then. If you have more free time on Tuesday and Friday than on other days, you can plan workouts or priority 3 activities at those times. Looking at the whole week will help you avoid being surprised by something you had forgotten was coming up.

2. Make and use to-do lists. Use a *to-do list* to record the things you want to accomplish. If you generate a daily or weekly to-do list on a separate piece of paper, you can look at all tasks and goals at once. This will help you consider time frames and priorities. You might want to prioritize your tasks and transfer them to appropriate places in your date book. Some people create daily to-do lists right on their date book pages. You can tailor a to-do list to an important event such as exam week or an especially busy day

when you have a family gathering or a presentation to make. This kind of specific to-do list can help you prioritize and accomplish an unusually large task load.

3. Post monthly and yearly calendars at home. Keeping a calendar on the wall will help you stay aware of important events. You can purchase one, print it from your computer, or draw it yourself, month by month, on plain paper. Use a yearly or a monthly version (Figure 4.4 shows part of a monthly calendar) and keep it where you can refer to it often. If you live with roommates or family, make the calendar a group project so that you stay aware of each other's plans. Knowing each other's schedules can also help you avoid scheduling problems such as one roommate scheduling a party the night before the other roommate's exam.

4. Schedule down time. When you're wiped out from too much activity, you don't have the energy to accomplish much with your time. A little **down time** will refresh you and improve your attitude. Even half an hour a day will help. Fill the time with whatever relaxes you—having a snack, reading, watching TV, playing a game or sport, walking, writing, or just doing nothing. Make down time a priority.

5. Be flexible. Since priorities determine the map of your day, week, month, or year, any priority shift can jumble your schedule. Be ready to reschedule your tasks as your priorities change. On Monday, a homework assignment due in a week might be priority 2. By Saturday, it has become priority 1. On some days a surprise priority such as a medical emergency or a family situation may pop up and force you to cancel everything else on your schedule. On other days a class may be canceled and you will have extra time on your hands. Adjust to whatever each day brings.

Down time
Quiet time set aside for relaxation and low-key activity.

FIGURE 4.4   Monthly calendar.

APRIL

SUNDAY	MONDAY	TUESDAY	WEDNESDAY	THURSDAY	FRIDAY	SATURDAY
					1	2
3 My Birthday	4 Paper due	5 Electronics lab due	6 Dynamics test	7 ASNE meeting 5:15 pm	8	9 Habitat for Humanity 8–5
10	11 Thermo-dynamics test	12 Lab study group meeting 7 pm	13	14	15 Ice cream social 4 pm	16 Concert & dinner
17	18	19	20	21 Thermo-dynamics test	22	23
24 Easter Services at 11 am	25	26 Lab study group meeting 7 pm	27	28	29	30

No matter how well you schedule your time, you will have moments when it's hard to stay in control. Knowing how to identify and avoid procrastination and other time traps will help you get back on track.

WHY IS PROCRASTINATION A PROBLEM?

Procrastination occurs when you postpone any important task that needs to be done. People procrastinate for different reasons. Having trouble with goal setting is one reason. People may project goals too far into the future, set unrealistic goals that are too frustrating to reach, or have no goals at all. People also procrastinate because they don't believe in their ability to complete a task or don't believe in themselves in general. As natural as these tendencies are, they can also be extremely harmful. If continued over a period of time, procrastination can develop into a habit that will dominate a person's behavior. Following are some ways to face your tendency to procrastinate and *just do it!*

> **Procrastination**
> The act of putting off something that needs to be done.

Strategies to Fight Procrastination

Weigh the benefits (to you and others) of completing the task versus the effects of procrastinating. What rewards lie ahead if you get it done? What will be the effects if you continue to put it off? Which situation has better effects? Chances are you will benefit more in the long term from facing the task head-on.

Set reasonable goals. Plan your goals carefully, allowing enough time to complete them. Unreasonable goals can be so intimidating that you do nothing at all. "Pay off the credit-card bill next month" could throw you. However, "Pay off the credit-card bill in six months" might inspire you to take action.

Get started. Going from doing nothing to doing something is often the hardest part of avoiding procrastination. Once you start, you may find it easier to continue.

Break the task into smaller parts. If it seems overwhelming, look at the task in terms of its parts. How can you approach it step by step? If you can concentrate on achieving one small goal at a time, the task may become less of a burden. To start, tell yourself, "I'll read the first two pages, and then continue."

Ask for help with tasks and projects at school, work, and home. You don't always have to go it alone. For example, if you have put off an intimidating assignment, ask your professor for guidance. Other sources of assistance could be friends, classmates, study groups, and engineering societies. If you need accommodations for a disability, don't assume that others know about it. Once you identify what's holding you up, see who can help you face the task.

Don't expect perfection. No one is perfect. Most people learn by starting at the beginning and wading through plenty of mistakes and confusion. It's better to try your best than to do nothing at all.

Procrastination is natural, but it can cause you problems if you let it get the best of you. When it does happen, take some time to think about the causes. What is it about this situation that frightens you or puts you off? Answering that question can help you address what causes lie underneath the procrastination. These causes might indicate a deeper problem that needs to be solved.

ENDNOTES

1. Lewis Carroll, *Alice's Adventures in Wonderland* (New York: Tom Doherty Associates, 1988), 50.

2. Paul R. Timm, Ph.D., *Successful Self-Management: A Psychologically Sound Approach to Personal Effectiveness* (Los Altos, CA.: Crisp Publications, 1987), 22–41.

3. Stephen Covey, *The Seven Habits of Highly Effective People* (New York: Simon & Schuster, 1989), 70–144, 309–318.

4. General Electric Company, "Our Mission," <http://www.ge.com/capital/rail/Europe/uk/brochure_mission.html> (3 April 2000).

5. ASME International, "About ASME," <http://www.asme.org/about/> (3 April 2000).

6. Mile High United Way, "Learn About Us," <http://www.unitedwaydenver.org/learnus/learnus.htm> (3 April 2000).

7. ASME International, "ASME Goals," <http://www.asme.org/asme/4.html> (5 May 2000).

Name _____ Date _____

CHAPTER 4 Applications

Opportunities to Apply What You Learn **KEY INTO YOUR LIFE**

Your Values

EXERCISE **4.1**

Begin to explore your values by rating the following values on a scale from 1 to 4, 1 being most important to you, and 4 being least important. If you have values that you don't see in the chart, list them in the blank spaces and rate them.

VALUE	RATING	VALUE	RATING
Knowing yourself		Mental health	
Physical health		Fitness and exercise	
Spending time with your family		Having an intimate relationship	
Helping others		Education	
Being well paid		Being employed	
Being liked by others		Free time/vacations	
Enjoying entertainment		Time to yourself	
Spiritual/religious life		Reading	
Keeping up with the news		Staying organized	
Being financially stable		Close friendships	
Creative/artistic pursuits		Self-improvement	
Lifelong learning		Facing your fears	

Considering your priorities, write your top five values here:

1. _____
2. _____
3. _____
4. _____
5. _____

EXERCISE | 4.2 | ## Why Are You Here?

Why did you decide to enroll in school? Do any of the reasons listed in the chapter fit you? Do you have other reasons all your own? Many people have more than one answer. Write up to five here.

_____

_____

_____

_____

_____

Take a moment to think about your reasons. Which reasons are most important to you? Why? Prioritize your reasons above by writing 1 next to the most important, 2 next to the second most important, etc.

How do you feel about your reasons? You may be proud of some. On the other hand, you may not feel comfortable with others. Which do you like or dislike and why?

_____

_____

_____

_____

_____

EXERCISE | 4.3 | ## Short-Term Scheduling

Take a close look at your schedule for the coming month, including events, important dates, and steps toward goals. On the calendar layout on page 80, fill in the name of the month and appropriate numbers for the days. Then record what you hope to accomplish, including the following:

- Due dates for papers, projects, and presentations
- Test dates
- Important meetings, medical appointments, and due dates for bill payments

- Birthdays, anniversaries, and other special occasions
- Steps toward long-term goals

This kind of chart will help you see the big picture of your month. To stay on target from day to day, check these dates against the entries in your date book and make sure that they are indicated there as well.

To-Do Lists

EXERCISE   4.4

Make a to-do list for what you have to do tomorrow. Include all tasks—priority 1, 2, and 3—and events.

TOMORROW'S DATE: _____

1. _____
2. _____
3. _____
4. _____
5. _____
6. _____
7. _____
8. _____
9. _____
10. _____

Use a coding system of your choice to indicate priority levels of both tasks and events. Place a check by the items that are important enough to note in your date book. Use this list to make your schedule for tomorrow in the date book, making a separate list for priority 3 items. At the end of the day, evaluate this system. Did the to-do list help you? How did it make a difference? If you liked it, use this exercise as a guide for using to-do lists regularly.

MONTH CHART

5

Critical and Creative Thinking

Tapping the Power of Your Mind

Your mind's powers show in everything you do, from the smallest chores (comparing prices on cereals at the grocery store) to the most complex situations (figuring out how to earn money after being laid off). Your mind is able to process, store, and create with the facts and ideas it encounters. Critical and creative thinking are what enable those skills to come alive. Understanding how your mind works is the first step toward critical thinking. When you have that understanding, you can perform the essential critical thinking task: asking important questions about ideas and information. This chapter will show you both the mind's basic actions and the thinking processes that use those actions. You will explore what it means to be an open-minded critical and creative thinker, able to ask and understand questions that promote your success in college, career, and life.

In this chapter, you will explore answers to the following questions:

* What is critical thinking?

* How does your mind work?

* How does critical thinking help you solve problems and make decisions?

* Why shift your perspective?

* Why plan strategically?

* How can you develop your creativity?

WHAT IS CRITICAL THINKING?

Critical thinking is thinking that goes beyond the basic recall of information. If the word *critical* sounds negative to you, consider that the dictionary defines its meaning as "indispensable" and "important." Critical thinking is important thinking that involves asking questions. This is called "essential questioning." Using critical thinking, you question established ideas, create new ideas, turn information into tools to solve problems and make decisions, and take the long-term view as well as the day-to-day view.

A critical thinker asks as many kinds of questions as possible. The following are examples of possible questions about a given piece of information: *Where did it come from? What could explain it? In what ways is it true or false, and what examples could prove or disprove it? How do I feel about it, and why? How is this information similar to or different from what I already know? Is it good or bad? What causes led to it, and what effects does it have?* Critical thinkers also try to transform information into something they can use. They ask themselves whether the information can help them solve a problem, make a decision, create something new, or anticipate the future. Such questions help the critical thinker learn, grow, and create.

Not thinking critically means not asking questions about information or ideas. A person who does not think critically tends to accept or reject information or ideas without examining them. Table 5.1 compares how a critical thinker and a non-critical thinker might respond to particular situations.

Asking questions (the focus of the table), considering without judgment as many responses as you can, and choosing responses that are as complete and accurate as possible are some primary ingredients that make up the skill of critical thinking. You must be willing to ask questions.

Critical Thinking Is a Skill

Anyone can develop the ability to think critically. Critical thinking is a skill that can be taught to students at all different levels of ability. One of the most crucial components of this skill is learning information. For instance, part of the skill of critical thinking is comparing new information with what you

Not thinking critically vs. thinking critically.   **TABLE 5.1**

YOUR ROLE	SITUATION	NON-QUESTIONING RESPONSE	QUESTIONING RESPONSE
Student	Professor is lecturing on the development of atomic weapons.	You assume that everything your professor tells you is true.	You consider what the professor says; you write down questions about issues you want to clarify; initiate discussion with the professor or other classmates.
Parent	Teacher discovers your child lying about something at school.	You're mad at your child and believe the teacher, or you think the teacher is lying.	You ask both teacher and child about what happened, and you compare their answers, evaluating who you think is telling the truth; you discuss the concepts of lying/honesty with your child.
Spouse/ Partner	Your partner feels that he or she no longer has quality time with you.	You think he or she is wrong and defend yourself.	You ask how long your partner has felt this way; you ask your partner and yourself why this is happening; you explore how you can improve the situation.
Employee	You are angry at your supervisor.	You ignore or avoid your supervisor.	You are willing to discuss the situation.
Neighbor	People different from you move in next door.	You ignore or avoid them; you think their way of living is strange.	You introduce yourself; you offer to help if they need it; you respectfully explore what's different about them.
Citizen	You encounter a homeless person.	You avoid the person and the issue.	You examine whether the community has a responsibility to the homeless, and if you find that it does, you explore how to fulfill that responsibility.
Consumer	You want to buy a car.	You decide on a brand-new car and don't think through how you will handle the payments.	You consider the different effects of buying a new car vs. buying a used car; you examine your money situation to see what kind of payment you can handle each month.

already know. Your prior knowledge provides a framework within which to ask questions about and evaluate a new piece of information. Without a solid base of knowledge, critical thinking is harder to achieve. For example, thinking critically about the statement "Shakespeare's character King Richard III is like an early version of Adolf Hitler" is impossible without basic knowledge of World War II and Shakespeare's play *Richard III*.

The skill of critical thinking focuses on generating questions about statements and information. To examine potential critical-thinking responses in more depth, explore the different questions that a critical thinker may have about one particular statement.

A Critical-Thinking Response to a Statement

Consider the following statement of opinion: *"My obstacles are keeping me from succeeding in school. Other people make it through school because they don't have to deal with the obstacles that I have."*

Non-questioning thinkers may accept an opinion such as this as an absolute truth, believing that their obstacles will hinder their success. As a result, on the road to achieving their goals, they may lose motivation to overcome those obstacles. In contrast, critical thinkers would take the opportunity to examine the opinion through a series of questions. Here are some examples of questions one student might ask.

> *"What exactly are my obstacles?* Examples of my obstacles are a heavy work schedule, single parenting, being in debt, and returning to school after ten years out."

> *"Who has problems that are different from mine?* I do have one friend who is going through problems worse than mine, and she's getting by. I also know another guy who doesn't have too much to deal with that I can tell, and he's struggling just like I am."

> *"Who has problems similar to mine?* Well, if I consider my obstacles specifically, I might be saying that single parents and returning adult students will all have trouble in school. That is not necessarily true. People in all kinds of situations may still become successful."

> *"Why do I think this?* Maybe I am scared of returning to school and adjusting to a new environment. Maybe I am afraid to challenge myself, which I haven't done in a long time. Whatever the cause, the effect is that I feel bad about myself and don't work to the best of my abilities, and that can hurt both me and my family who depends on me."

> *"What is an example of someone who has had success despite having to overcome obstacles?* What about Oseola McCarty, the cleaning woman who saved money all her life and raised $150,000 to create a scholarship at the University of Southern Mississippi? She didn't have what anyone would call advantages, such as a high-paying job or a college education."

> *"What conclusion can I draw from my questions?* From thinking about my friend and about Oseola McCarty, I would say that people can successfully overcome their obstacles by working hard, focusing on their abilities, and concentrating on their goals."

> *"How do I evaluate the effects of this statement?* I think it's harmful. When we say that obstacles equal difficulty, we can damage our desire to try to overcome those obstacles. When we say that successful people don't have obstacles, we might overlook that some very successful people have to deal with hidden disadvantages such as learning disabilities or abusive families."

The Value of Critical Thinking

Critical thinking has many important advantages. Following are some of the positive effects, or benefits, of putting energy into critical thinking.

You will increase your ability to perform thinking processes that help you reach your goals. Critical thinking is a learned skill, just like shooting a basketball or using a new software program on the computer. As with any other skill, the more you use it, the better you become. The more you ask questions, the better you think. The better you think, the more effective you will be when completing schoolwork, managing your personal life, and performing on the job.

You can produce knowledge, rather than just reproduce it. The interaction of new information with what you already know creates new knowledge. The usefulness of such knowledge can be judged by how you apply it to new situations. For example, it won't mean much for a civil engineering student just to design a truss on an exam unless she can make judgments about the appropriate truss configuration on her summer job.

You can be a valuable employee. You certainly won't be a failure in the workplace if you follow directions. However, you will be even more valuable if you think critically and ask strategic questions about how to make improvements, large or small. Questions could range from "Is there a better way to deliver phone messages?" to "What new product can we innovate to stay competitive with new technology?" An employee who shows the initiative to think critically will be more likely to earn responsibility and promotions.

You can increase your creativity. You cannot be a successful critical thinker without being able to come up with new and different questions to ask, possibilities to explore, and ideas to try. Creativity is essential in producing what is new. Being creative generally improves your outlook, your sense of humor, and your perspective as you cope with problems. Later in this chapter, you will look at ways to awaken and increase your natural creativity.

In engineering, you will exercise critical thinking on a constant basis. As you strive to solve problems and make new products to meet the needs of society, you will continually employ the scientific method:

- Determine the problem.
- Identify possible solutions (so-called alternatives).
- Gather the data (costs, equipment needs, time) associated with each alternative.
- Evaluate the alternatives, considering all of the data.
- Pick the best alternative as the solution.

Solving problems in engineering requires that you ask critical questions. Questions help you decide where to go for information, what analyses to perform, what tests to conduct. The more you improve your thinking through practice and experience, the better you will be at coming up with questions about the world, or your area of study, and finding methods for answering those questions.

In the next section, you will read about the seven basic actions your mind performs when asking important questions. These actions are the basic blocks you will use to build the critical-thinking processes you will explore later in the chapter.

"We do not live to think but, on the contrary, we think in order that we may succeed in surviving."

JOSE ORTEGA Y GASSETT

HOW DOES YOUR MIND WORK?

Critical thinking depends on a thorough understanding of the workings of the mind. Your mind has some basic moves, or actions, that it uses to understand relationships among ideas and concepts. Sometimes it uses one action by itself, but most often it uses two or more in combination.

Brain research has advanced rapidly in the past decade. The discovery of new technologies and new uses for old technologies have led to discoveries about memory, moods, and the learning process. For instance, researchers have used brain-scanning technology to show how parts of the brain respond to depression. This in turn has helped other researchers develop medications that work on a cellular level in brain tissue to effectively treat depression.

Researchers also use brain-scanning techniques to study a person's brain during learning. For instance, brain scans have shown that while learning to play the piano, the brain recruited areas of the cerebral cortex to help in the learning process. Once the learning was complete and the function became automatic, like riding a bicycle, those borrowed areas went back to their normal functions. This helps to explain how the mind works to learn new information.

Mind Actions: The Thinktrix

You can identify your mind's actions using a system called the Thinktrix, originally conceived by educators Frank Lyman, Arlene Mindus, and Charlene Lopez[1] and developed by numerous other instructors. They studied how students think and named seven mind actions that are the basic building blocks of thought. These actions are not new to you, although some of their names may be. They represent the ways in which you think all the time.

Through exploring these actions, you can go beyond just thinking and learn *how* you think. This will help you take charge of your own thinking. The more you know about how your mind works, the more control you will have over thinking processes such as problem solving, decision making, creating, and strategic planning.

Following are explanations of each of the mind actions. Each explanation names the action, defines it, and explains it with examples. As you read, write your own examples in the blank spaces provided. Each action is also represented by an picture or *icon* that helps you visualize and remember it.

Recall: Facts, sequence, and description. This is the simplest action. When you **recall** you describe facts, objects, or events, or put them into sequence.

The icon: A string tied around a finger is a familiar image of recall or remembering.

Examples:

* Naming the steps of a geometry proof, in order
* Remembering the valence electron arrangement for calcium, chloride, and nitrogen

Your example: Recall some important events this month.

_____

_____

Similarity: Analogy, likeness, comparison. This action examines what is **similar** about one or more things. You might compare situations, ideas, people, stories, events, or objects.

The icon: Two alike objects, in this case triangles, indicate similarity.

Examples:

⬗ Comparing notes with another student to see what facts and ideas you have both considered important

⬗ Analyzing the arguments you've had with your partner this month and seeing how they all seem to be about the same problem

Your example: Tell what is similar about the numbers 2, 4, 8, 12, and 16.

_____

_____

Difference: Distinction, contrast, comparison. This action examines what is **different** about two or more situations, ideas, people, stories, events, or objects, contrasting them with one another.

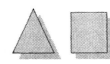

The icon: Two differing objects, in this case a triangle and a square, indicate difference.

Examples:

⬗ Seeing how the engines differ in race cars and production automobiles
⬗ Contrasting a weekday where you work half day and go to school half day with a weekday when you attend class and then have the rest of the day to study

Your example: Explain what it is about one course that makes it easier to learn the material than in another course.

_____

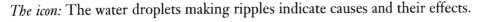

Cause and effect: Reasons, consequences, prediction. Using this action, you look at what has **caused** a fact, situation, or event, and/or what **effects,** or consequences, come from it. In other words, you examine both what led up to something and what will follow because of it.

The icon: The water droplets making ripples indicate causes and their effects.

Examples:

⬗ You see how staying up late at night causes you to oversleep, which has the effect of your being late to class. This causes you to miss some of the material, which has the further effect of your having problems on the test.
⬗ When you pay your phone and utility bills on time, you create effects such as a better credit rating, uninterrupted service, and a better relationship with your service providers.

Your example: Name probable causes for the solar cycle's effects on satellite communications.

_____

_____

Example to Idea: Inductive reasoning, generalization, classification, conceptualization. From one or more **examples** (facts or events), you develop a general **idea** or ideas. Grouping facts or events into patterns may allow you to make a general statement about several of them at once. Classifying a fact or event helps you build knowledge. This mind action moves from the specific to the general.

The icon: The arrow and "Ex" pointing to a light bulb on their right indicate how an example or examples lead to the idea (the light bulb, lit up).

Examples:

* Molecules such as hydrochloric acid, sulfuric acid, and acetic acid all easily lose a proton (examples). Therefore, all molecules with a certain structure are acids (idea).
* You see a movie and you decide it is mostly about pride.

Your example: You drop a pencil and it falls down; you see an apple fall from a tree. Name the idea.

_____

_____

Idea to Example: Deductive reasoning, categorization, substantiation, proof. In a reverse of the previous action, you take an **idea** or ideas and think of **examples** (events or facts) that support or prove that idea. This mind action moves from the general to the specific.

The icon: In a reverse of the previous icon, this one starts with the light bulb and has an arrow pointing to "Ex." This indicates that you start with the idea, the lit bulb, and then branch into the example or examples that support the idea.

Examples:

* When you write a paper, you start with a thesis statement, which communicates the central idea: "Engineers make the world work." Then you gather examples to back up that idea: Electricity forms the foundation of modern technological society and is made possible through the efforts of electrical, mechanical, civil, chemical, and environmental engineers. Clean water has raised the average life expectancy significantly since the start of the twentieth century because of civil and environmental engineers. Transportation (including air, water, and land) allows us ease of access around the entire globe and is due to aerospace, mechanical, and civil engineers.
* You talk to your professor about changing your major, giving examples that support your idea: You have worked in the field you want to change

to, you have fulfilled some of the requirements for that major already, and you are unhappy with your current course of study.

Your example: Air pressure changes with altitude changes (idea). Name an example you might experience that supports this idea.

Evaluation: Analysis, value, judgment, rating. Here you **judge** whether something is useful or not useful, important or unimportant, good or bad, or right or wrong by identifying and weighing its positive and negative effects (pros and cons). Be sure to consider the specific situation at hand (a cold drink might be good on the beach in August, not so good in the snowdrifts in January). With the facts you have gathered, you determine the value of something in terms of both predicted effects and your own needs. Cause and effect analysis always accompanies evaluation.

The icon: A set of scales out of balance indicates how you weigh positive and negative effects to arrive at an evaluation.

Examples:

- You decide to try taking later classes for a semester. You schedule classes in the afternoons and spend your nights on the job. You find that instead of getting up early to use the morning time, you tend to sleep in and then get up not too long before you have to be at school. From those harmful effects, you evaluate that it doesn't work for you. You decide to schedule earlier classes next time.
- Someone offers you a chance to cheat on a test. You evaluate the potential effects if you are caught. You also evaluate the long-term effects on you of not actually learning the material. You decide that it isn't worth your while to participate in the plan to cheat.

Your example: Evaluate your mode of transportation to school.

You may want to use a *mnemonic device*—a memory tool—to remember the seven mind actions. You can make a sentence of words that each start with a mind action's first letter. Here's an example: "Really Smart Dogs Cook Eggs In Enchiladas" (the first letter of each word stands for one of the mind actions).

How Mind Actions Build Thinking Processes

The seven mind actions are the fundamental building blocks that your mind uses every day. Note that you will rarely use them one at a time in a step-by-step process, as they are presented here. You will usually combine them, overlap them, and repeat them more than once, using different actions for different situations. For example, when you want to say something nice to the members of your study group, you might consider past comments that had an effect *similar* to what you want to accomplish. When a test question asks you to explain where the basic tenets of engineering ethics were violated, you might list *examples* that show your *idea* of engineering ethics lapses.

When you combine mind actions in working toward a specific goal, you are performing a thinking process. The next few sections will explore some of the most important critical-thinking processes: solving problems, making decisions, shifting your perspective, and planning strategically. Each thinking process helps you succeed by directing your critical thinking toward the achievement of your goals. Figure 5.3, appearing later in the chapter, shows all of the mind actions and thinking processes together and reminds you that the mind actions form the core of the thinking processes.

HOW DOES CRITICAL THINKING HELP YOU SOLVE PROBLEMS AND MAKE DECISIONS?

Problem solving and decision making are probably the two most crucial and common thinking processes used in engineering. Each one requires various mind actions. They overlap somewhat, because every problem that needs solving requires you to make a decision. Each process will be considered separately here. You will notice similarities in the steps involved in each.

Although both of these processes have multiple steps, you will not always have to work your way through each step. As you become more comfortable with solving problems and making decisions, your mind will automatically click through the steps you need whenever you encounter a problem or decision. Also, you will become more adept at evaluating which problems and decisions need serious consideration and which can be taken care of more quickly and simply.

Problem Solving

Problem solving starts with asking questions. Asking questions is the fundamental step in inquiry. Problems to solve can range from very small, such as how to avoid losing your car keys, to very large, such as how to design transportation systems to enhance sustainable development. A solution may come quickly or require many months of analysis and testing. How quickly a solution is reached may depend on two things: (1) the urgency of the problem and (2) the complexity of the problem. However, if you use the steps of the following problem-solving process to think critically, you have the best chance of coming up with a favorable solution.

You can apply this problem-solving plan to any situation or issue that you want to resolve. Using the following steps will maximize the number of possible solutions you generate and will allow you to explore each one as fully as possible.

1. State the problem clearly. What are the facts? *Recall* the details of the situation. Be sure to name the problem specifically, without focusing on causes or effects. For example, a student might state this as a problem:

> "I have always thought that one man of tolerable abilities may work great changes, and accomplish great affairs among mankind, if he first forms a good plan."
>
> BENJAMIN FRANKLIN

"I'm not understanding the class material." However, that may be a *cause* of the actual problem at hand: "I'm failing my calculus quizzes."

2. Analyze the problem. What is happening that, in your opinion, needs to change? In other words, what *effects* does the situation have that cause a problem for you? What *causes* these effects? Look at the *causes and effects* that surround the problem. Continuing the example of the calculus student, if some effects of failing quizzes include poor grades in the course and disinterest, some causes may include poor study habits, poor test-taking skills, lack of sleep, or not understanding the material. Look at the urgency of the problem: "What is the consequence of my failing these quizzes?" "Will I fail the class?" "Will this adversely impact my plan to study biomedical engineering?"

3. Brainstorm possible solutions. **Brainstorming** helps loosen up your thinking and creativity. When you brainstorm ideas and answers without judging them, you remove a major barrier to creativity: fear that your answer will be wrong. That is the beauty of brainstorming—there are no right or wrong answers. This gives you the freedom to let your mind come up with all kinds of possibilities, some useful, some useless. Again, ask yourself: "What are possible causes of my failing grade?" Now, think up every cause you can, focusing just on causes, not effects or solutions.

Brainstorming
The spontaneous, rapid generation of ideas or solutions, undertaken by a group or an individual, often as part of a problem-solving process.

4. Explore each solution. Why might your solution work? Why not? Might a solution work partially, or in a particular situation? *Evaluate* ahead of time the pros and cons, or the positive and negative effects, of each plan. Create a chain of causes and effects in your head, as far into the future as you can, to see where you think this solution would lead. The calculus student might consider the effects of improved study habits, more sleep, tutoring, or dropping the class.

5. Choose and implement the solution you decide is best. Decide how you will put your solution to work. Then, implement your solution. The calculus student could decide on a combination of improved study habits and tutoring.

6. Evaluate the solution that you acted upon, looking at its *effects.* What are the positive and negative effects of what you did? In terms of your needs, was it a useful solution or not? Could the solution use any adjustments or changes that would make it more useful? Would you do the same again or not? Evaluating his choice, the calculus student may decide that the effects are good but that his fatigue still causes a problem.

7. Continue to refine the solution. Problem solving is always a process. You may have opportunities to apply the same solution over and over again. Evaluate repeatedly, making changes that you decide make the solution better. The calculus student may decide to continue to study more regu-

larly but, after a few weeks of tutoring, could opt to trade in the tutoring time for extra studying on his own. He may decide to take what he has learned from the tutor so far and apply it to his increased study efforts.

Using this process will enable you to solve personal, educational, and workplace problems in a thoughtful, comprehensive way. Figure 5.1 is a "think link" that demonstrates a way to visualize the flow of problem solving. Figure 5.2 contains a sample of how one person used this plan to solve a problem.

Decision Making

Decisions are choices. Although every problem-solving process involves making a decision (when you decide which solution to try), not all decisions involve solving problems. Making a choice, or decision, requires thinking critically through all of the possible choices and evaluating which will work best for you and for the situation. Decisions large and small come up daily, hourly, even every few minutes. Do you call your landlord when the heat isn't coming on? Do you drop a course? Should you stay in a relationship? Can you work part time without interfering with school?

FIGURE 5.1

Problem-solving plan.

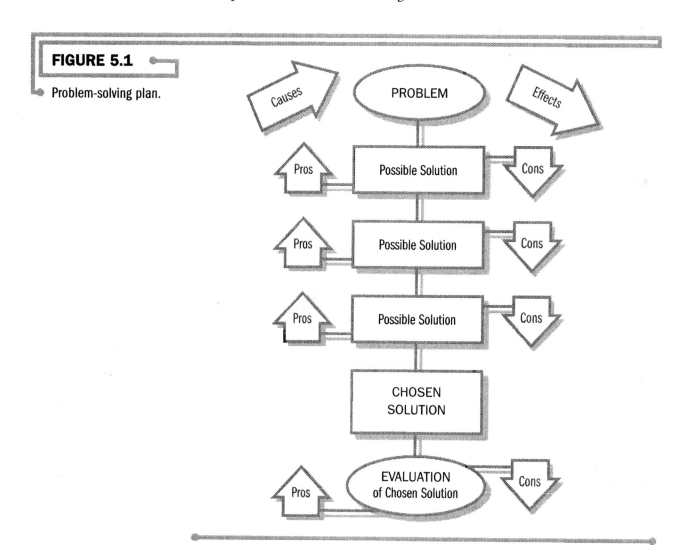

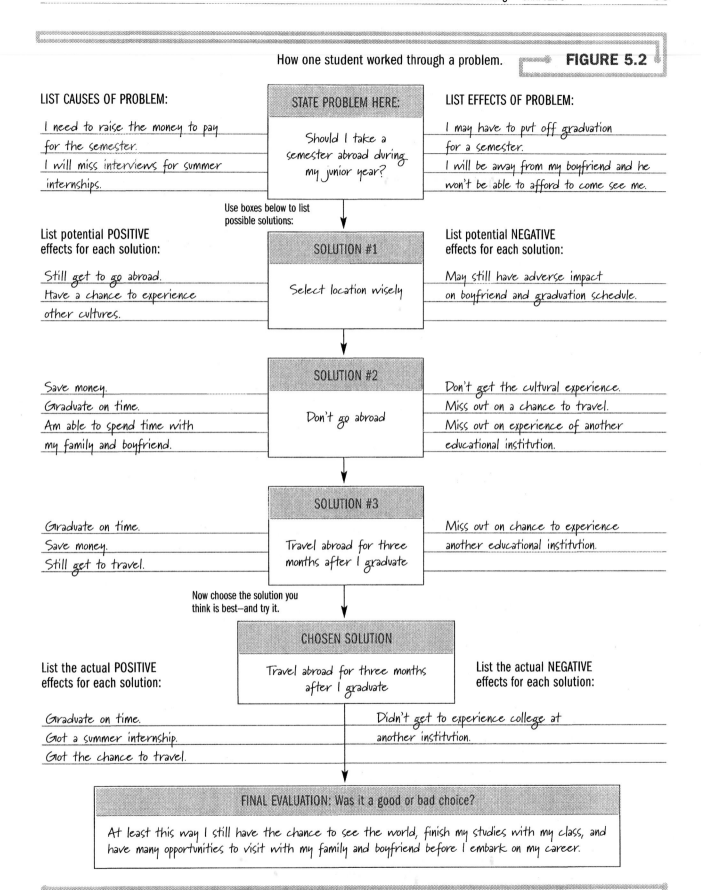

How one student worked through a problem.   **FIGURE 5.2**

LIST CAUSES OF PROBLEM:

I need to raise the money to pay
for the semester.
I will miss interviews for summer
internships.

STATE PROBLEM HERE:

Should I take a
semester abroad during
my junior year?

LIST EFFECTS OF PROBLEM:

I may have to put off graduation
for a semester.
I will be away from my boyfriend and he
won't be able to afford to come see me.

Use boxes below to list
possible solutions:

**List potential POSITIVE
effects for each solution:**

Still get to go abroad.
Have a chance to experience
other cultures.

SOLUTION #1

Select location wisely

**List potential NEGATIVE
effects for each solution:**

May still have adverse impact
on boyfriend and graduation schedule.

SOLUTION #2

Don't go abroad

Save money.
Graduate on time.
Am able to spend time with
my family and boyfriend.

Don't get the cultural experience.
Miss out on a chance to travel.
Miss out on experience of another
educational institution.

SOLUTION #3

Travel abroad for three
months after I graduate

Graduate on time.
Save money.
Still get to travel.

Miss out on chance to experience
another educational institution.

Now choose the solution you
think is best—and try it.

CHOSEN SOLUTION

Travel abroad for three months
after I graduate

**List the actual POSITIVE
effects for each solution:**

Graduate on time.
Got a summer internship.
Got the chance to travel.

**List the actual NEGATIVE
effects for each solution:**

Didn't get to experience college at
another institution.

FINAL EVALUATION: Was it a good or bad choice?

At least this way I still have the chance to see the world, finish my studies with my class, and
have many opportunities to visit with my family and boyfriend before I embark on my career.

Source: Adapted from a heuristic developed by Frank T. Lyman Jr., Ph.D., University of Maryland, 1983.

Before you begin the decision-making process, evaluate the level of the decision you are making. Do you have to decide what to have for lunch (usually a minor issue), or whether to quit a good job (often a major life change)? Some decisions are little, day-to-day considerations that you can take care of quickly on your own. Others require thoughtful evaluation, time, and perhaps the input of others you trust. The following is a list of steps to take in order to think critically through a decision.

1. **Decide on a goal.** Why is this decision necessary? In other words, what result do you want from this decision, and what is its value? Considering the *effects* you want can help you formulate your goal. For example, say a student currently attends a small private college. Her goal is to become a marine engineer. The school has a good program, but her financial situation has changed and has made this school too expensive for her.

2. **Establish needs.** *Recall* the needs of everyone (or everything) involved in the decision. The student needs a school with a full marine engineering program; she and her parents need to cut costs (her father changed jobs and her family cannot continue to afford the current school); she needs to be able to transfer credits.

3. **Name, investigate, and evaluate available options.** Brainstorm possible choices, and then look at the facts surrounding each. *Evaluate* the good and bad effects of each possibility. Weigh these effects and judge which is the best course of action. Here are some possibilities that the student in the college example might consider:

   * Continue at the current college. **Positive effects:** I wouldn't have to adjust to a new place or to new people. I could continue my course work as planned. **Negative effects:** I would have to find a way to finance most of my tuition and costs on my own, whether through loans, grants, or work. I'm not sure I could find time to work as much as I would need to, and I don't think I would qualify for as much aid as I now need.

   * Transfer to the state college. **Positive effects:** I could reconnect with people there that I know from high school. Tuition and room costs would be cheaper than at my current school. I could transfer credits. **Negative effects:** I would still have to work some or find minimal financial aid. The marine engineering program is small and not very strong.

   * Transfer to the community college. **Positive effects:** They have many of the courses I need as prerequisites for the marine engineering curriculum. The school is twenty minutes from my parents' house, so I could live at home and avoid paying housing costs. Credits will transfer. The tuition is extremely reasonable. **Negative effects:** I don't know anyone there. I would be less independent. The school doesn't offer a bachelor's degree.

4. **Decide on a plan of action and pursue it.** Make a choice based on your evaluation, and act on your choice. In this case the student might decide to go to the community college for two years and then transfer back to a four-year school to earn a bachelor's degree in marine engi-

neering. Although she might lose some independence and contact with friends, the positive effects are money saved, opportunity to spend time on studies rather than working to earn tuition money, and the availability of classes that match the marine engineering program requirements.

5. **Evaluate the result.** Was it useful? Not useful? Some of both? Weigh the positive and negative effects. The student may find with her transfer decision that it can be hard living at home, although her parents are adjusting to her independence and she is trying to respect their concerns as parents. Fewer social distractions result in her getting more work done. The financial situation is much more favorable. All things considered, she evaluates that this decision was a good one.

Making important decisions can take time. Think through your decision thoroughly, considering your own ideas as well as those of others you trust, but don't hesitate to act once you have your plan. You cannot benefit from your decision until you act upon it and follow through.

WHY SHIFT YOUR PERSPECTIVE?

Seeing the world only from your **perspective,** or point of view, is inflexible, limiting, and frustrating to both you and others. You probably know how hard it can be to relate to someone who cannot understand where you are coming from—a co-worker who's annoyed that you leave early on Thursdays for physical therapy, a parent who doesn't see why you can't take a study break to visit, a friend who can't understand why you would date someone of a different race. Seeing beyond one's own perspective can be difficult, especially when life problems and fatigue take their toll.

> **Perspective**
> A mental point of view or outlook, based on a cluster of related assumptions, incorporating values, interests, and knowledge.

On the other hand, when you shift your own perspective to consider someone else's, you open the lines of communication. Trying to understand what other people feel, need, and want makes you more responsive to them. They then may feel respected by you and respond to you in turn. For example, if you want to add or drop a course and your advisor says it's impossible, not waiting to hear you out, the last thing you may feel like doing is pouring your heart out. On the other hand, if your advisor asks to hear your point of view, you may sense that your needs are respected. Because the advisor wants to hear from you, you feel valued; that may encourage you to respond, or even to change your mind.

Every time you shift your perspective, you can also learn something new. There are worlds of knowledge and possibilities outside your individual existence. You may learn that what you eat daily may be against someone else's religious beliefs. You may discover people who don't fit a stereotype. Shifting your perspective is invaluable in helping you find fresh solutions. In engineering, a fresh view is extremely helpful in enhancing creativity.

Asking questions like these will help you maintain flexibility and openness in your perspective.

- What is similar and different about this person/belief/method and me/my beliefs/my methods?

- What positive and negative effects come from this different way of being/acting/believing? Even if this perspective seems to have negative effects for me, how might it have positive effects for others, and therefore have value?

- What can I learn from this different perspective? Is there anything I could adopt for my own life—something that would help me improve who I am or what I do? Is there anything I wouldn't do myself but that I can still respect and learn from?

Shifting your perspective is at the heart of all successful communication. Each person is unique. Even within a group of people similar to yourself, there will be a great variety of perspectives. Whether you see that each world community has different customs or you understand that a friend can't go out on weekends because he spends that time with his mother, you have increased your wealth of knowledge and shown respect to others. Being able to shift perspective and communicate more effectively may mean the difference between success and failure in today's diverse working world.

WHY PLAN STRATEGICALLY?

Strategy
A plan of action designed to accomplish a specific goal.

If you've ever played a game of chess or checkers, participated in a wrestling or martial arts match, or had a drawn-out argument, you have had experience with **strategy.** In those situations and many others, you continually have to think through and anticipate the moves the other person is about to make. Often you have to think about several possible options that person could put into play, and you consider what you would counter with should any of those options occur. In competitive situations, you try to outguess the other person with your choices. The extent of your strategic skills can determine whether you will win or lose.

Strategy is the plan of action, the method, the "how" behind any goal you want to achieve. Specifically, strategic planning means having a plan for the future, whether you are looking at the next week, month, year, ten years, or fifty years. It means exploring the future positive and negative effects of the choices you make and actions you take today. You are planning strategically right now just by being in school. You made a decision that the requirements of attending college are a legitimate price to pay for the skills, contacts, and opportunities that will help you in the future. As a student, you are challenging yourself to achieve. You are learning to set goals for the future, analyze what you want in the long term, and prepare for the job market to increase your career options. Being strategic with yourself means challenging yourself as you would challenge a competitor, urging yourself to work toward your goals with conviction and determination.

What are the benefits, or positive effects, of strategic planning?

Strategy is an essential skill in the workplace. A software company that wants to develop a successful e-commerce product needs to examine the anticipated trends in electronic business. A lawyer needs to think through every aspect of the client's case, anticipating how to respond to any allegation the opposing side will bring up in court. Strategic planning creates a vision into the future that allows the planner to anticipate all kinds of possibilities and, most importantly, to be prepared for them.

Strategic planning powers your short-term and long-term goal setting. Once you have set goals, you need to plan the steps that will help you achieve those goals over time. For example, a strategic thinker who wants to own a home in five years' time might drive a used car and cut out luxuries, put a small amount of money every month into a mutual fund, and keep an eye on current mortgage percentages. In class, a strategic planner will think critically about the material presented, knowing that information is most useful later on if it is clearly understood.

Strategic planning helps you keep up with technology. As technology develops more and more quickly, some jobs become obsolete and others are created. It's possible to spend years in school training for a career area that will be drying up when you are ready to enter the work force. When you plan strategically, you can take a broader range of courses or choose a major and career that are expanding. This will make it more likely that your skills will be in demand when you graduate.

Effective critical thinking is essential to strategic planning. If you aim for a certain goal, what steps will move you toward that goal? What positive effects do you anticipate these steps will have? How do you evaluate your past experiences with planning and goal setting? What can you learn from similar or different previous experiences in order to take different steps today? Critical thinking runs like a thread through all of your strategic planning.

Here are some tips for becoming a strategic planner:

Develop an appropriate plan. What approach will best achieve your goal? What steps toward your goal will you need to take one year, five years, ten years, or twenty years from now?

Anticipate all possible outcomes of your actions. What are the positive and negative effects (pros and cons) that may occur?

Ask the question "how?" How do you achieve your goals? How do you learn effectively and remember what you learn? How do you develop a productive idea on the job? How do you distinguish yourself at school and at work?

Use human resources. Talk to people who are where you want to be, whether professionally or personally. What caused them to get there? Ask them what they believe are the important steps to take, degrees to have, training to experience, knowledge to gain.

In each thinking process seen in Figure 5.3, you use your creativity to come up with ideas, examples, causes, effects, and solutions. You have a capacity to be creative, whether you are aware of it or not. Open up your mind and awaken your creativity. It will enhance your critical thinking and make life more enjoyable.

FIGURE 5.3

The wheel of thinking.

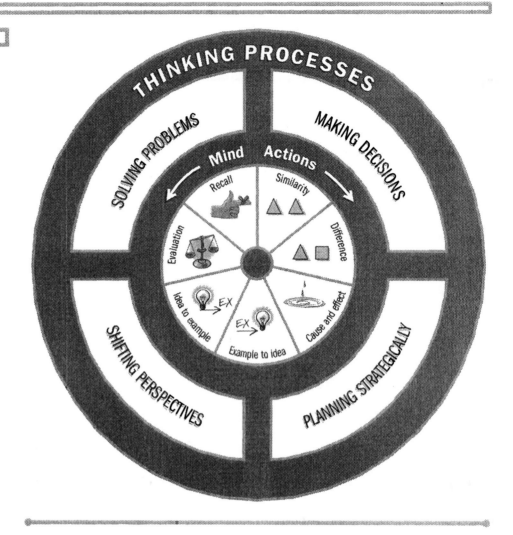

HOW CAN YOU DEVELOP YOUR CREATIVITY IN ENGINEERING?

Creativity
The ability to produce something new through imaginative skill.

Everyone is creative. Although the word "creative" may seem to refer primarily to artists, writers, musicians, and others who work in fields whose creative aspects are in the forefront, **creativity** comes in many other forms. It is the power to create anything, whether it is a solution, idea, approach, tangible product, work of art, system, program—anything at all. To help you expand your concept of creativity, here are some examples of day-to-day creative thinking:

- Figuring out an alternative plan when your study partner unexpectedly cancels on you
- Planning how to coordinate your work and class schedules
- Talking through a problem with a professor, and finding a way to understand each other

Creative innovations introduced by all kinds of people continually expand and change the world. Here are some that have had an impact:

- Sir Isaac Newton, who in contemplating the fall of an apple discovered the law of gravity, a fundamental building block of physics.
- Art Fry and Spencer Silver invented the Post-It™ note in 1980, enabling people to save paper and protect documents by using removable notes.
- Henry Ford introduced the assembly-line method of automobile construction, making cars cheap enough to be available to the average citizen.
- Galileo transformed a telescope into a microscope, allowing inspection of lifeforms and particles invisible to the naked eye and significantly advancing medicine.
- Admiral Grace Murray Hopper developed the first computer compiler, enabling us to program computers in languages such as English, French, and German instead of using mathematical symbols.

Even though these particular innovations had wide-ranging effects, the characteristics of these influential innovators can be found in all people who exercise their creative capabilities.

Characteristics of Creative People in Engineering

Creative people think in fresh new ways that improve the world and increase productivity, consistently responding to change with new ideas. Roger van Oech, an expert on creativity, highlights this kind of flexibility.[2] "I've found that the hallmark of creative people is their mental flexibility," he says. "Like race-car drivers who shift in and out of different gears depending on where they are on the course, creative people are able to shift in and out of different types of thinking depending on the needs of the situation at hand. . . . they're doggedly persistent in striving to reach their goals."

Creative people combine ideas and information in ways that form completely new solutions, ideas, processes, uses, or products. Children often can tap into this creative freedom more easily than adults. Whether they make up a new game, wear a bowl as a hat, or create forts from chairs and blankets, they create naturally without worrying that their ideas might not be "right." See if you can retrieve some of that creative freedom from your childhood when you use creative techniques.

Creativity in engineering leads to many new products and services. Although many such products and services occur accidentally, through what is called *serendipity*, it takes creativity to realize that the accidental discovery or result is valuable. Serendipity is common in engineering. It is defined as "the gift of finding valuable or agreeable things not sought for."[3]

Examples of creativity in science and technology include:

Velcro by George de Mestral. De Mestral accidentally discovered Velcro when he returned home from a walk and noticed a cocklebur stuck tightly to the fabric of his clothing. On close examination, he noticed how well the bur's hooks held onto the fabric and used that concept to develop Velcro.

Penicillin by Sir Alexander Fleming. In 1928, Fleming worked in a bacteriology laboratory preparing influenza cultures in petri dishes. He noticed a clear area in the dish where a piece of mold had fallen. He isolated the mold and found it belonged to the genus *Penicillium*. It was just chance that this mold fell in his petri dish, but he was observant enough to notice and question it. He is quoted as saying, "The story of penicillin has a certain romance to it and helps to illustrate the amount of chance or fortune, or fate, or destiny, call it what you will, in anybody's career."[4]

These types of discoveries are not dependent on accidents alone: creativity is needed to think of new ways to do things and to make sense of what you observe. Louis Pasteur expressed it this way: "In the fields of observation, chance favors only the prepared mind."

Innovation comes in many forms. For the engineers who created the Mars landing team, *Pathfinder* and *Sojourner*, a scarcity of time and money were the creative factors. Older tried-and-true methods had to be thrown out as too expensive, and new innovations were developed.

Brainstorming Toward a Creative Answer

You are brainstorming when you approach a problem by letting your mind free-associate and come up with as many possible ideas, examples, or solutions as you can, without immediately evaluating them as good or bad. Brainstorming is also referred to as "divergent thinking"—you start with the issue or problem and then let your mind diverge, or go in as many different directions as it wants, in search of ideas or solutions. You can use brainstorming for problem solving, decision making, preparing to write an essay, or any time you want to open your mind to new possibilities. Here are some rules for successful brainstorming:[5]

Don't evaluate or criticize an idea right away. Write down your ideas so that you remember them. Evaluate later, after you have had a chance to think about them. Try to avoid criticizing other people's ideas as well. Students often become stifled when their ideas are evaluated during brainstorming. Notice your tendency to say that things are right or wrong, black or white, and instead let things be gray—unknown.

Focus on quantity; don't worry about quality until later. Try to generate as many ideas or examples as you can. The more thoughts you generate, the better the chance that one may be useful. Brainstorming works well in groups. Group members can become inspired by, and make creative use of, one another's ideas.

Let yourself consider wild and wacky ideas. Trust yourself to fall off the edge of tradition when you explore your creativity. Sometimes the craziest ideas end up being the most productive, positive, workable solutions around.

Remember, creativity can be developed if you have the desire and patience. Be gentle with yourself in the process. Most people are harsher with themselves and their ideas than is necessary. Your creative expression will become more free with practice.

Success in the Real World

William Wulf

President, National Academy of Engineering

I am tempted to say that I have been very "lucky" in my career—I have been a professor at two great universities, founder of a successful software company, a government official, and now the President of the National Academy of Engineering—an organization whose members are among the most accomplished engineers in the U.S. But "lucky" isn't quite the right word, and a simple list of positions doesn't capture why it's been so much fun.

"Lucky" isn't the right word because my engineering education prepared me to succeed in a variety of situations. But let me start at the beginning. My father and uncles were engineers, and so in some ways I was programmed to be one too. But frankly, for my first two years of college I was an indifferent student. But then, in the summer between my sophomore and junior years, I got *hooked* on engineering.

In fact, I can remember the exact moment I got hooked on engineering. I had a summer job as a draftsman at the Teletype Corporation in Chicago. The group I was working for was designing, among other things, a device that read punched plastic cards and dialed a phone number encoded on them. For several weeks the team had wrestled with the problem of the cards occasionally binding as they went through the reader.

Although it wasn't my job, one day I looked at the reader and saw both the root of the problem and a simple, inexpensive, *elegant* fix for it. I mocked up the solution with a bit of cardboard and drafting tape and it worked beautifully. My boss let me have a metal version built by the shop, and it too worked perfectly.

As the result of that insight I enjoyed the praise of my fellow and much senior engineers, I got a bit of a bonus in my paycheck, and I still get a kick from thinking about the thousands of people that used that dialer trouble free. However, what hooked me on engineering was the creative thrill of seeing the *elegant* solution to the problem.

I learned that day that the dull stereotype of engineers is simply bogus! Engineering is, in fact, one of the most creative professions I know. Looking back on my career, I have been fortunate to have had many of those creative moments—and I remember each one vividly!

Some of those insights have led to products, others led to research results, others resolved man-

agement and organizational issues, and still others led to government programs and policies. But whatever the application, it was my engineering education and its wonderful combination of objective analysis, openness to new ideas, and the sense of taste for the elegant design that prepared me. And in each case, seeing the creative, effective, elegant solution was *fun!*

Under the picture on my Web site I say that I live in mortal fear that someday they will find out that they pay me to have so much fun! Fortunately, they haven't figured it out yet.

Success in the Real World

Barrett Caldwell

Associate Professor, Department of Industrial Engineering, University of Wisconsin-Madison

Kids normally remember Christmas Eve because of the presents, but I think my most memorable Christmas Eve as a child was December 24, 1968. My parents let me stay up late to watch the Apollo 8 broadcast from the orbit of the moon. That night, I decided I wanted to be an astronaut, to work for NASA, and to do space flight. As I got older, I thought that the best way for me to fulfill these dreams was to be an engineer. I went to a high school that emphasized liberal arts, but I liked engineering, because engineers solved problems, they didn't just talk about them. Engineering isn't just about doing well in math or physics, or thinking in equations (even though I did all of those). I learned that engineering was a way of looking at the world, and not being satisfied with things as they were. Engineers were not just creative in the sense that they created things, but that good engineering meant being able to solve a problem by looking at it from different perspectives and trying possible solutions creatively until you found something that worked.

I went to graduate school in social psychology, which confuses a lot of people. Part of my reasoning was that I had been interested in psychology since high school, but I also wanted to learn more about the people for whom I would be designing spacecraft, and how to improve their lives in space. In the end, I think it was a better combination than I could have imagined. My graduate work taught me a lot about the importance of context, and how the social and organizational and cultural context affects the range of what engineers can—and should—accomplish. For better or for worse, people look to engineers to improve the quality of our lives—more comfortable, more productive, safer, more interesting lives.

Most people don't really know what engineering is like, or what engineers really do on a day-to-day basis. Quite honestly, I don't think most people understand the pleasures of being an engineer. They don't want to spend their time thinking about and solving problems; they don't enjoy the creativity of applying tools and scientific principles to do something that hasn't been done before. But an

engineer needs to understand that a large part of the problem-solving process is recognizing which problems to solve, and how to design and create systems, not just isolated components. These are probably some of the most important things an engineer can learn about the importance of his contributions to the world. I like saying that I'm a systems engineer: I want to make sure that things work together. I want to know that people can use tools efficiently, to do the tasks that need to be done. I want to help them communicate and coordinate better, and share knowledge with each other better. I even get to work with NASA, and help people go to Mars someday.

Creativity and Critical Thinking

Critical thinking and creativity work hand in hand. Critical thinking is inherently creative, because it requires you to take the information you are given and come up with original ideas or solutions to problems. For example, you can brainstorm to generate possible causes of a certain effect. If the effect you are examining is fatigue in afternoon classes, you might come up with possible causes such as lack of sleep, too much morning caffeine, a diet heavy in carbohydrates, a natural tendency toward low energy at that time, or a professor who doesn't inspire you. Through your consideration of causes and solutions, you have been thinking both creatively and critically.

Creative thinkers and critical thinkers have similar characteristics—both consider new perspectives, ask questions, don't hesitate to question accepted assumptions and traditions, and persist in the search for answers. Only through thinking critically and creatively can you freely question, brainstorm, and evaluate in order to come up with the most fitting ideas, solutions, decisions, arguments, and plans.

You use critical-thinking mind actions throughout everything you do in school and in your daily life.

> "The world of reality has its limits. The world of imagination is boundless."
>
> **JEAN JACQUES ROUSSEAU**

ENDNOTES

1. Frant T. Lyman, Jr., Ph.D., "Think-Pair-Share, Thinktrix, Thinklinks, and Weird Facts: An Interactive System for Cooperative Thinking," in *Enhancing Thinking Through Cooperative Learning*, ed. Neil Davidson and Toni Worsham (New York: Teachers College Press, 1992), 169–181.

2. Roger von Oech, *A Kick in the Seat of the Pants* (New York: Harper & Row Publishers, 1986) 5–21.

3. R. M. Roberts, *Serendipity: Accidental Discoveries in Science* (New York: John Wiley & Sons, 1989), ix.

4. Ibid., 164.

5. Dennis Coon, *Introduction to Psychology: Exploration and Application*, 6th ed. (St. Paul: West Publishing Company, 1992), 295.

CHAPTER 5   Applications

KEY INTO YOUR LIFE   *Opportunities to Apply What You Learn*

EXERCISE   5.1   Brainstorming on the Idea Wheel

Your creative mind can solve problems when you least expect it. Many people report having sudden ideas while exercising, driving, or showering; upon waking; or even when dreaming. When the pressure is off, the mind is often more free to roam through uncharted territory and bring back treasures.

To make the most of this mind-float, grab ideas right when they surface. If you don't, they roll back into your subconscious as if on a wheel. Since you never know how big the wheel is, you can't be sure when that particular idea will roll to the top again. That's one of the reasons why writers carry notebooks—they need to grab thoughts when they come to the top of the wheel.

Name a problem, large or small, to which you haven't yet found a satisfactory solution. Do a brainstorm without the time limit. Be on the lookout for ideas, causes, effects, solutions, or similar problems coming to the top of your wheel. The minute it happens, grab this book and write your idea next to the problem. Take a look at your ideas later and see how your creative mind may have pointed you toward some original and workable solutions. You may want to keep a book by your bed to catch ideas that pop up before, during, or after sleep.

Problem: _____

Ideas: _____

_____

_____

_____

_____

_____

_____

_____

_____

Group Problem Solving

As a class, brainstorm a list of problems in your lives. Write the problems on the board or on a large piece of paper attached to an easel. Include any problems you feel comfortable discussing with others. Such problems may be in the categories of schoolwork, relationships, job stress, discrimination, parenting, housing, procrastination, and others. Divide into groups of two to four with each group choosing or being assigned one problem to work on. Use the empty problem-solving flowchart on the next page to fill in your work.

1. Identify the problem. As a group, state your problem specifically, without causes ("I'm not attending all of my classes" is better than "lack of motivation"). Then, look at the causes and effects that surround it. Record the effects that the problem has on your lives. List what causes the problem. Remember to look for "hidden" causes (you may perceive that traffic makes you late to school, but the hidden cause might be that you don't get up early enough to have adequate commuting time in the morning).

2. Brainstorm possible solutions. Determine the most likely causes of the problem; from those causes, derive possible solutions. Record all the ideas that group members offer. After 10 minutes or so, each group member should choose one possible solution to explore independently.

3. Explore each solution. In thinking independently through the assigned solution, each group member should (a) weigh the positive and negative effects, (b) consider similar problems, (c) determine whether the problem requires a different strategy from other problems like it, and (d) describe how the solution affects the causes of the problem. Evaluate your assigned solution. Is it a good one? Will it work?

4. Choose your top solution(s). Come together again as a group. Take turns sharing your observations and recommendations, then take a vote: Which solution is the best? You may have a tie or may combine two different solutions. Either way is fine. Different solutions suit different people and situations. Although it's not always possible to reach agreement, try to find the solution that works for most of the group.

5. Evaluate the solution you decide is best. When you decide on your top solution or solutions, discuss what would happen if you went through with it. What do you predict would be the positive and negative effects of this solution? Would it turn out to be a truly good solution for everyone?

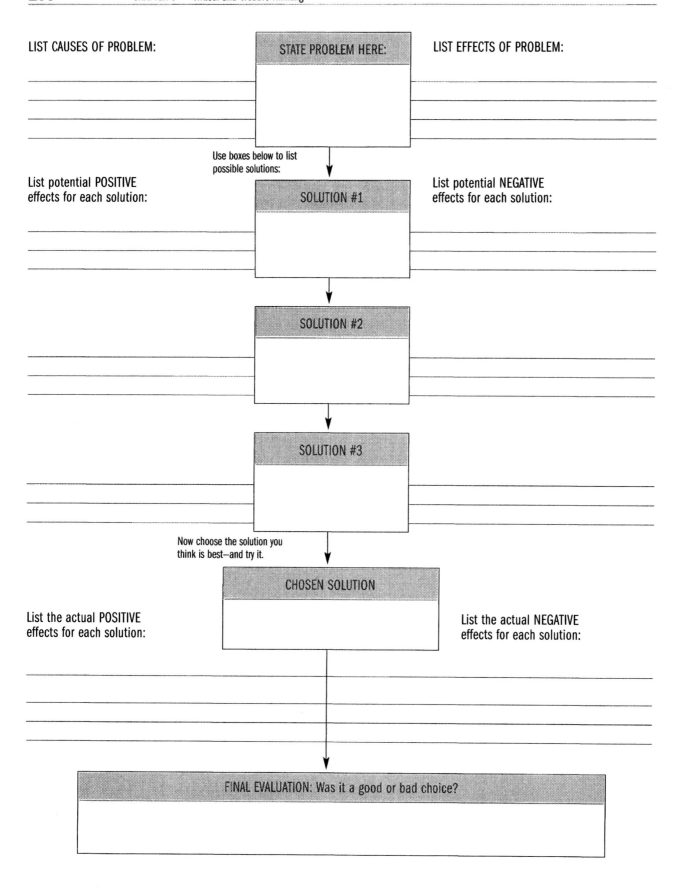

LIST CAUSES OF PROBLEM:

STATE PROBLEM HERE:

LIST EFFECTS OF PROBLEM:

Use boxes below to list possible solutions:

List potential POSITIVE effects for each solution:

SOLUTION #1

List potential NEGATIVE effects for each solution:

SOLUTION #2

SOLUTION #3

Now choose the solution you think is best—and try it.

CHOSEN SOLUTION

List the actual POSITIVE effects for each solution:

List the actual NEGATIVE effects for each solution:

FINAL EVALUATION: Was it a good or bad choice?

6

Reading and Study Skills

The society you live in revolves around the written word. As the Condition of Education 1996 report states, "In recent years, literacy has been viewed as one of the fundamental tools necessary for successful economic performance in industrialized societies. Literacy is no longer defined merely as a basic threshold of reading ability, but rather as the ability to understand and use printed information in daily activities, at home, at work, and in the community."[1]

If you read thoroughly and understand what you read, and if you achieve your study goals, you can improve your capacity to learn and understand. In this chapter you will learn how you can overcome barriers to successful reading and benefit from defining a purpose each time you read. You will explore the annotation study technique and see how critical reading can help you maximize your understanding of any text. Finally, the chapter will provide an overview of library and Web resources.

In this chapter, you will explore answers to the following questions:

- What are some challenges of reading?
- What kind of reading will you do in engineering?
- Why define your purpose for reading?
- What are reading strategies for engineering courses?
- How can you read critically?
- What resources do your library and the Web offer?

WHAT ARE SOME CHALLENGES OF READING?

Whatever your skill level, you will encounter challenges that make reading more difficult, such as an excess of reading assignments, difficult texts, distractions, a lack of speed and comprehension, and vocabulary. Following are some ideas about how to meet these challenges. Note that if you have a reading disability, if English is not your primary language, or if you have limited reading skills, you may need additional support and guidance. Most colleges provide services for students through a reading center or tutoring program. Take the initiative to seek help if you need it. Many accomplished learners have benefited from help in specific areas.

Dealing With Reading Overload

Reading overload is part of almost every college experience. On a typical day, you may be faced with reading assignments that look like this:

- An entire textbook chapter containing formulas, equations, and moles (Chemistry)
- An original research study on mathematical modeling (Calculus)
- Part of Chapter 3, Chapter 4, and a lab (Introduction to Engineering Computing)

Reading all this and more leaves little time for anything else unless you read selectively and skillfully. You can't control your reading load. You can, however, improve your reading skills. The material in this chapter will present techniques that can help you read and study as efficiently as you possibly can, while still having time left over for other things.

Working Through Difficult Engineering Texts

While many engineering textbooks are useful teaching tools, some can be poorly written and organized. Students using texts that aren't well written may blame themselves for the difficulty they're experiencing. Because texts are often written with the purpose of challenging the intellect, even well-written and organized texts may be difficult and dense to read. Generally, the further you advance in your education, the more complex your required reading is likely to be. For example, your thermodynamics professor may assign a chapter on steam cycles of coal-fired power plants. When is the last time you heard the terms *super-saturated steam* and *condenser* in normal conversation? You may feel at times as though you are reading a foreign language as you encounter new concepts, words, and terms.

Assignments can also be difficult when the required reading is from primary sources rather than from texts. *Primary sources* are original documents rather than another writer's interpretation of these documents. They include:

- historical documents
- works of literature (novels, poems, and plays)
- scientific studies, including lab reports and accounts of experiments
- technical journal articles

The academic writing found in journal articles and scientific studies is different from other kinds of writing. Some academic writers assume that readers understand sophisticated concepts. They may not define basic terms, provide background information, or supply a wealth of examples to support their ideas. As a result, concepts may be difficult to understand.

Making your way through poorly written or difficult reading material is hard work that can be accomplished through focus, motivation, commitment, and skill. The following strategies may help.

Approach your reading assignments head-on. Be careful not to prejudge them as impossible or boring before you even start to read.

Accept the fact that some texts may require some extra work and concentration. Set a goal to make your way through the material and learn, whatever it takes.

When a primary source discusses difficult concepts that it does not explain, put in some extra work to define such concepts on your own. Ask your professor or other students for help. Consult reference materials in that particular subject area, other class materials, dictionaries, and encyclopedias. You may want to make this process more convenient by creating your own mini-library at home. Collect reference materials that you use often, such as a dictionary, a thesaurus, a writer's style handbook, and maybe an atlas or computer manual. You may also benefit from owning reference materials in your particular areas of study. "If you find yourself going to the library to look up the same reference again and again, consider purchasing that book for your personal or office library," advises library expert Sherwood Harris.[2]

"No barrier of the senses shuts me out from the sweet, gracious discourse of my book friends. They talk to me without embarrassment or awkwardness."

HELEN KELLER

Success in the Real World

De Ann Redlin

Aerospace Engineering Student, University of Colorado at Boulder

Preparing for an exam should generally be a review of the material that has been covered in class. Use the textbook and class notes in tandem to reinforce the knowledge you have already gained. Whatever you do, do not just memorize the material. Memorization may not be the best way to engrain complicated concepts and equations into your mind. You should be able to use your knowledge of the subject to understand concepts and derive equations.

The only way to get the knowledge that you need to pass an exam is to go to class every scheduled day. Reading the text beforehand gives you an idea of what you need clarified during the lecture by the professor. To get more out of reading the textbook, take notes while doing so; even short notes in the margin are helpful when you look back at the book in search of an obscure concept.

During class, you should take notes on what the professor is describing. Take these notes in your own words and not those of the professor, so that you can feel confident that you understand what is being discussed. Writing the material down is sometimes the best way to gain an understanding of it—especially if you are a visual learner. If you are unable to describe the concept in your own words, then you probably need to ask a question. Your questions or someone else's questions can help you and everyone in the class to better understand the concepts.

More important, you must be confident in your knowledge of the material. This only comes from learning throughout the course of time and not during the long night before the exam.

Look for order and meaning in seemingly chaotic reading materials. Finding order within chaos is an important skill, not just in the mastery of reading, but also in life. This skill can give you power by helping you "read" (think through) work dilemmas, personal problems, and educational situations.

Managing Distractions

With so much happening around you, it's often hard to keep your mind on what you are reading. Distractions take many forms. Some are external: the sound of a telephone, a friend who sits next to you at lunch and wants to talk, your roommate watching television. Other distractions come from within. As you try to study, you may be thinking about your financial situation, an argument you had with a friend or partner, a lab due in Circuits, or a site on the Internet that you want to visit.

Identify the Distraction and Choose a Suitable Action

Pinpoint what's distracting you before you decide what kind of action to take. If the distraction is *external* and *out of your control*, such as construction outside your building or a noisy group in the library, try to move away from it. If the distraction is *external* but *within your control*, such as the television, telephone, or children, take action. For example, if the television or phone is a problem, turn off the TV or unplug the phone for an hour.

If the distraction is *internal*, there are a few strategies to try that may help you clear your mind. You may want to take a break from your studying and tend to one of the issues that you are worrying about. Physical exercise may relax you and bring back your ability to focus. For some people, studying while listening to music helps to quiet a busy mind. For others, silence may do the trick. If you need silence to read or study and cannot find a truly quiet environment, consider purchasing sound-muffling headphones or even earplugs.

Find the Best Place and Time to Read

Any reader needs focus and discipline in order to concentrate on the material. Finding a place and time that minimize outside distractions will help you achieve that focus. Here are some suggestions:

Read alone unless you are working with a study group. Roommates, family members, friends, or others who are not in study mode may interrupt your concentration. If you prefer to read alone, establish a relatively interruption-proof place and time, such as an out-of-the-way spot at the library or an after-class hour in an empty classroom. If you study at home and live with other people, you may want to place a "Quiet" sign on the door. Some students benefit from reading with one or more other students. If this helps you, plan to schedule a group reading meeting where you read sections of the assigned material and then break to discuss them.

Find a comfortable location. Many students study in the library on a hard-backed chair. Others prefer a library easy chair, a chair in their room, or even the floor. The spot you choose should be comfortable enough for hours of reading, but not so comfortable that you fall asleep. Also, make sure that you have adequate lighting and aren't too hot or too cold.

Choose a regular reading place and time. Choose a spot or two you like and return to it often. Also, choose a time when your mind is alert and focused. Some students prefer to read just before or after the class for which the reading is assigned. Eventually, you will associate preferred places and times with focused reading.

If it helps you concentrate, listen to soothing background music. The right music can drown out background noises and relax you. However, the wrong music can make it impossible to concentrate; for some people, silence is better. Experiment to learn what you prefer; if music helps, stick with the type that works best. A personal headset makes listening possible no matter where you are.

Turn off the television. For most people, reading and TV don't mix.

Success in the Real World

Ramon Pizarro

Patent Attorney and Counselor at Law

From my perspective, obtaining an education in engineering has been at the heart of what many would consider as a non-traditional application of my training as an engineer. I was born in 1961 in the town of Rancagua, Chile. At that time it seemed quite clear to my family that we would live our lives in Chile, just like many other generations of Pizarros and Galleguillos (my mother's maiden name). However, 1970 marked the beginning of radical political change in Chile. These changes forced my parents into making the decision to leave Chile to seek a more stable place in which to raise their five children. The search led my family to the United States.

While my father is a metallurgical engineer (M.S. Metallurgical Engineering, Colorado School of Mines, 1967), and my family understood the importance of English as an essential second language, my transition into the English-speaking world and American culture was not smooth. The transition would start with the building of an English vocabulary, which would lead into the obstacle of having to extinguish the Spanish accent from my English.

At the age of 10 I knew that I wanted to be a mechanical engineer. I think that my decision was motivated by my fascination with machines and how they accomplish their jobs. This included anything from bicycles to tractors to boats to airplanes. I wanted to know how things worked. I was lucky in that my interests at that time could be satisfied in a field of study that did not depend heavily on a mastery of the English language. However, my fascination with machines opened the door to what lay behind the creation of these machines, and that was the creativity and ingenuity that had allowed people to apply math and science to arrive at these machines.

I then decided that I enjoyed the "creative process" more than I enjoyed the study of the abstract scientific principles of science and engineering, or the drawn-out process of taking a finished design to ongoing production. It was at this point that I decided to become a patent attorney. This decision meant that I had to face my weaknesses in the English language, to take on a profession that depended heavily on my mastery of the language.

In facing this challenge, I had to decide whether I wanted to leave a traditional engineering career that had allowed me the comfort of avoiding an English-intensive profession and risk failure in pursuit of a new profession, which at the time seemed to me to be as foreign as Chile may be to many Americans. To garner the courage to leave the comfort of engineering,  I reflected on how far I had progressed in learning English so as to assimilate with the rest of American culture. I also reflected on the fact that engineering and the very problems associated with assimilating into American culture had given me powerful problem-solving skills that would improve my chances of succeeding in a new field, whether intrinsically scientific or not.

In other words, as I tried to decide whether I should leap into the next chapter in my career, I realized that it was because of the obstacles that I had come across in adopting a new language and culture that I had gained the courage and confidence to move on to the next step. Also, I saw that the problem-solving skills I had honed through engineering further reinforced my confidence in my ability to take on the new problems that would undoubtedly be a part of learning and striving to master a new field.

Building Comprehension and Speed

Most students lead busy lives, carrying heavy academic loads while perhaps working a job or even caring for a family. It's difficult to make time to study at all, let alone handle the enormous reading assignments for your different classes. Increasing your reading comprehension and speed will save you valuable time and effort.

Rapid reading won't do you any good if you can't remember the material or answer questions about it. However, reading too slowly can be equally inefficient because it often eats up valuable study time and gives your mind space to wander. Your goal is to read for maximum speed *and* comprehension. Focus on comprehension first, because greater comprehension is the primary goal and also promotes greater speed.

Methods for Increasing Reading Comprehension

Following are some specific strategies for increasing your understanding of what you read:

Continually build your knowledge through reading and studying. More than any other factor, what you already know before you read a passage will determine your ability to understand and remember important ideas. Previous knowledge, including vocabulary, facts, and ideas, gives you a **context** for what you read.

Context
Written or spoken knowledge that can help to illuminate the meaning of a word or a passage.

Establish your purpose for reading. When you establish what you want to get out of your reading, you will be able to determine what level of understanding you need to reach and, therefore, on what you need to focus.

Remove the barriers of negative self-talk. Instead of telling yourself that you cannot understand, think positively. Tell yourself: *I can learn this material. I am a good reader.* And, then, if you do need help, get it.

Think critically. Ask yourself questions. Do you understand the sentence, paragraph, or chapter you just read? Are ideas and supporting examples clear to you? Could you clearly explain what you just read to someone else?

Methods for Increasing Reading Speed

The following suggestions will help increase your reading speed.

- Try to read groups of words rather than single words.
- Avoid pointing your finger to guide your reading, since this will slow your pace.
- Try swinging your eyes from side to side as you read a passage, instead of stopping at various points to read individual words.
- When reading narrow columns, focus your eyes in the middle of the column and read down the page. With practice, you'll be able to read the entire column width.
- Avoid **vocalization** when reading.

Vocalization
The practice of speaking the words and/or moving your lips while reading.

* Avoid thinking each word to yourself as you read it, a practice known as *subvocalization*. Subvocalization is one of the primary causes of slow reading speed.

WHAT KIND OF READING WILL YOU DO IN ENGINEERING?

Readings in engineering will differ from liberal arts courses in three ways.

1. You will need to learn a large amount of new vocabulary. Any engineering topic that you study will have new terms to describe phenomena unique to that discipline. For example, in a basic electrical engineering circuits course, you will learn words like *resistance*, *capacitance*, and *inductance*. Many times, you will need to become conversant with acronyms, such as HVAC (heating, ventilation, and air conditioning), LED (light-emitting diode), and ASTM (American Society for Testing and Materials).

2. The content is generally not written in a narrative style. Therefore, following the flow of the text is more challenging. Engineering books, if written in typical technical writing style, can be dry and a drudgery to plow through. Fortunately, there are many technical and textbook writers who are able to present engineering information in lively and interesting ways. Hopefully, these writers will be the ones you are required to read. If not, just take extra time for your reading and ask for help interpreting the "foreign" language you are learning.

3. The content is concentrated, and the text is full of information, diagrams, and formulas. There usually is not any plot in engineering texts, or as described above, any easy narrative flow. In addition, you are required to read and understand symbols, math formulas and equations, diagrams of models, and graphs that are used to explain the materials. You will be memorizing new terms and models in order to learn more complex concepts. Graphics, not written text, are often used to represent ideas.

Now, you understand better the challenges and types of reading in engineering. The next important step is to examine why you are reading any given piece of material.

WHY DEFINE YOUR PURPOSE FOR READING?

As with all other aspects of your education, asking important questions will enable you to make the most of your efforts. When you define your purpose, you ask yourself *why* you are reading a particular piece of material. One way to do this is by completing this sentence: "In reading this material, I intend to define/learn/answer/achieve . . ." With a clear purpose in mind, you can decide how much time and what kind of effort to expend on various reading assignments. Nearly 375 years ago, Francis Bacon, the English philosopher, recognized that . . .

Some books are to be tasted, others to be swallowed, and some few to be chewed and digested; that is, some books are to be read only in parts, others to be read but not curiously; and some few to be read wholly, and with diligence and attention.

Achieving your reading purpose requires adapting to different types of reading materials. Being a flexible reader—adjusting your reading strategies and pace—will help you to adapt successfully.

Purpose Determines Reading Strategy

With purpose comes direction; with direction comes a strategy for reading. Following are four reading purposes, examined briefly. You may have one or more for each piece of reading material you approach.

Purpose 1: Read to Evaluate Critically. Critical evaluation involves approaching the material with an open mind, examining causes and effects, evaluating ideas, and asking questions that test the strength of the writer's argument and that try to identify assumptions. Critical reading is essential for you to demonstrate an understanding of material that goes beyond basic recall of information. You will read more about critical reading later in the chapter.

Purpose 2: Read for Comprehension. Much of the studying you do involves reading for the purpose of comprehending the material. The two main components of comprehension are *general ideas* and *specific facts/examples.* These components depend on one another. Facts and examples help to explain or support ideas, and ideas provide a framework that helps the reader to remember facts and examples.

General Ideas. General-idea reading is rapid reading that seeks an overview of the material. You may skip entire sections as you focus on headings, subheadings, and summary statements in search of general ideas.

Specific Facts/Examples. At times, readers may focus on locating specific pieces of information—for example, the ultimate strength of various types of steel. Often, a reader may search for examples that support or explain more general ideas—for example, the causes of global warming. Because you know exactly what you are looking for, you can skim the material at a rapid rate. Reading your texts for specific information may help before taking a test.

> "In books, I could travel anywhere, be anybody, understand worlds long past and imaginary colonies in the future."
>
> RITA DOVE

Purpose 3: Read for Practical Application. A third purpose for reading is to gather usable information that you can apply toward a specific goal. When you read a computer software manual, an instruction sheet for assembling a gas grill, or a cookbook recipe, your goal is to learn how to do something. Reading and action usually go hand in hand.

Purpose 4: Read for Pleasure. Some materials you read for entertainment, such as *Sports Illustrated* magazine or the latest John Grisham courtroom thriller. Entertaining reading may also go beyond materials that seem obviously designed to entertain. Whereas some people may read a Jane Austen novel for comprehension, as in a class assignment, others may read Austen books for pleasure.

Purpose Determines Pace

George M. Usova, senior education specialist and graduate professor at The Johns Hopkins University, explains: "Good readers are flexible readers. They read at a variety of rates and adapt them to the reading *purpose* at hand, the *difficulty* of the material, and their *familiarity* with the subject area."[3] As Table 6.1 shows, good readers link the pace of reading to their reading purpose.

Recognizing obstacles to effective reading and defining the various purposes for reading lay the groundwork for effective *studying*—the process of mastering the concepts and skills contained in your texts.

TABLE 6.1	TYPE OF MATERIAL	READING PURPOSE	PACE
Linking purpose to pace.	**Academic readings** • Textbooks • Original sources • Articles from scholarly journals • Online publications for academic readers • Lab reports • Required fiction	• Critical analysis • Overall mastery • Preparation for tests	• Slow, especially if the material is new and unfamiliar
	Manuals • Instructions • Recipes	• Practical application	• Slow to medium
	Journalism and nonfiction for the general reader • Nonfiction books • Newspapers • Magazines • Online publications for the general public	• Understanding of general ideas, key concepts, and specific facts for personal understanding and/or practical application	• Medium to fast
	Nonrequired Fiction	• Understanding of general ideas, key concepts, and specific facts for enjoyment	• Variable, but tending toward the faster speeds

Source: Adapted from Nicholas Reid Schaffzin, *The Princeton Review Reading Smart* (New York: Random House, 1996), 15.

READING STRATEGIES FOR ENGINEERING COURSES

As an engineering student, you will be reading calculus, chemistry, physics, and computer science textbooks, lab manuals, and on-line course supplementary materials in your first year of college. In addition, you will read one or two humanities/social science textbooks. During your sophomore, junior, and senior years, textbook reading will consist of material on fluids, heat transfer, energy and material balances, circuits, and structures. In other words, most of your reading is going to be technical in nature.

Reading technical material is very different from reading text that is descriptive or narrative, such as that found in arts and sciences or business classroom textbooks. Therefore, reading strategies that college students often employ to be successful in arts and sciences or business classes need to be adapted for use in engineering courses.

Math, science, and engineering texts contain vast amounts of information that build upon material presented in previous chapters. Paragraphs are filled with terms that are often unfamiliar, blocks of text are interspersed with numerical formulas, sections illustrated with problems, charts, diagrams, and drawings. This type of material requires a slow to medium pace of reading to adequately comprehend the information.

When studying some engineering sources, textbooks can be secondary sources of information. Primary sources can be classroom notes and on-line supplementary material. Textbooks become secondary sources of information in classes that require significant hours of lab time, such as a fluid mechanics, circuits, or surveying course, or when the book provides limited explanation of material covered in class. Engineering students should consult manuals or additional books listed in the course syllabus and go to professors' office hours to bridge the gaps in learning.

Previewing the Chapter

Previewing or surveying the chapter before you read it gives you an idea of what information will be presented. This process includes reading headings, sub-headings, and chapter summaries. Instead of writing questions for headings and sub-headings as you would for arts and sciences or business courses, jotting down ideas covered in the chapter will suffice. It is important to note that many engineering textbooks do not have chapter summaries, just additional problems at the end of the chapter.

Engineering chapters contain a lot of information. Try reading a third or a half of the chapter at a time in order to process the information in chunks. Breaking down information into parts and reviewing those parts during short periods of time enhances learning. This technique is known as **time-spaced learning.** Another reading technique that can be of great benefit to engineering students is **annotation.**

Time-spaced learning
Reviewing information during short periods of time.

Annotation
Making notes in the margin of the text.

Annotation

A strategy that is effective for reading engineering textbooks is annotation. Annotation, also called note-making, refers to making notes in the margins of the text as you read. There are different ways to annotate texts depending on whether the selection is from a textbook or manual, literature, or a critical essay. In engineering courses, annotations are done in textbooks or lab manuals. Figure 6.1 shows an example of annotation in a chemistry textbook.[4]

Annotation is an active learning process. You must be alert and engaged in order to do it. Annotating helps you learn how to pick out main ideas or the most important points versus the less important details. It also helps you to understand. In order to condense a concept and put it down in your own words, you must first understand it. Finally, annotating helps you to remember. The simple act of writing things out helps you to remember. Explaining them to yourself helps even more.

FIGURE 6.1

Annotations in a chemistry textbook.

11.2 Energy Changes and the Solution Process **425**

packs. When the pack is squeezed, the pouch breaks and the solid dissolves, either raising or lowering the temperature (Figure 11.2).

Hot packs:	$CaCl_2(s)$	$\Delta H_{soln} = -81.3$ kJ/mol
	$MgSO_4(s)$	$\Delta H_{soln} = -91.2$ kJ/mol
Cold packs:	$NH_4NO_3(s)$	$\Delta H_{soln} = +25.7$ kJ/mol

exo — rise in temp solute.
endo — fall in temp solute.

(a) (b)

FIGURE 11.2 **(a)** Dissolution of $CaCl_2$ in water is exothermic, causing the temperature of the water to rise from its initial value of 25°C. **(b)** Dissolution of NH_4NO_3 is endothermic, causing the temperature of the water to fall from its initial value.

The exact values of the heats of solution for different substances result from an interplay of the three kinds of interactions mentioned earlier:

Intermolecular Interactions

$SS: \Delta H = +$ } *require*
$SlSL: \Delta H = +$ } *energy to spread*
$SSL: \Delta H = -$

Solvent–solvent interactions: Energy is required (positive ΔH) to overcome intermolecular forces between solvent molecules because the molecules must be separated and pushed apart to make room for solute particles.

Solute–solute interactions: Energy is required (positive ΔH) to overcome intermolecular forces holding solute particles together in a crystal. For an ionic solid, this is the lattice energy (Section 6.4). Substances with higher lattice energies therefore tend to be less soluble than substances with lower lattice energies.

Solvent–solute interactions: Energy is released (negative ΔH) when solvent molecules cluster around solute particles and solvate them. For ionic substances in water, the amount of hydration energy released is generally greater for smaller cations than for larger ones because water molecules can approach the positive nuclei of smaller ions more closely and thus bind more tightly. Similarly, hydration energy generally increases as the charge on the ion increases.

The first two kinds of interactions are endothermic, requiring an input of energy to spread apart solvent molecules and to break apart crystals. Only the third interaction is exothermic, as attractive intermolecular forces develop between solvent and solute. The sum of the three interactions determines

Sum 3 interactions →
ΔH

Solv Solv = requires NRG
Solv Solv = requires NRG
Solv Solv = releases NRG

HOW CAN YOU READ CRITICALLY?

Your textbooks will often contain features that highlight important ideas and help you determine questions to ask while reading. As you advance in your education, however, many reading assignments will not be so clearly marked, especially if they are primary sources. You will need critical-reading skills in order to select the important ideas, identify examples that support them, and ask questions about the text without the aid of any special features or tools.

Critical reading enables you to consider reading material carefully, developing a thorough understanding of it through evaluation and analysis. A critical reader is able to discern what in a piece of reading material is true or useful, such as when using material as a source for an essay. A critical reader can also compare one piece of material to another and evaluate which makes more sense, which proves its thesis more successfully, or which is more useful for the reader's purpose.

Ask Questions Based on the Mind Actions

The essence of critical reading, as with critical thinking, is asking questions. Instead of simply accepting what you read, seek a more thorough understanding by questioning the material as you go along. Using the mind actions of the Thinktrix (see Chapter 5) to formulate your questions will help you understand the material.

What parts of the material you focus on will depend on your purpose for reading. For example, if you are writing a paper on the causes of bridge failures, you might spend your time focusing on how certain causes fit your thesis. If you are comparing two pieces of writing that contain opposing arguments, you may focus on picking out their central ideas and evaluating how well the writers use examples to support these ideas.

You can question any of the following components of reading material:

- The central idea of the entire piece
- A particular idea or statement
- The examples that support an idea or statement
- The proof of a fact
- The definition of a concept

Following are some ways to critically question your reading material, based on the mind actions. Apply them to any component you want to question by substituting the component for the words "it" and "this."

Similarity:	What does this remind me of, or how is it similar to something else I know?	
Difference:	What different conclusions are possible? How is this different from my experience?	
Cause and Effect:	Why did this happen, or what caused this? What are the effects or consequences of this?	

What effect does the author want to have, or what is the purpose of this material?

What effects support a stated cause?

Example to Idea: How would I classify this, or, what is the best idea to fit this example(s)?

How would I summarize this, or what are the key ideas?

What is the thesis or central idea?

Idea to Example: What evidence supports this, or what examples fit this idea?

Evaluation: How would I evaluate this? Is it valid or pertinent?

Does this example support my thesis or central idea?

Shift Your Perspective

Your understanding of perspective will help you understand that many reading materials are written from a particular perspective. Perspective often has a strong effect on how the material is presented. For example, if a recording artist and a music censorship advocate were to each write a piece about a controversial song created by that artist, their different perspectives would result in two very different pieces of writing.

To analyze perspective, ask questions like the following:

What perspective is guiding this? What are the underlying ideas that influence this material?

Who wrote this, and what may be the author's perspective? For example, an article on tire tread separation written by an employee of a tire manufacturer may differ from that written by an engineer who serves as an expert witness in automotive fatality cases.

What does the title of the material tell me about its perspective? For example, a piece entitled "Automobile dealers not informing public of correct inflation values for tires" may intend to be persuasive, whereas "Should a nylon layer be present between the steel belts and external rubber on tires?" would be expected to be informational.

How does the material's source affect its perspective? An article in *The Wall Street Journal* may attempt to present both sides of a controversial story whereas one published in the tire manufacturer's in-house newsletter would be expected to be favorable to the tire manufacturer's point of view.

Read for Understanding

Reading critically allows you to investigate what you read so that you can reach the highest possible level of understanding. Think of your reading process as an archaeological dig. The first step is to excavate a site and uncover the artifacts. In reading, this corresponds to your initial preview and reading of the material. As important as the excavation is, the process would be incomplete if you stopped there and just took home a bunch of items covered in dirt. The second half of the process is to investigate each item, evaluate what all of those items mean, and to derive new knowledge and ideas from what you discover. Critical reading allows you to complete that crucial second half of the process.

As you work through all of the different requirements of critical reading, remember that critical reading takes *time* and *focus*. Finding a time, place, and purpose for reading, covered earlier in the chapter, is crucial to successful critical reading. Give yourself a chance to gain as much as possible from what you read.

No matter where or how you prefer to study, your school's library (or libraries) can provide many useful services to help you make the most of classes, reading, studying, and assignments.

LIBRARY AND WEB RESOURCES

Your library can help you search for all kinds of information. First, learn about your library, its resources, and its layout. While some schools have only one library, other schools have a library network that includes one or more central libraries and smaller, specialized libraries that focus on specific academic areas. Often, your college will have an engineering library. Take advantage of library tours, training sessions, and descriptive pamphlets. Spend time walking around the library on your own. If you still have questions, ask a librarian. A simple question can save hours of searching. The following sections will help you understand how your library operates.

General Reference Works

General reference works give you an overview and lead you to more specific information. These works cover topics in a broad, nondetailed way. General reference guides are found in the front of most libraries and are often available on CD-ROM, a compact disk that contains millions of words and images. Among the works that fall into this category are:

- encyclopedias—for example, the multivolume *Encyclopedia Britannica*
- almanacs—*The World Almanac and Book of Facts*
- dictionaries—*Webster's New World College Dictionary*
- biographical reference works—*Webster's Biographical Dictionary*
- bibliographies—*Books in Print*

Specialized Reference Works

Look at *specialized reference works* to find more specific facts. Specialized reference works include encyclopedias and dictionaries that focus on a narrow field. The short summaries you will find there focus on critical ideas. Bibliographies that accompany the articles point you to the names and works

"With one day's reading a man may have the key in his hands."

EZRA POUND

of recognized experts. Examples of specialized references include the *International Encyclopedia of Robotics*, the *Encyclopedia of Computer Science and Technology*, and the *Dictionary of Electronics and Nucleonics*.

Library Book Catalog

Found near the front of the library, the *book catalog* lists every book the library owns. The listings usually appear in three separate categories: authors' names, book titles, and subjects. Not too long ago, most libraries stored their book catalog on index-sized cards in hundreds of small drawers. Today, many libraries have replaced these cards with computers. Using a terminal that has access to the library's computer records, you can search by specific author, title, and subject.

The computerized catalog in your college library is probably connected to the holdings of other college and university libraries. This gives you an on-line search capacity, which means that if you don't find the book you want in your local library, you can track it down in another library and request it through an interlibrary loan. *Interlibrary loan* is a system used by many colleges to allow students to borrow materials from a library other than the one at their school. Students request materials through their own library, where the materials are eventually delivered by the outside library. When you are in a rush, keep in mind that interlibrary loan may take a substantial amount of time.

Periodical Indexes

Periodicals are magazines, journals, and newspapers that are published on a regular basis throughout the year. Examples include *Time, Business Week*, and *Science*. Many libraries display periodicals that are a year or two old and convert older copies to microfilm or microfiche (photocopies of materials reduced greatly in size and printed on film readable in a special reading machine—microfilm is a strip of film, and microfiche refers to individual leaves of film). Finding articles in publications involves a search of periodical indexes. The most widely used general index is the *Reader's Guide to Periodical Literature*, which is available on CD-ROM and in book form. The *Reader's Guide* indexes articles in more than 100 general-interest magazines and journals.

Electronic Research

You will also find complete source material through a variety of electronic sources, including the Internet, on-line services, and CD-ROM. Here is a sampling of the kind of information you will find:

- complete articles from thousands of journals and magazines
- complete articles from newspapers around the world

- government data on topics as varied as agriculture, transportation, and labor
- business documents, including corporate annual reports

Your library is probably connected to the *Internet*, a worldwide computer network that links government, university, research, and business computers along the Information Superhighway. Tapping into the *World Wide Web*—a tool for searching the huge libraries of information stored on the Internet—gives you access to billions of written words and graphic images. The Internet is so vast that this book contains a Web Resources appendix (Appendix B) to help you explore it. After reading this appendix, you will have many tools to aid you on your journeys along the information superhighway. If your college has its own Internet home page, start by spending some time browsing through it.

Although most libraries do not charge a fee to access the Internet, they may charge when you connect to commercial on-line services. Ask your librarian about all fees and restrictions. Libraries also have electronic databases on CD-ROM. A database is a collection of data—or, in the case of most libraries, a list of related resources that all focus on one specific subject area—arranged so that you can search through it and retrieve specific items easily. For example, the DIALOG information system includes hundreds of small databases in specialized areas. CD-ROM databases are generally smaller than on-line databases and are updated less frequently. However, there is never a user's fee.

ENDNOTES

1. U. S. Department of Education, National Center for Education Statistics, *The Condition of Education 1996*, NCES 96-304, by Thomas M. Smith (Washington, D. C.: U. S. Government Printing Office, 1996), 84.

2. Sherwood Harris, *The New York Public Library Book of How and Where to Look It Up* (Englewood Cliffs, NJ: Prentice Hall, 1991), 13.

3. George M. Usova, *Efficient Study Strategies: Skills for Successful Learning* (Pacific Grove, CA: Brooks/Cole Publishing Company, 1989), 45.

4. J. McMurry and R. C. Fay, *Chemistry*, 2nd ed. (New York: Prentice Hall, 1998), 425.

5. Teresa Audesirk and Gerald Audesirk, *Life on Earth* (Upper Saddle River, NJ: Prentice Hall, 1997), 55–56.

Name   **Date**

KEY INTO YOUR LIFE *Opportunities to Apply What You Learn*

| EXERCISE | 6.1 | **Studying a Text Page** |

The following pages are from the chapter titled "Formulas, Equations and Moles" in the second edition of J. McMurry and R. C. Fay, *Chemistry: A Prentice Hall Text*. Using what you learned in this chapter about study techniques, complete the questions on this page.

a. Identify the headings on the pages.

_____

_____

b. What do the headings tell you about the content of the pages?

_____

_____

c. The examples in these pages are incorporated in the text for what specific purpose?

_____

_____

d. Figure 3.6 is an example of what strategy?

_____

_____

e. Figure 3.7 is an example of what two strategies?

_____

_____

f. Using a marker pen, highlight key phrases and sentences. Write short marginal notes to help you review the material later.

_____

_____

g. After reading these pages, list four key concepts that you will need to study:

1. _____

2. _____

3. _____

4. _____

(a)   **(b)**   **(c)**

FIGURE 3.6   The procedure for diluting a concentrated solution. **(a)** The volume to be diluted is withdrawn and placed in an empty volumetric flask. **(b)** Solvent is then added to a level just below the calibration mark, and the flask is shaken. **(c)** More solvent is added to reach the calibration mark, and the solution is inverted a few times to ensure mixing.

In practice, dilutions are carried out as shown in Figure 3.6. The volume to be diluted is withdrawn with a pipet, placed in an empty volumetric flask of the chosen volume, and diluted to the calibration mark on the flask.

EXAMPLE 3.12   How would you prepare 500.0 mL of 0.2500 M NaOH solution starting from a concentration of 1.000 M?

BALLPARK SOLUTION   Because the concentration decreases by a factor of four after dilution (from 1.000 M to 0.2500 M), the volume must increase by a factor of four. Thus, to prepare 500.0 mL of solution, we should start with 500.0/4 = 125.0 mL.

DETAILED SOLUTION   The problem gives initial and final concentrations (M_i and M_f) and final volume (V_f) and asks for the initial volume (V_i) that we need to dilute. Rewriting the equation $M_i \times V_i = M_f \times V_f$ as $V_i = (M_f/M_i) \times V_f$ gives the answer:

$$V_i = \frac{M_f}{M_i} \times V_f = \frac{0.2500\ M}{1.000\ M} \times 500.0\ mL = 125.0\ mL$$

We therefore need to place 125.0 mL of 1.000 M NaOH solution in a 500.0 mL volumetric flask and fill to the mark with water.

▶ **PROBLEM 3.16**   What is the final concentration if 75.0 mL of a 3.50 M glucose solution is diluted to a volume of 400.0 mL?

▶ **PROBLEM 3.17**   Sulfuric acid is normally purchased at a concentration of 18.0 M. How would you prepare 250.0 mL of 0.500 M aqueous H_2SO_4?

$$\frac{V_f}{V_i}\ M_i\ =\ M_f$$

$$\frac{400\ ML}{75\ ML}\ 35\ M = 4.16M$$

3.9   Solution Stoichiometry

We remarked in Section 3.7 that molarity can act as a conversion factor between numbers of moles of solute and the volume of a solution. If we know the volume and molarity of a solution, we can calculate the number of moles of solute. If we know the number of moles of solute and molarity, we can find the volume.

Stoichiometry is used as a conversion factor.

Source: CHEMISTRY, by McMurray & Fay, © 1998. Reprinted by permission of Prentice-Hall, Inc., Upper Saddle River, NJ.

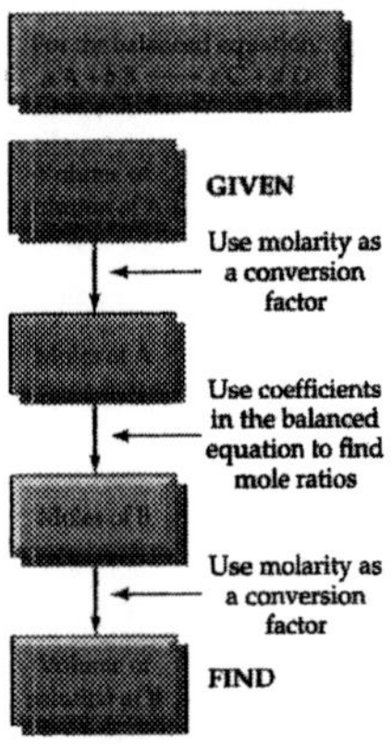

GIVEN

Use molarity as
a conversion
factor

Use coefficients
in the balanced
equation to find
mole ratios

Use molarity as
a conversion
factor

FIND

FIGURE 3.7 A flow diagram
summarizing the use of
molarity as a conversion factor
between moles and volume in
stoichiometry calculations.

Molarity can be used to
determine either moles
or volume.

As indicated by the flow diagram in Figure 3.7, a knowledge of **molarity** is critical for carrying out stoichiometry calculations on substances in solution. Molarity makes it possible to calculate the volume of one solution needed to react with a given volume of another solution. This sort of calculation is particularly important in acid–base chemistry, as shown in Example 3.13.

EXAMPLE 3.13   Stomach acid, a dilute solution of HCl in water, can be neutralized by reaction with sodium hydrogen carbonate, $NaHCO_3$, according to the equation

$$HCl(aq) + NaHCO_3(aq) \longrightarrow NaCl(aq) + H_2O(l) + CO_2(g)$$

How many milliliters of 0.125 M $NaHCO_3$ solution are needed to neutralize 18.0 mL of 0.100 M HCl?

BALLPARK SOLUTION   The balanced equation shows that HCl and $NaHCO_3$ react in a 1:1 molar ratio, and we are told that the concentrations of the two solutions are about the same. Thus, the volume of the $NaHCO_3$ solution must be about the same as that of the HCl solution.

DETAILED SOLUTION   Since we need to know the numbers of moles to solve stoichiometry problems, we first have to find how many moles of HCl there are in 18.0 mL of a 0.100 M solution by multiplying volume times molarity:

$$\text{Moles of HCl} = 18.0 \text{ mL} \times \frac{1 \text{ L}}{1000 \text{ mL}} \times \frac{0.100 \text{ mol}}{1 \text{ L}} = 1.80 \times 10^{-3} \text{ mol HCl}$$

Next, check the coefficients of the balanced equation to find that each mole of HCl reacts with 1 mol of $NaHCO_3$, and then calculate how many milliliters of 0.125 M $NaHCO_3$ solution contains 1.80×10^{-3} mol:

$$1.80 \times 10^{-3} \text{ mol HCl} \times \frac{1 \text{ mol } NaHCO_3}{1 \text{ mol HCl}} \times \frac{1 \text{ L solution}}{0.125 \text{ mol } NaHCO_3} = 0.0144 \text{ L solution}$$

Thus, 14.4 mL of the 0.125 M $NaHCO_3$ solution is needed to neutralize 18.0 mL of the 0.100 M HCl solution.

▶ **PROBLEM 3.18**   What volume of 0.250 M H_2SO_4 is needed to react with 50.0 mL of 0.100 M NaOH? The equation is

$$H_2SO_4(aq) + 2 NaOH(aq) \longrightarrow Na_2SO_4(aq) + 2 H_2O(l)$$

▶ **PROBLEM 3.19**   What is the molarity of an HNO_3 solution if 68.5 mL is needed to react with 25.0 mL of 0.150 M KOH solution?

3.10 Titration

There are two ways to make a solution of known molarity. The first and most obvious way is to make the solution carefully, using an accurately weighed amount of solute dissolved in solvent to an accurately calibrated volume. Often, though, it's more convenient to make up a solution quickly, using an

Focusing on Your Purpose for Reading

EXERCISE **6.2**

Read the following paragraphs on kinetic and potential energy and the first law of thermodynamics taken from *Life On Earth* by Teresa Audesirk and Gerald Audesirk.[5] When you have finished, answer the questions below.

a. Reading for critical evaluation. Evaluate the material by answering these questions:

Were the ideas clearly supported by examples? If you feel one or more were not supported, give an example.

_____

_____

_____

_____

Did the author make any assumptions that weren't examined? If so, name one or more.

_____

_____

_____

_____

Do you disagree with any part of the material? If so, which part, and why?

_____

_____

_____

_____

Do you have any suggestions for how the material could have been presented more effectively?

_____

_____

_____

_____

Among the fundamental characteristics of all living organisms is the ability to guide chemical reactions within their bodies along certain pathways. The chemical reactions serve many functions, depending on the nature of the organism: to synthesize the molecules that make up the organism's body, to reproduce, to move, even to think. Chemical reactions either require or release **energy**, which can be defined simply as *the capacity to do work*, including synthesizing molecules, moving things around, and generating heat and light. In this chapter we discuss the physical laws that govern energy flow in the universe, how energy flow in turn governs chemical reactions, and how the chemical reactions within living cells are controlled by the molecules of the cell itself. Chapters 7 and 8 focus on photosynthesis, the chief "port of entry" for energy into the biosphere, and glycolysis and cellular respiration, the most important sequences of chemical reactions that release energy.

Energy and the Ability to Do Work

As you learned in Chapter 2, there are two types of energy: **kinetic energy** and **potential energy**. Both types of energy may exist in many different forms. Kinetic energy, or *energy of movement*, includes light (movement of photons), heat (movement of molecules), electricity (movement of electrically charged particles), and movement of large objects. Potential energy, or *stored energy*, includes chemical energy stored in the bonds that hold atoms together in molecules, electrical energy stored in a battery, and positional energy stored in a diver poised to spring (Fig. 4-1). Under the right conditions, kinetic energy can be transformed into potential energy, and vice versa. For example, the diver converted kinetic energy of movement into potential energy of position when she climbed the ladder up to the platform; when she jumps off, the potential energy will be converted back into kinetic energy.

To understand how energy flow governs interactions among pieces of matter, we need to know two things: (1) the quantity of available energy and (2) the usefulness of the energy. These are the subjects of the laws of thermodynamics, which we will now examine.

The Laws of Thermodynamics Describe the Basic Properties of Energy

All interactions among pieces of matter are governed by the two **laws of thermodynamics**, physical principles that define the basic properties and behavior of energy. The laws of thermodynamics deal with "isolated systems," which are any parts of the universe that cannot exchange either matter or energy with any other parts. Probably no part of the universe is completely isolated from all possible exchange with every other part, but the concept of an isolated system is useful in thinking about energy flow.

The First Law of Thermodynamics States That Energy Can Neither Be Created nor Destroyed

The **first law of thermodynamics** states that within any isolated system, energy can neither be created nor destroyed, although it can be changed in form (for example, from chemical energy to heat energy). In other words, within an isolated system *the total quantity of energy remains constant*. The first law is therefore often called the law of conservation of energy. To use a familiar example, let's see how the first law applies to driving your car (Fig. 4-2). We can consider that your car (with a full tank of gas), the road, and the surrounding air roughly constitute an isolated system. When you drive your car, you convert the potential chemical energy of gasoline into kinetic energy of movement and heat energy. The total amount of energy that was in the gasoline before it was burned is the same as the total amount of this kinetic energy and heat.

An important rule of energy conversions is this: Energy always flows "downhill," from places with a high concentration of energy to places with a low concentration of energy. This is the principle behind engines. As we described in Chapter 2, temperature is a measure of how fast molecules move. The burning gasoline in your car's engine consists of molecules moving at extremely high speeds: a high concentration of energy. The cooler air outside the engine consists of molecules moving at much lower speeds: a low concentration of energy. The molecules in the engine hit the piston harder than the air molecules outside the engine do, so the piston moves upward, driving the gears that move the car. Work is done. When the engine is turned off, it cools down as heat is transferred from the warm engine to its cooler surroundings. The molecules on both sides of the piston move at the same speed, so the piston stays still. No work is done.

b. Reading for practical application. Imagine you have to give a presentation on this material the next time the class meets. On a separate sheet of paper, create an outline or think link that maps out the key elements you would discuss.

c. Reading for comprehension. Answer the following questions to determine the level of your comprehension.

Name the two types of energy.

_____

_____

Which one "stores" energy?

_____

_____

_____

_____

Can kinetic energy be turned into potential energy?

_____

_____

_____

_____

What is the term that describes the basic properties and behaviors of energy?

_____

Mark the following statements as true (T) or false (F).

_____   Within any isolated system, energy can be neither created nor destroyed.

_____   Energy always flows downhill, from high concentration levels to low.

_____   All interactions among pieces of matter are governed by two laws of thermodynamics.

_____   Some parts of the universe are isolated from other parts.

7

Note-Taking and Writing

Harnessing the Power of Words and Ideas

Words, joined to form ideas, are tools that have enormous power. Whether you write an essay, a memo to a supervisor, or a love letter over e-mail, words allow you to take your ideas out of the realm of thought and give them a form that other people can read and consider. You can harness their power for your own. Set a goal for yourself: Strive continually to improve your knowledge of how to use words to construct understandable ideas.

This chapter will teach you the note-taking skills you need to record information successfully. It will show you how to express your written ideas completely and how good writing is linked to clear thinking. In class or at work, taking notes and writing well will help you stand out from the crowd.

In this chapter, you will explore answers to the following questions:

- How can note-taking help you?
- Which note-taking system should you use?
- How can you write faster when you take notes?
- Why does good writing matter?
- What are the elements of effective writing?
- What is the writing process?
- What are the types of writing assignments you might have during your engineering education?

HOW DOES TAKING NOTES HELP YOU?

Notes help you learn when you are in class, doing research, or studying. Since it is virtually impossible to take notes on everything you hear or read, the act of note-taking encourages you to decide what is worth remembering. The positive effects of note-taking include:

- Your notes provide material that helps you study information and prepare for tests.
- When you take notes, you become an active, involved listener and learner.
- Note-taking helps increase your observation skills.
- Notes help you think critically and organize ideas.
- The information you learn in class or lab may not appear in any text; you will have no way to study it without writing it down.
- If it is difficult for you to process information while in class, having notes to read and make sense of later can help you learn.
- Note-taking is a skill for life that you will use on the job and in your personal life.

Recording Information in Class

Your notes have two purposes: First, they should reflect what you hear in class, and second, they should be a resource for studying, writing, or comparing with your text material.

Preparing to Take Class Notes

Taking good class notes depends on good preparation, including the following:

- If your professor assigns reading on a lecture topic, you may choose to complete the reading before class so that the lecture becomes more of a review than an introduction.

- Use separate pieces of $8\frac{1}{2}$-by-11-inch paper for each class. If you use a three-ring binder, punch holes in papers your professor hands out and insert them immediately following your notes for that day.

- Take a comfortable seat where you can easily see and hear, and be ready to write as soon as the professor begins speaking.

- Choose a note-taking system that helps you handle the professor's speaking style. While one professor may deliver organized lectures at a normal speaking rate, another may jump from topic to topic or talk very quickly.

- Set up a support system with a student in each class. That way, when you are absent, you can get the notes you missed.

What to Do During Class

Because no one has the time to write down everything, the following strategies will help you choose and record what you feel is important, in a format that you can read and understand later.

- Date each page. When you take several pages of notes during a lecture, add an identifying letter or number to the date on each page: 11/27 A, 11/27 B, . . . or 11/27—1 of 3, 11/27—2 of 3.

- Add the specific topic of the lecture at the top of the page. For example:

    11/27A—Thermal Behavior of Gases

- If your professor jumps from topic to topic during a single class, try starting a new page for each new topic.

- Ask yourself critical-thinking questions as you listen: Do I need this information? Is the information important or is it just a digression? Is the information fact or opinion? If it is opinion, is it worth remembering?

- Record whatever a professor emphasizes (see Figure 7.1 for details).

- Continue to take notes during class discussions and question-and-answer periods. What your fellow students ask about may help you as well.

- Leave one or more blank spaces between points. This white space will help you review your notes, because information will appear in self-contained sections.

- Draw pictures and diagrams that help illustrate ideas.

- Indicate material that is especially important with a star, with underlining, with a highlighter pen, or by writing words in capital letters.

- If you cannot understand what the professor is saying, leave a space and place a question mark in the margin. Then ask the professor to explain it again after class, or discuss it with a classmate. Fill in the blank when the idea is clear.

- Take notes until the professor stops speaking. Students who stop writing a few minutes before the class is over can miss critical information.

- Make your notes as legible, organized, and complete as possible. Your notes are useful only if you can read and understand them.

> "Omit needless words. . . . This requires not that the writer make all his sentences short, or that he avoid all detail and treat his subjects only in outline, but that every word tell."
>
> WILLIAM STRUNK, JR.

FIGURE 7.1

How to pick up on professor cues.

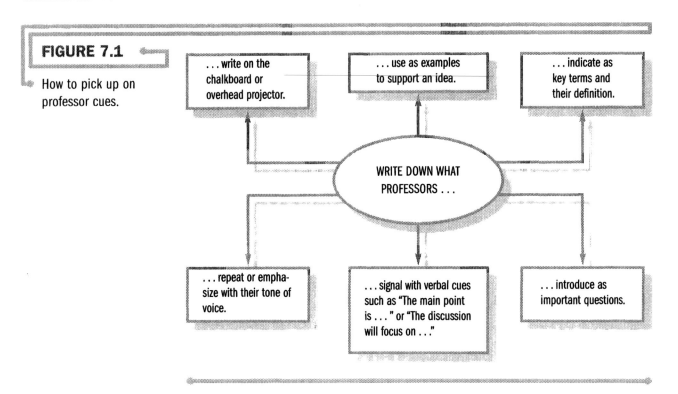

Make Notes a Valuable After-Class Reference

Class notes are a valuable study tool when you review them regularly. To help you do this, recopy your notes after class. This will help clarify points and assist your memory.

Try to begin your review within a day of the lecture. Read over the notes to learn the information, clarify abbreviations, fill in missing information, and underline or highlight key points. Try to review each week's notes at the end of that week. Think critically about the material, in writing, study group discussions, or quiet reflective thought. You might also try summarizing your notes, either as you review them or from memory.

You can take notes in many ways. Different note-taking systems suit different people and situations. Explore each system and choose what works for you.

WHAT NOTE-TAKING SYSTEM SHOULD YOU USE?

You will benefit most from the system that feels most comfortable to you. As you consider each system, remember the learning-styles profile you compiled in Chapter 3. The most common note-taking systems include outlines, the adapted Cornell note-taking system, and think links (also called concept maps).

Taking Notes in Outline Form

When a reading assignment or lecture seems well organized, you may choose to take notes in outline form. *Outlining* shows the relationships among ideas and their supporting examples through the use of line-by-line phrases set off by various indentations.

FIGURE 7.2

Sample formal outline.

Impulse and Momentum

I. Key Ideas
  A. Impulse and Momentum: Forces that act between colliding objects
    1. Impulse: impulse force = average value of force times time interval
    2. Momentum: vector quantity = body's mass times velocity
  B. Conservation of Momentum: "Law of conservation of momentum"—Acceleration and change in total momentum of system determined by net external force on system.
II. Key Equations
  A. Momentum of a particle $p = mv$
  B. Impulse and Momentum
    1. Impulse $= F_{av} \Delta t = m\Delta v = \Delta(mv) = \Delta p$
    2. Conservation of momentum $= p = p_1 + p_2 =$ constant

Adapted from Granvil C. Kyker, Jr., *Study Guide: Paul A Tipler College Physics* (New York: Worth, 1987), 81-82.

Formal outlines indicate ideas and examples using Roman numerals, capital and lower-case letters, and numbers. When you are pressed for time, such as during class, you can use an informal system of consistent indenting and dashes instead. Formal outlines also require at least two headings on the same level—that is, if you have a II A you must also have a II B. Figure 7.2 shows an outline on impulse and momentum.

Guided Notes

From time to time, a professor may give you a guide, usually in the form of an outline, to help you take notes in the class. This outline may be on a page that you receive at the beginning of the class, on the board, or on an overhead projector.

Although *guided notes* help you follow the lecture and organize your thoughts during class, they do not replace your own notes. Because they are more of a basic outline of topics than a comprehensive coverage of information, they require that you fill in what they do not cover in detail. If you tune out in class because you think that the guided notes are all you need, you will most likely miss important information.

When you receive guided notes on paper, write directly on the paper if there is room. If not, use a separate sheet and write on it the outline categories that the guided notes suggest. If the guided notes are on the board or overhead, copy them down, leaving plenty of space in between for your own notes.

Using the Adapted Cornell Note-Taking System

The Cornell note-taking system was developed about 45 years ago by Walter Pauk at Cornell University. Pauk created this method primarily to help students improve their note-taking skills in arts and sciences courses. The lecture material in these courses is based upon topics, main ideas, and supporting details. These types of lectures can present an overwhelming amount of material during a 45-minute class.

Note-taking in engineering and math/science courses is very different from note-taking in arts and sciences classes. Lecture material consists mostly of concepts, principles or theorems, formulas, and problems. The information given in these courses needs to be expanded, not condensed. Therefore, the Cornell method has been adapted specifically for math/science and engineering courses to reflect the nature of the content of information presented in these classes. Here is how you would take notes using this system. Figure 7.3 provides an example from a calculus course.

Section 1—the note-taking column (right-hand side of the paper): This section of the paper is to be used to *record* notes during class. Your notes may be written in an informal outline or summary form.

Section 2—the recall or expansion column (left-hand column): This section is to be left blank during class. After class, within 24 to 48 hours, fill in missing steps of problems, add more detailed explanations or formulas, and write down references to page numbers from the book.

Section 3—the bottom of the left-hand column: This is to be filled in after Section 2. Section 3 could contain a reminder about solving a problem or a possible test question.

Creating a Think Link or Concept Map

Concept mapping is a visual study strategy, introduced during the early 1970s, that shows the relationship between ideas or concepts in a hierarchical order. It is an effective strategy and a viable alternative to outlining. Concept maps are also known as *mind maps* or *think links*. Mapping allows you to organize and integrate large amounts of information in a concise way. It allows you to diagram ideas using shapes and lines that link ideas and supporting details and examples. The visual design makes the connections easy to see, and the use of shapes and pictures extends the material beyond just words. Many learners respond well to the power of **visualization.** You can use concept maps to brainstorm ideas for paper topics as well.

The different types of maps include flow charts, process maps (actually a form of flow charting that shows sequential steps in a process without any branching or decision points), and free-form concept maps.

Visualization
The interpretation of verbal ideas through the use of mental visual images.

Adapted Cornell note-taking method for engineering and math/sciences courses—example.   **FIGURE 7.3**

CALCULUS 2

Recall/Expanding Column

Note-Taking Column

Domain and Range of Function

Given: $f(x) = \frac{1}{2}x - \frac{7}{2}$

Find $f^{-1}(x)$ and compose f and f^{-1} to show that $f(f^{-1}(x)) = f^{-1}f(x) = x$

Also state the domain and range of f and f^{-1}.

$$f(x) = \frac{1}{2}x - \frac{7}{2}$$

D: All Reals
R: All Reals

No restrictions on the domain and range of this function

1. Begin with $f(x) = y$ $\therefore x = \frac{1}{2}y - \frac{7}{2}$

2. Interchange x and y. $x = \frac{1}{2}y - \frac{7}{2}$

3. Solve for y.
$2x = y - 7$
$2x + 7 = y$

After Step 2
Multiply both sides by 2 and distribute

$$2(x) = (\frac{1}{2}y - \frac{7}{2})2$$

$$2x = y - 7$$

4. Let $y = f^{-1}(x)$ $\therefore f^{-1}(x) = 2x + 7$

D: All Reals
R: All Reals

No restrictions on the domain and the range of this function

Replace x with $2x+7$ in f. $\longleftrightarrow$

Also, $\frac{1}{2}(2x + 7) - \frac{7}{2}$

$= x + \frac{7}{2} - \frac{7}{2}$

$= x$

5. Next, show that
$f(f^{-1}(x)) = x$
$f(2x + 7) = \frac{1}{2}(2x + 7) - \frac{7}{2} = x$

Replace x with $\frac{1}{2}x - \frac{7}{2}$ in f^{-1} $\longleftrightarrow$

Also, $2(\frac{1}{2}x - \frac{7}{2}) + 7$

$= x - 7 + 7$

$= x$

Reminder: Composing f and f^{-1} in either order gives us the identity function.

6. Finally, show that
$f^{-1}(f(x)) = x$
$f^{-1}(\frac{1}{2}x - \frac{7}{2}) = 2(\frac{1}{2}x - \frac{7}{2}) + 7 = x$

We have verified that both composites give the identity function.

The basic process of concept mapping for any course, technical or not, involves four steps:

Step 1: List main ideas and supporting details that you would like incorporated in your map. These ideas would be areas that the professor emphasized during class.

Step 2: Based upon the information you have to study, determine what type of map you will draw.

Step 3: Draw your map using your notes and place main ideas and details in an hierarchical order.

Step 4: Recreate your map two to three times from memory.

In engineering and math/science courses, concept maps are slightly different. Concept maps in these courses should include theorems, principles, and formulas. In addition, steps to a problem can be broken down. Examples of a flow chart for chemistry (Figure 7.4) and a free-form concept map for physics (Figure 7.5) follow.

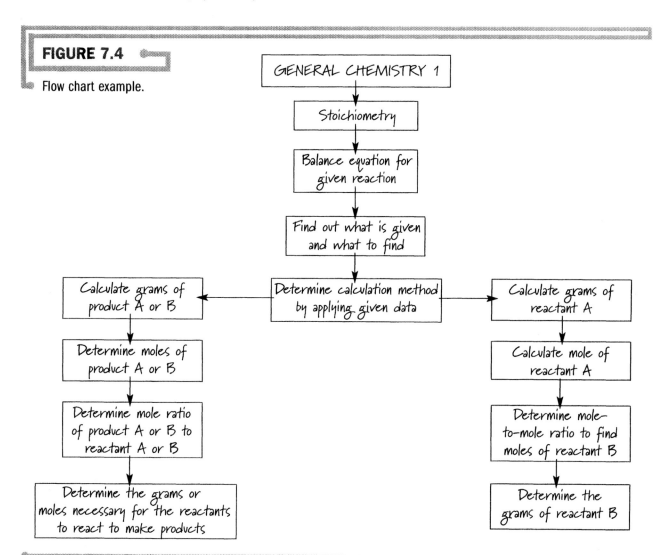

FIGURE 7.4

Flow chart example.

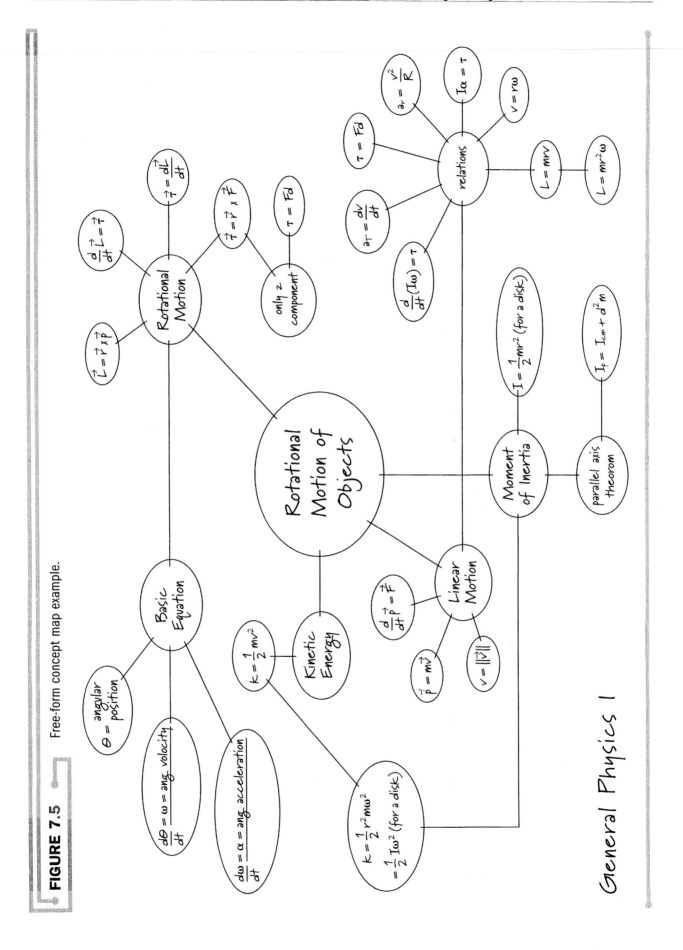

FIGURE 7.5   Free-form concept map example.

HOW CAN YOU WRITE FASTER WHEN TAKING NOTES?

When taking notes, many students feel they can't keep up with the professor. Using some personal shorthand (not standard secretarial shorthand) can help to push the pen faster. *Shorthand* is writing that shortens words or replaces them with symbols. Because you are the only intended reader, you can misspell and abbreviate words in ways that only you understand.

The only danger with shorthand is that you might forget what your writing means. To avoid this problem, review your shorthand notes while your abbreviations and symbols are fresh in your mind. If there is any confusion, spell out words as you review.

Here are some suggestions that will help you master this important skill:

1. Use the following standard abbreviations in place of complete words:

w/	with	cf	compare, in comparison to
w/o	without	ff	following
→	means; resulting in	Q	question
←	as a result of	p.	page
↑	increasing	*	most importantly
↓	decreasing	<	less than
∴	therefore	>	more than
∵	because	=	equals
≈	approximately	%	percent
+ or &	and	Δ	change
−	minus; negative	2	to; two; too
NO. or #	number	vs	versus; against
i.e.	that is,	eg	for example
etc.	and so forth	c/o	care of
ng	no good	lb	pound

2. Shorten words by removing vowels from the middle of words:

prps	=	purpose
Crvtte	=	Corvette (as on a vanity license plate for a car)

3. Substitute word beginnings for entire words:

assoc	=	associate; association
info	=	information

4. Form plurals by adding s:

prblms	=	problems
prntrs	=	printers

5. Make up your own symbols and use them consistently:

b/4	=	before
2thake	=	toothache

6. Learn to rely on key phrases instead of complete sentences ("German—nouns capitalized" instead of "In the German language, all nouns are capitalized.")

While note-taking focuses on taking in ideas, writing focuses on expressing them. Next you will explore the roles that writing can play in your life.

WHY DOES GOOD WRITING MATTER?

Good writing requires and reflects clear thinking. Therefore, a clear thought process is the best preparation for a well-written document, and a well-written document shows the reader a clear thought process. Good writing also depends on reading. The more you expose yourself to the work of other writers, the more you will develop your ability to express yourself well. Not only will you learn more words and ideas, but you will also learn about all the different ways a writer can put words together in order to express ideas. In addition, critical reading generates new ideas inside your mind, ideas you can use in your writing.

In school, courses you take may require you to write essays or papers in order to communicate your knowledge and thought process. In order to express yourself successfully in those essays and papers, you need good writing skills. Knowing how to write and express yourself is essential outside of school as well.

Professors, supervisors, and other people who see your writing judge your thinking ability based on what you write and how you write it. Your writing represents you. Over the next few years you may write papers, essays, answers to essay test questions, lab reports, job application letters, resumes, business proposals and reports, memos to co-workers, and letters to customers and suppliers. Good writing skills help you achieve the goals you set out to accomplish with each writing task. In engineering, good writing presents unique challenges because of the technical nature of the material.

WHAT ARE THE ELEMENTS OF EFFECTIVE WRITING?

Every writing situation is different, dependent upon three elements. Your goal is to understand each element before you begin to write:

- Your purpose: What do you want to accomplish with this particular piece of writing?
- Your topic: What is the subject about which you will write?
- Your audience: Who will read your writing?

Figure 7.6 shows how these elements are interdependent. As a triangle needs three points to be complete, a piece of writing needs these three elements.

Writing Purpose

Writing without having set your purpose first is like driving without deciding where you want to go. You'll get somewhere, but chances are it won't be where you needed to be. Therefore, when you write, always define what you want to accomplish before you start.

There are many different purposes for writing. However, the two purposes you will most commonly use in class work and on the job are to inform and to persuade.

The purpose of *informative writing* is to present and explain ideas. A research paper on how hospitals use donated blood to save lives informs readers without trying to mold opinion. The writer presents facts in an unbiased way, without introducing a particular point of view.

Persuasive writing has the purpose of convincing readers that your point of view is correct. Often, persuasive writing seeks to change the mind of the reader. For example, as a member of the student health committee, you write a newspaper column attempting to persuade readers to give blood. Examples of persuasive writing include newspaper editorials, business proposals, and books and magazine articles with a point of view.

Additional possible writing purposes include *entertaining* the reader and *narrating* (describing an image or event to the reader). Although most of your writing in school will inform or persuade, you may occasionally need to enter-

FIGURE 7.6

The three elements of writing.

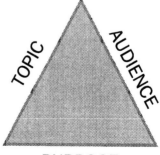

tain or narrate as well. Sometimes purposes will even overlap—you might write an informative essay that entertains at the same time.

Knowing Your Audience

In almost every case, a writer creates written material so that it can be read by others. The two partners in this process are the writer and the audience. Knowing who your **audience** is will help you communicate successfully.

> **Audience**
> The reader or readers of any piece of written material.

Key Questions About Your Audience

In school, your primary audience is your professors. Professors use your papers to evaluate the depth of your knowledge. For many assignments, professors will want you to assume that they are typical readers rather than informed professors. Writing for typical readers usually means that you should be as complete as possible in your explanations.

At times you may write papers that intend to address informed professors or a specific reading audience other than your professors. In such cases, you may ask yourself some or all of the following questions, depending on which are relevant to your topic.

* What are my readers' ages, cultural backgrounds, interests, and experiences?
* What are their roles? Are they professors, students, employers, customers?
* How much do they know about my topic? Are they experts in the field or beginners?
* Are they interested, or do I have to convince them to read what I write?
* Can I expect my audience to have an open or closed mind?

After you answer the questions about your audience, take what you have discovered into consideration as you write.

Your Commitment to Your Audience

Your goal is to organize your ideas so that readers can follow them. Suppose, for example, you are writing an informative research paper for a non-expert audience on using on-line services to get a job. One way to accomplish your goal is to first explain what these services are and the kinds of help they offer, then describe each service in detail, and finally conclude with how these services will change job hunting in the 21st century.

Effective and successful writing involves following the steps of the *writing process.*

WHAT IS THE WRITING PROCESS?

The writing process provides an opportunity for you to state and refine your thoughts until you have expressed yourself as clearly as possible. Critical thinking plays an important role every step of the way. The four main parts of the process are planning, drafting, revising, and editing.

Success in the Real World

Alexis C. Swoboda

P.E., Petroleum Engineer, U.S. Department of the Interior, Bureau of Land Management

Little did I know that although I am trained as and work as a petroleum engineer, writing has been and continues to be very important in my career and in my life. In fact, it is surprising how pivotal writing and other forms of communicating are in one's career.

I love to read. In fact, my key recollection of my summers was walking to the public library every day and checking out books to read at home. Reading led to writing. By the time I got to college, I had written class notes, book reports, essays, term papers, stories, and science reports. In college, I wrote class notes, research papers and projects, compositions, and more.

Throughout my engineering work experience, I have realized that writing is critical to career success. Technical writing is almost a science in itself; one needs to write precisely and with clarity, yet in terms that are understandable to a non-technical audience. In my career, I have written by myself and have worked with teams to write proposals, studies, project reports, agendas, meeting minutes, quarterly reports, trip reports, annual reports, reports to stockholders, business letters, master plans, and now, e-mail. I have given presentations using slides and charts and graphs. I have reviewed the written work of my colleagues and associates.

I have written articles and papers for publication, usually with a co-author. By working together to prepare finished products, we not only researched our topic, we also prepared a strategy, discussed our direction, wrote and rewrote our own and each other's parts of the paper, assembled all of the parts, and corrected our mistakes so that our finished product was polished and professional. We not only learned about editing and writing, we also learned about teamwork, cooperation, and negotiation.

Through my volunteer activities, I have become even more involved in writing—even in magazine editing and publishing. Through that process, I learned about the mechanics of planning themes, soliciting articles from prospective authors, and reviewing articles for publication.

So, for those students out there who think writing is an art they do not have to master, my words of advice are: learn everything that you can about writing and other forms of communication. Being able to communicate well is far more important in your career than you can possibly imagine while you are in college.

Planning

Planning gives you a chance to think about what to write and how to write it. Planning involves brainstorming for ideas, defining and narrowing your topic by using prewriting strategies, conducting research if necessary, writing a thesis statement, and writing a working outline. Although the steps in preparing to write are listed in sequence, in real life the steps overlap one another as you plan your document.

Open Your Mind Through Brainstorming

Whether your professor assigns a partially defined topic (computer pioneer Admiral Grace Murray Hopper) or a general category within which you make your own choice (major engineering accomplishments), you should brainstorm to develop ideas about what you want to write. Brainstorming is a creative technique that involves generating ideas about a subject without making judgments. You may want to look at the section on creativity in Chapter 5 for more details.

First, let your mind be open to possibilities! Write down ideas on the assigned subject that come to mind, in no particular order. Then, organize that list into an outline or concept map that helps you see the possibilities more clearly. To make an outline or concept map, separate list items into general ideas or categories and sub-ideas or examples with the ideas they support.

Figure 7.7 shows a portion of an outline that a student, Corissa Young, wrote about how she decided to be an aerospace engineer.

Narrow Your Topic Through Prewriting Strategies

When your brainstorming has generated some possibilities, you can narrow your topic. Focus on the sub-ideas and examples from your initial brainstorming session. Because they are relatively specific, they will be more likely to point you toward possible topics.

Choose one or more sub-ideas or examples that you like and explore them using prewriting strategies such as brainstorming, freewriting, and asking journalists' questions.[1] **Prewriting strategies** will help you decide which of your possible topics you would most like to pursue.

> **Prewriting strategies**
> Techniques for generating ideas about a topic and finding out how much you already know before you start your research and writing.

FIGURE 7.7

Part of a brainstorming outline.

Events/experiences early in life influenced my choice of engineering major.

—Family/parents—teachers

—Teacher influence—i.e. school

—Interest in math and science

—Challenger explosion

   —Couldn't believe it happened

   —Wanted to make sure it didn't happen again

   —Decided to become an aerospace engineer

Brainstorming. The same process you used to generate ideas will also help you narrow your topic further. Generate thoughts about the possibility you have chosen and write them down. Then, organize them into categories, noticing any patterns that appear. See if any of the sub-ideas or examples seem as if they might make good topics.

Freewriting. Another stream-of-consciousness technique that encourages you to put down ideas on paper as they occur to you is called *freewriting*. When you freewrite, you write whatever comes to mind without censoring your ideas or worrying about grammar, spelling, punctuation, or organization. Freewriting helps you think creatively and gives you an opportunity to begin weaving in information that you know. Freewrite on the sub-ideas or examples you have created to see if you want to pursue any of them. Here is a sample of freewriting:

> pondered for a long time on my decision as to what I was going to be when I grew up. I had always had a strong interest in math and science and my teachers encouraged me in these abilities. These teachers, in consultation with my parents, made sure I had the math, starting with algebra and going through calculus, and the sciences, including chemistry and physics, that I needed in high school in order to pursue an engineering field in college. I was particularly influenced by the Challenger explosion in 1986. I was shocked that the accident had actually happened, baffled that all of those engineers and scientists could collectively make what turned out to be such a bad decision, wanted to be sure that something like that never happened again, and decided that the way to fix it was to become an aerospace engineer.

Asking journalists' questions. When journalists start working on a story, they ask themselves Who? What? Where? When? Why? and How? You can use these journalists' questions to focus your thinking. Ask these questions about any sub-idea or example to discover what you may want to discuss. For example:

Who?	Who influenced me the most in my decision to pursue aerospace engineering?
What?	What specific event happened to crystallize my focus?
When?	When did this event happen?
Where?	Where was I when I made my decision?
Why?	Why was this an important event in my life? Why did this event change my life?
How?	How did I make this decision to be an aerospace engineer?

As you prewrite, don't forget to focus on the paper length, due date of your assignment, and any other requirements (such as topic area or purpose). These requirements influence your choice of a final topic. For example, if you had a month to write an informative 20-page paper on dragonflies and how their wings relate to aircraft design, you might choose to discuss the aerodynamic characteristics of dragonflies, including their wing configuration and rapid directional control. If you were given a week to write a five-page persuasive essay, you might write about how aerospace wing design should be influenced by studies on dragonflies.

Prewriting will help you develop a topic broad enough to give you something with which to work but narrow enough to be manageable. Prewriting also helps you see what you know and what you don't know. If your assignment requires more than you already know, you may need to do research.

Conduct Research

Much of the writing you do in college, such as when you must write a short report for a freshman course or a short essay for an exam, will rely on what you already know about a subject. In these cases, prewriting strategies may generate all the ideas and information you need. In other writing situations, outside sources are necessary. Try doing your research in stages. In the first stage, look for a basic overview that can help you write a thesis statement. In the second stage, go into more depth in your research, tracking down information that will help you fill in the gaps and complete your thoughts.

Write a Thesis Statement

Your work up until this point has prepared you to write a *thesis statement*, the central message you want to communicate. The thesis statement states your subject and point of view, reflects your writing purpose and audience, and acts as the organizing principle of your paper. It tells your readers what they should expect to read. Here is an example from Corissa's paper:

Topic	Why I chose aerospace engineering
Purpose	To inform and narrate
Audience	Professor and students in class
Thesis statement	Watching the space shuttle Challenger blow up when I was in elementary school made me decide that I wanted to be an aerospace engineer.

A thesis statement is just as important in a short document, such as a letter, as it is in a long paper. For example, when you write a job application letter, a clear thesis statement will help you tell the recruiter why you deserve the job.

> "Clear a space for the writing voice. . . . you cannot will this to happen. It is a matter of persistence and faith and hard work. So you might as well just go ahead and get started."
>
> **ANNE LAMOTT**

Write a Working Outline

The final step in the preparation process involves writing a working outline. Use this outline as a loose guide instead of a finalized structure. As you draft your paper, your ideas and structure may change many times. Only through allowing changes and refinements to happen can you get closer and closer to what you really want to say. Some students prefer a more formal outline structure, while others like to use a concept map. Choose whatever form suits you best.

Create a Checklist

Use the checklist in Table 7.1 to make sure your preparation is complete. Under "Date Due," create your own writing schedule, giving each task an intended completion date. Work backward from the date the assignment is due and estimate how long it will take to complete each step. Refer to Chapter 4 for time-management skills that will help you schedule your writing process.

As you develop your schedule, keep in mind that you'll probably move back and forth between tasks. You might find yourself doing two and even three things on the same day. Stick to the schedule as best you can, while balancing the other demands of your busy life, and check off your accomplishments on the list as you complete them.

Drafting

Some people aim for perfection when they write a first draft. They want to get everything right—from word choice to tone to sentence structure to paragraph organization to spelling, punctuation, and grammar. Try to resist this tendency, because it may lead you to shut the door on ideas before you even know they are there.

A *first draft* involves putting ideas down on paper for the first time—but not the last! You may write many different versions of the assignment until you like what you see. Each version moves you closer to communicating

TABLE 7.1	DATE DUE	TASK	IS IT COMPLETE?
Preparation checklist.		Brainstorm	
		Define and narrow	
		Use prewriting strategies	
		Conduct research if necessary	
		Write thesis statement	
		Write working outline	
		Complete research	

exactly what you want to say in the way you want to say it. The process is like starting with a muddy pond and gradually clearing the mud away until your last version is a clear body of water, showing the rocks and the fish underneath the surface. Think of your first draft as a way of establishing the pond before you start clearing it up.

The elements of writing a first draft are freewriting, crafting an introduction, organizing the ideas in the body of the paper, formulating a conclusion, and citing sources.

Freewrite Your Draft

If the introduction, body, and conclusion are the three parts of the sandwich, freewriting is the process of searching the refrigerator for the ingredients and laying them all out on the table. Take everything that you have developed in the planning stages and freewrite a very rough draft. Don't censor yourself. For now, don't consciously think about your introduction, conclusion, or structure within the paper body. Focus on getting your ideas out of the realm of thought and onto the paper, in whatever form they prefer to be at the moment.

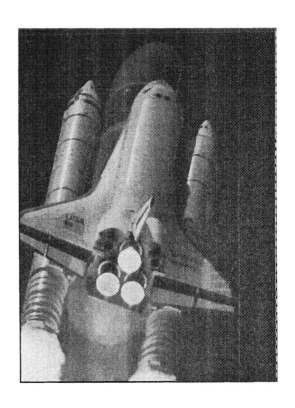

When you have the beginnings of a paper in your hands, you can start to shape it into something with a more definite form. First, work on how you want to begin your paper.

Write an Introduction

The introduction tells your readers what the rest of the paper will contain. Including the thesis statement is essential. Here, for example, is a draft of an introduction for Corissa's paper about an event/experience early in life that influenced her choice of an engineering major. The thesis statement is underlined at the end of the paragraph:

> t was early in the morning at school when my third grade teacher announced that we were going to be able to watch the launch of the Space Shuttle Challenger on TV. I was really interested in the planets and space travel. The shuttle started to go and then all of a sudden something went wrong. <u>Watching the Space Shuttle Challenger blow up when I was in elementary school made me decide that I wanted to be an aerospace engineer.</u>

When you write an introduction, you might try to draw the reader in with an anecdote—a story that is directly related to the thesis. You can try other

Hooks
Elements—including facts, quotes, statistics, questions, stories, or statements—that catch the reader's attention and encourage her to continue to read.

hooks, such as a relevant quotation, dramatic statistics, and questions that encourage critical thinking. Whatever strategy you choose, be sure it is linked to your thesis statement. In addition, try to state your purpose without referring to its identity as a purpose. For example, in your introductory paragraph, state "Computer technology is infiltrating every aspect of engineering," instead of, "In this paper, my purpose is to prove that computer technology is infiltrating every aspect of engineering."

After you have an introduction that seems to set up the purpose of your paper, work on making sure the body fulfills that purpose.

Create the Body of a Paper

The body of the paper contains your central ideas and supporting evidence. *Evidence*—proof that informs or persuades—consists of the facts, statistics, examples, and expert opinions that you know or have gathered during research.

Look at the array of ideas and evidences within your draft in its current state. Think about how you might group certain items of evidence with the particular ideas they support. Then, when you see the groups that form, try to find a structure that helps you to organize them into a clear pattern. Here are some strategies to consider.

- Arrange ideas by time. Describe events in order or in reverse order.
- Arrange ideas according to importance. You can choose to start with the idea that carries the most weight and move to ideas with less value or influence. You can also move from the least important to the most important idea.
- Arrange ideas by problem and solution. Start with a specific problem, then discuss one or more solutions.

Write the Conclusion

Your conclusion is a statement or paragraph that provides closure for your paper. Aim to summarize the information in the body of your paper, as well as to critically evaluate what is important about that information. Try one of the following devices:

- a summary of main points (if material is longer than three pages)
- a story, a statistic, a quote, a question that makes the reader think
- a call to action
- a look to the future

As you work on your conclusion, try not to introduce new facts or restate what you feel you have proved ("I have successfully proven that violent cartoons are related to increased violence in children"). Let your ideas as they are presented in the body of the paper speak for themselves. Readers should feel that they have reached a natural point of completion.

Credit Authors and Sources

When you write a paper using any materials other than your own thoughts and recollections, the ideas you gathered in your research become part of your own writing. This does not mean that you can claim these ideas as your own or fail to attribute them to someone. You need to credit authors for their ideas and words in order to avoid **plagiarism.**

To prevent plagiarism, learn the difference between a quotation and a paraphrase. A *quotation* uses a source's exact words, which should be set off from the rest of the text by quotation marks. A *paraphrase* is a restatement of the quotation in your own words, using your own sentence structure. *Restatement* means to completely rewrite the idea, not just to remove or replace a few words. A paraphrase may not be acceptable if it is too close to the original.

Even an acceptable paraphrase requires a citation of the source of the ideas within it. Take care to credit any source that you quote, paraphrase, or use as evidence. To credit sources, write a footnote or endnote that describes the source. Use the format preferred by your professor. Writing handbooks such as the *APA Publication Manual* contain acceptable formats.

> **Plagiarism**
> The act of using someone else's exact words, figures, unique approach, or specific reasoning without giving appropriate credit.

Revising

When you *revise*, you critically evaluate the word choice, paragraph structure, and style of your first draft to see how it works. Any draft, no matter how good, can always be improved. Be thorough as you add, delete, replace, and reorganize words, sentences, and paragraphs. You may want to print out your draft and then spend time making notes and corrections on that hard copy before you make changes on a typewritten or computer printed version.

In addition to revising on your own, some of your classes may include peer review (having students read each other's work and offer suggestions). A peer reviewer can tell you what comes across well and what may be confusing. Having a different perspective on your writing is extremely valuable. Even if you don't have an organized peer-review system, you may want to ask a classmate to review your work as a favor to you.

The elements of revision include being a critical writer, evaluating paragraph structure, and checking for clarity and conciseness.

Be a Critical Writer

Critical thinking is as important in writing as it is in reading. Thinking critically when writing will help you move your papers beyond restating what you have researched and learned. Of course, your knowledge is an important part of your writing. What will make your writing even more important and unique, however, is how you use critical thinking to construct your own new ideas and knowledge from what you have learned.

The key to critical writing is asking the question, "So what?" For example, if you were writing a paper on nutrition, you might discuss a variety of good eating habits. Asking "So what?" could lead you into a discussion of *why* these habits are helpful or what positive effects they have. If you were writing a paper on Newton's views on mechanics, you might list the main ideas you noticed that he had on the subject. Then, asking "So what?" could lead you to evaluate why Newton's ideas are so important to our understanding of mechanics today.

As you revise, ask yourself questions that can help you think through ideas and examples, come up with your own original insights about the material, and be as complete and clear as possible. Use the mind actions to guide you. Here are some examples of questions you may ask:

Are these examples clearly connected to the idea?

Are there any similar concepts or facts I know of that can add to how I support this?

What else can I recall that can help to support this idea?

In evaluating any event or situation, have I clearly indicated the causes and effects?

What new idea comes to mind when I think about these examples or facts?

How do I evaluate any effect/fact/situation? Is it good or bad, useful or not?

What different arguments might a reader think of that I should address here?

Finally, critical thinking can help you evaluate the content and form of your paper. As you start your revision, ask yourself the following questions:

- Will my audience understand my thesis and how I've supported it?
- Does the introduction prepare the reader and capture attention?
- Is the body of the paper organized effectively?
- Is each idea fully developed, explained, and supported by examples?
- Are my ideas connected to one another through logical transitions?
- Do I have a clear, concise, simple writing style?
- Does the paper fulfill the requirements of the assignment?
- Does the conclusion provide a natural ending to the paper?

Check for Clarity and Conciseness

Aim to say what you want to say in the clearest, most efficient way possible. A few well-chosen words will do your ideas more justice than a flurry of language. Try to eliminate extra words and phrases. Rewrite wordy phrases in a more concise, conversational way. For example, you can write "if" instead of "in the event that," or "now" instead of "at this point in time." "Capriciously, I sauntered forth to the entryway and pummeled the door that loomed so majestically before me," might become, "I skipped to the door and knocked loudly."

Editing

In contrast to the critical thinking of revising, *editing* involves correcting technical mistakes in spelling, grammar, and punctuation, as well as checking style consistency for elements such as abbreviations and capitalization. Editing comes last, after you are satisfied with your ideas, organization, and style of writing. If you use a computer, you might want to use the grammar-check and spell-check functions to find mistakes. A spell-checker helps, but you still need to check your work on your own. While a spell-checker won't pick up the mistake in the following sentence, someone who is reading for sense will:

They are not hear on Tuesdays.

Look also for *sexist language*, which characterizes people based on their gender. Sexist language often involves the male pronoun *he* or *his*. For example, "An executive often spends hours each day going through his electronic mail" implies that executives are always men. A simple change will eliminate the sexist language: "Executives often spend hours each day going through their electronic mail," or, "An executive often spends hours each day going through electronic mail." Try to be sensitive to words that leave out or slight women. *Mail carrier* is preferable to *mailman; student* to *coed.*

Proofreading is the last stage of editing, occurring when you have a final version of your paper. Proofreading means reading every word and sentence in the final version to make sure it is accurate. Look for technical mistakes, run-on sentences, and sentence fragments. Be alert for incorrect word usage and references that aren't clear.

Teamwork can be a big help as you edit and proofread, because another pair of eyes may see errors that you didn't notice on your own. If possible, have someone look over your work. Ask for feedback on what is clear and what is confusing. Then ask the reader to edit and proofread for errors.

A Final Checklist

You are now ready to complete your revising and editing checklist. All the tasks listed in Table 7.2 should be complete when you submit your final paper.

Your final paper reflects all the hard work you put in during the writing process.

> "See revision as 'envisioning again.' If there are areas where there is a blur or vagueness, you can simply see the picture again and add the details that will bring your work closer to your mind's picture."
>
> **NATALIE GOLDBERG**

DATE DUE	TASK	IS IT COMPLETE?
	Check the body of the paper for clear thinking and adequate support of ideas	
	Finalize introduction and conclusion	
	Check word spelling and usage	
	Check grammar	
	Check paragraph structure	
	Make sure language is familiar and concise	
	Check punctuation	
	Check capitalization	
	Check transitions	
	Eliminate sexist language	

TABLE 7.2

Revising and editing checklist.

TYPES OF WRITING ASSIGNMENTS IN ENGINEERING COURSES

Engineering writing assignments are more like technical writing assignments than literature reviews, essays, and research papers that you would write in arts and sciences and business courses. Writing assignments in engineering include, but are not limited to, lab notebooks, lab reports, group design projects, progress reports to clients, and oral presentations.

Laboratory Notebooks

As an engineering student, during lab you will be recording data and observations for future reference by yourself or others. For classes such as chemistry, a laboratory research notebook is usually required. Two copies of your observations may be needed, one to turn in to your lab instructor and one for you to keep.

Tips for Writing in Laboratory Notebooks

1. Use the first two pages as the table of contents.
2. Following the table of contents, number subsequent right-hand pages consecutively in ink.
3. Write data and observations on the **right-hand** page, in ballpoint **ink.**
4. Never erase an entry. To change an entry, draw a line through it and then enter the corrected fact. It is a good idea to write a brief explanation to explain the correction.
5. Enter all data immediately as it is obtained. **Do not** record values on scrap paper or try to remember them.
6. Make entries neatly, in printed rather than cursive writing, for clarity. Record all numbers to the correct number of significant figures and units. Tabular form is usually the best way to organize data.

Lab Reports

Lab reports can be quite time consuming. If you turn in your labs on time, make sure they are well-written, and check that the results are reasonable, you should do well in lab classes. Here are some helpful hints for preparing lab reports.

Helpful Hints for Writing Lab Reports

1. Don't use pronouns! (Incorrect: *I took the readings every 10 seconds.* Correct: *The readings were taken every 10 seconds.)*
2. Follow directions and answer **all** the questions.
3. Make sure that the voice for your lab reports is passive, even though some professors have dropped this requirement. *(The oscilloscope screen showed a sawtooth curve.)*

4. Type and save your lab reports.

5. Read over what you have written to make sure the report is clear and concise for the reader.

6. Run spell-check to make sure everything is spelled correctly.

7. Label charts, plots, diagrams, and tables. Do not assume that the reader will be able to understand all information that is displayed.

Short Reports/Progress Reports

Students who are designing projects for clients may have to write short reports or progress reports to give updates. When writing a short report (two to five pages), you might want to structure your report as follows:

* Describe your project.
* Emphasize the status of your project.
* Note problems that you have encountered.
* Note changes made to the project.
* Indicate when you expect to complete the project.
* Note costs that may be incurred.

Group Design Project Presentation

Students in engineering take design courses in either their freshman or sophomore year and usually again in their senior year. Typically, students write a written report about the design project and also give it as an oral presentation. Sometimes professors will give you an outline or format to show how you should present the project. In case your professor has not provided a format, below is a sample format.

ORAL PRESENTATION OUTLINE

Topic presented

Overview of the presentation

Introduction

   A. state the problem

   B. explain the experiment

   C. present the goals

Background information (necessary to solve the problem)

Conclusions

Further areas of research to be explored

Technical Paper Format

Technical papers on engineering subjects usually fit into a prescribed formula, although that formula may differ slightly depending on your field of specialization. A typical paper would be written with the following sections:

Summary

A concise restatement of the material that covers the main points.

Abstract: The beginning of the paper, an approximately 150-word **summary** of the entire paper.

Key findings: A short summary of the key findings of the paper.

Introduction: The context or motivation for investigating the problem.

Methodology: The methodology that you used to examine and solve the problem.

Conclusions: The findings of the analysis, as well as any recommendations for further work or analysis.

ENDNOTE

1. Analysis based on Lynn Quitman Troyka, *Simon & Schuster Handbook for Writers* (Upper Saddle River, NJ: Prentice Hall, 1996), 22–23.

Name   Date

CHAPTER 7   Applications

Opportunities to Apply What You Learn   KEY INTO YOUR LIFE

Evaluate Your Notes

EXERCISE | 7.1

Choose one particular class period from the last two weeks. Ask a classmate to photocopy his or her notes from that class period for you. Then evaluate your notes by comparing them with your classmate's. Think about the following questions:

- Do your notes make sense?
- How is your handwriting?
- Do the notes cover everything that was brought up in class?
- Are there examples to back up ideas?
- What note-taking system is used?
- Will these notes help you study?

Write your evaluation here:

_____

_____

_____

_____

_____

_____

_____

_____

What ideas or techniques from your classmate's notes do you plan to use in the future?

_____

_____

_____

_____

Adapted Cornell Note-Taking

Read the chemistry notes below and complete the left-hand column.

Recall Column	Note-Taking Column
	Kinetics

First Order Rxn

- EX: radioactive decay
- Rate Law rate = $K[A]$
- Integrated Rate Law:
  $\log A_t = -^{kt}/2,303 + \log A_0$
- Half-life: $t\,1/2 = ^{.693}/K$

Second Order Rxn

- EX $2HI \leftrightarrow H_2 + I_2$
- Rate law rate = $K[A]^2$
- Integrated Rate Law:
  $1/A_t = Kt + 1/A_0$
- Half-life: $t1/2 = 1/KA_0$

Reaction Mechanism

- $A + B \rightarrow C + D$ rate = $K[B][L]$
  $B + L \leftrightarrow E$
    Collision of $B + L$ is rate determining step
- $2\,A + B \rightarrow L + D$ rate = $K[A]^2$
  $B + L \rightarrow E$
    Rate determined step: $A + A \rightarrow A_2$ then
        $A_2 + B \rightarrow L + D$
          $B + L \rightarrow E$

Arrhenius Equation

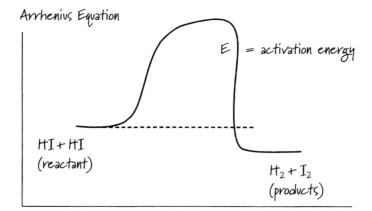

E = activation energy

HI + HI
(reactant)

$H_2 + I_2$
(products)

- Catalyst decreases Ea
  Homogeneous—same phrase
  heterogeneous—diff. phrase

Prewriting

Choose a topic you are interested in and know something about—for example, using Internet search engines, selecting a laptop computer, the consumption of alcohol on college campuses, or handling stress in college. Narrow your topic, then use the following prewriting strategies to discover what you already know about the topic and what you would need to learn if you had to write an essay about the subject for one of your classes. (If necessary, continue this prewriting exercise on a separate sheet of paper.)

Brainstorm your ideas:

_____

_____

_____

_____

_____

_____

_____

_____

Freewrite:

_____

_____

_____

_____

_____

_____

_____

Ask journalists' questions:

_____

_____

_____

_____

_____

_____

_____

_____

EXERCISE 7.4   **Writing a Thesis Statement**

Write two thesis statements for each of the following topics. The first statement should try to inform the reader, while the second should try to persuade. In each case, writing a thesis statement will require that you narrow the topic:

● The rising cost of a college education

Thesis with an informative purpose:

_____

_____

_____

Thesis with a persuasive purpose:

_____

_____

_____

● Taking care of your body and mind

Thesis with an informative purpose:

_____

_____

_____

Thesis with a persuasive purpose:

_____

_____

_____

● Choosing a career

Thesis with an informative purpose:

_____

_____

_____

Thesis with a persuasive purpose:

_____

_____

_____

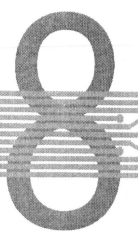

Listening, Memory, and Test Taking

Taking In, Retaining, and Demonstrating Knowledge

College exposes you daily to facts, opinions, and ideas. It is up to you to take in, retain, and demonstrate knowledge of what you learn, for use in or out of school. You can accomplish these goals through active listening, focused use of your memory skills, and thorough preparation for taking tests.

Listening is one of the primary ways of taking in information. Memory skills can help you retain what you've listened to so that you can recall it for a paper, a discussion, or a test. After you've listened and remembered, test taking is your key to demonstrating what you have learned to your professor or others. In this chapter, you will learn strategies to improve your ability to take in, remember, and show knowledge of what you have learned.

In this chapter, you will explore answers to the following questions:

● How can you become a better listener?

● How does memory work?

● How can you improve your memory?

● How can tape recorders help you listen, remember, and study?

● How can preparation help improve test scores?

● What strategies can help you succeed on tests?

● How can you learn from test mistakes?

HOW CAN YOU BECOME A BETTER LISTENER?

The act of hearing isn't quite the same as the act of listening. While *hearing* refers to sensing spoken messages from their source, *listening* involves a complex process of communication. Successful listening results in the speaker's intended message reaching the listener. In school, and at home, poor listening results in communication breakdowns and mistakes, and skilled listening promotes progress and success.

Ralph G. Nichols, a pioneer in listening research, studied 200 students at the University of Minnesota over a nine-month period. His findings, summarized in Table 8.1, demonstrate that effective listening depends as much on a positive attitude as on specific skills.[1]

Listening is a teachable—and learnable—skill. Improving your learning skills involves managing listening challenges and becoming an active listener. Although becoming a better listener will help in every class, it is especially important in subject areas that are difficult for you.

Manage Listening Challenges

Classic studies have shown that immediately after listening, students are likely to recall only half of what was said. This is partly due to particular listening challenges, including divided attention and distractions, the tendency to shut out the message, the inclination to rush to judgment, and partial hearing loss or learning disabilities.[2] To help create a positive listening environment, in both your mind and your surroundings, explore how to manage these challenges.

Divided Attention and Distractions

Internal and external distractions often divide your attention. *Internal distractions* include anything from hunger to headache to personal worries. Something the speaker says may also trigger a recollection that may cause your mind to drift. In contrast, *external distractions* include noises (whispering,

LISTENING IS HELPED BY . . .	LISTENING IS HINDERED BY . . .	TABLE 8.1
making a conscious decision to work at listening; viewing difficult material as a listening challenge.	caring little about the listening process; tuning out difficult material.	What helps and hinders listening.
fighting distractions through intense concentration.	refusing to listen at the first distraction.	
continuing to listen when a subject is difficult or dry, in the hope that one might learn something interesting.	giving up as soon as one loses interest.	
withholding judgment until hearing everything.	becoming preoccupied with a response as soon as a speaker makes a controversial statement.	
focusing on the speaker's theme by recognizing organizational patterns, transitional language, and summary statements.	getting sidetracked by unimportant details.	
adapting note-taking style to the unique style and organization of the speaker.	always taking notes in outline form, even when a speaker is poorly organized, leading to frustration.	
pushing past negative emotional responses and forcing oneself to continue to listen.	letting an initial emotional response shut off continued listening.	
using excess thinking time to evaluate, summarize, and question what one just heard and anticipating what will come next.	thinking about other things and, as a result, missing much of the message.	

honking horns, screaming sirens) and even excessive heat or cold. It can be hard to listen in an overheated room that is putting you to sleep.

Your goal is to reduce distractions and focus on what you're hearing. Sitting where you can see and hear clearly will help you listen well. Dress comfortably and try not to go to class hungry or thirsty.

Shutting Out the Message

Instead of paying attention to everything the speaker says, many students fall into the trap of focusing on specific points and shutting out the rest of the message. Creating a positive listening environment includes accepting responsibility for listening. The professor communicates information to you, but no one can force you to listen. You are responsible for taking in that information. Professors often cover material from outside the textbook during class and then test on that material. If you work to take in the whole message in class, you will be able to read over your notes later and think critically about what is most important.

The Rush to Judgment

People tend to stop listening when they hear something they don't like. If you rush to judge what you've heard, your focus turns to your personal reaction rather than the content of the speaker's message. Judgments also involve reactions to the speakers themselves. If you do not like your professors or if you have preconceived notions about their ideas or cultural background, you may decide that their words have little value.

Work to recognize and control your judgments. Being aware of what you tend to judge will help you avoid putting up a barrier against incoming messages that clash with your opinions or feelings. Try to see education as a continuing search for evidence, regardless of whether it supports or negates your point of view.

Partial Hearing Loss and Learning Disabilities

Good listening techniques don't solve every listening problem. Students who have a partial hearing loss have a physical explanation for why listening is difficult. If you have some level of hearing loss, seek out special services that can help you listen in class. You may require special equipment or might benefit from tutoring. You may be able to arrange to meet with your professor outside of class to clarify your notes.

Other disabilities, such as attention deficit disorder (ADD) or a problem with processing heard language, can cause difficulties with both focusing on and understanding that which is heard. People with such disabilities have varied ability to compensate for and overcome them. If you have a disability, don't blame yourself for having trouble listening. Your counseling center, student health center, advisor, and professors should be able to give you particular assistance in working through your challenges.

> "No one cares to speak to an unwilling listener. An arrow never lodges in a stone; often it recoils upon the sender of it."
>
> ST. JEROME

HOW DOES MEMORY WORK?

You need an effective memory in order to use the knowledge you take in throughout your life. Human memory works like a computer. Both have essentially the same purpose: to encode, store, and retrieve information.

During the *encoding stage*, information is changed into usable form. On a computer, this occurs when keyboard entries are transformed into electronic symbols and stored on a disk. In the brain, sensory information becomes impulses that the central nervous system reads and codes. You are encoding, for example, when you study a list of chemistry formulas.

During the *storage stage*, information is held in memory (the mind's version of a computer hard drive) for later use. In this example, after you complete your studying of the formulas, your mind stores them until you need to use them.

During the *retrieval stage*, memories are recovered from storage by recall, just as a saved computer program is called up by name and used again. In this example, your mind would retrieve the chemistry formulas when you had to take a test or solve a problem.

Memories are stored in three different storage banks. The first, called *sensory memory*, is an exact copy of what you see and hear, and lasts for a second or less. Certain information is then selected from sensory memory and moved into *short-term memory*, a temporary information storehouse that lasts no more than 10 to 20 seconds. You are consciously aware of material in your short-term memory. While unimportant information is quickly dumped, important information is transferred to *long-term memory*—the mind's more permanent storehouse.

Having information in long-term memory does not mean that you will be able to recall it when needed. Particular techniques can help you improve your recall.

HOW CAN YOU IMPROVE YOUR MEMORY?

Your physics professor is giving a test tomorrow on angular momentum. You feel confident, since you spent hours last week memorizing the formulas. Unfortunately, by the time you take the test, you may remember very little. That's because most forgetting occurs within minutes after memorization.

In a classic study conducted in 1885, researcher Herman Ebbinghaus memorized a list of meaningless three-letter words such as CEF and LAZ. Within one short hour he measured that he had forgotten more than 50 percent of what he learned. After two days, he knew less than 30 percent. Although his recall of the syllables remained fairly stable after that, the experiment shows how fragile memory can be, even when you take the time and energy to memorize information.[3]

People who have superior memories may have an inborn talent for remembering. More often, though, they have mastered techniques for improving recall. Remember that techniques aren't a cure-all for memory difficulties, especially for those who may have learning disabilities. If you have a disability, the following memory techniques may help you but may not be enough. Seek specific assistance if you consistently have trouble remembering.

Memory Improvement Strategies

As a student, your job is to understand, learn, and remember information, from general concepts to specific details. The following suggestions will help improve your recall.

Develop a Will to Remember

Why can you remember the lyrics to dozens of popular songs but not the inert gases on the periodic table? Perhaps this is because you want to remember them, you connect them with a visual image, or you have an emotional tie to them. To achieve the same results at school or on the job, tell yourself that what you are learning is important and that you need to remember it. Saying these words out loud can help you begin the active, positive process of memory improvement.

Understand What You Memorize

Make sure that everything you want to remember makes sense. Something that has meaning is easier to recall than something that is gibberish. This basic principle applies to everything you study—from physics and chemistry to music and anthropology.

Recite, Rehearse, and Write

When you *recite* material, you repeat it aloud in order to remember it. Reciting helps you retrieve information as you learn it and is a crucial step in studying (see Chapter 6). *Rehearsing* is similar to reciting, but is done in silence, in your mind. It involves the process of repeating, summarizing, and associating information with other information. *Writing* is rehearsing on paper. The act of writing solidifies the information in your memory.

Separate Main Points from Unimportant Details

If you use critical-thinking skills to select and focus on the most important information, you can avoid overloading your mind with extra clutter. To focus on key points, highlight only the most important information in your texts and write notes in the margins about central ideas. When you review your lecture notes, highlight or rewrite the most important information to remember.

Study During Short but Frequent Sessions

Research shows that you can improve your chances of remembering material if you learn it more than once. To get the most out of your study sessions, spread them over time, in what is called *time-spaced learning*. A pattern of short sessions followed by brief periods of rest is more effective than continual studying with little or no rest. Even though you may feel as though you accomplish a lot by studying for an hour without a break, you'll probably remember more from three 20-minute sessions. Try sandwiching study time into breaks in your schedule, such as when you have time between classes. Some of the advantages of time-spaced learning are greater retention and recall of information, less fatigue while learning, and better use of knowledge between learning periods.

Separate Material into Manageable Sections

When material is short and easy to understand, studying it from start to finish may work. For longer material, you may benefit from dividing it into logical sections, mastering each section, putting all the sections together, and then testing your memory of all the material. Actors take this approach when learning the lines of a play, and it can work just as well for students.

Use Visual Aids

Any kind of visual representation of study material can help you remember. You may want to convert material into a think link or outline. Write material in any visual shape that helps you recall it and link it to other information.

Flash-cards are a great visual memory tool. They give you short, repeated review sessions that provide immediate feedback. Make them from 3-by-5-inch index cards. Use the front of the card to write a word, idea, or phrase you want to remember. Use the back side for a definition, explanation, and other key facts. Figure 8.1 shows two flashcards for studying psychology.

Here are some additional suggestions for making the most of your flash cards:

* Use the cards as a self-test. Divide the cards into two piles: the material you know and the material you are learning. You may want to use rubber bands to separate the piles.

* Carry the cards with you and review them frequently. You'll learn the most if you start using cards early in the course, well ahead of exam time.

* Shuffle the cards and learn information in various orders. This will help avoid putting too much focus on some information and not enough on others.

* Test yourself in both directions. First, look at the terms or ideas and provide definitions or explanations. Then turn the cards over and reverse the process.

Mnemonic Devices

Certain show business performers entertain their audiences by remembering the names of 100 strangers or flawlessly repeating 30 ten-digit phone numbers. These performers probably have superior memories, but genetics alone can't produce these results. They also rely on memory techniques, known as **mnemonic** devices (pronounced neh MAHN ick) to help them.

Mnemonic devices
Memory techniques that involve associating new information with information you already know.

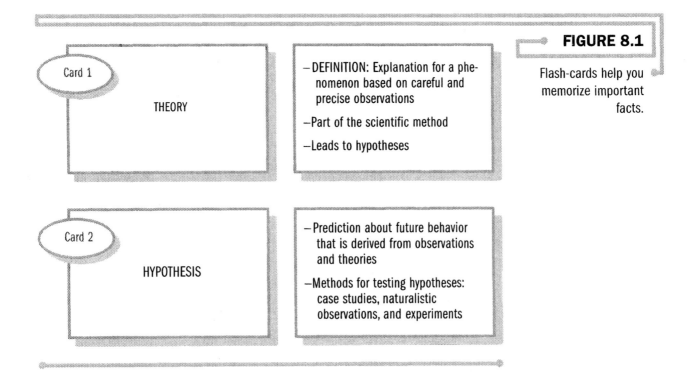

FIGURE 8.1

Flash-cards help you memorize important facts.

Card 1

THEORY

—DEFINITION: Explanation for a phenomenon based on careful and precise observations

—Part of the scientific method

—Leads to hypotheses

Card 2

HYPOTHESIS

—Prediction about future behavior that is derived from observations and theories

—Methods for testing hypotheses: case studies, naturalistic observations, and experiments

Mnemonic devices work by connecting information you are trying to learn with simpler information or information that is familiar. Instead of learning new facts by rote (repetitive practice), associations give you a hook on which to hang these facts and retrieve them. Mnemonic devices make information familiar and meaningful through unusual, unforgettable mental associations and visual pictures.

Here's an example to prove the power of mnemonics. Suppose you want to remember the names of the first six presidents of the United States. The first letters of their last names—Washington, Adams, Jefferson, Madison, Monroe, and Adams—together read W A J M M A. To remember them, you might add an "e" after the "J" and create a short nonsense word, "wajemma." To remember their first names—George, John, Thomas, James, James, and John—you might set the names to the tune of "Happy Birthday" or any musical tune that you know.

Visual images and acronyms are a few of the more widely used kinds of mnemonic devices. Apply them to your own memory challenges.

> "The true art of memory is the art of attention."
>
> SAMUEL JOHNSON

Create Visual Images and Associations

Visual images are easier to remember than images that rely on words alone. In fact, communication through visual images goes back to the prehistoric era, when people made drawings that still exist on cave walls. It's no accident that the phrase "a picture is worth a thousand words" is so familiar. The best mental pictures often involve colors, three-dimensional images, action scenes, and exaggerated, funny, or ridiculous images. Especially for visual learners, turning information into mental pictures helps improve memory.

Create Acronyms

Acronym
A word formed from the first letters of a series of words, created in order to help you remember the series.

Another helpful association method involves the use of the **acronym.** The acronym "Roy G. Biv" often helps students remember the colors of the spectrum. Roy G. Biv stands for **R**ed, **O**range, **Y**ellow, **G**reen, **B**lue, **I**ndigo, **V**iolet. In history, you can remember the big-three Allies during World War II—Britain, America, and Russia—with the acronym BAR.

When you can't create a name like Roy G. Biv, create an acronym from an entire sentence, in which the first letter of each word in the sentence stands for the first letter of each memorized term. When science students want to remember the list of planets in order of their distance from the sun, they learn the sentence: My very elegant mother just served us nine pickles. (Mercury, Venus, Earth, Mars, Jupiter, Saturn, Uranus, Neptune, and Pluto.)

Improving your memory requires energy, time, and work. By using the specific memory techniques described in this chapter, you will be able to learn more in less time—and remember what you learn long after exams are over.

HOW CAN TAPE RECORDERS HELP YOU LISTEN, REMEMBER, AND STUDY?

The selective use of a tape recorder can provide helpful backup to your listening and memory skills and to your study materials. It's important, though, not to let tape recording substitute for active participation. Not all students like to use tape recorders, but if you choose to do so, here are some guidelines and a discussion of potential effects.

Guidelines for Using Tape Recorders

Ask the professor whether he or she permits tape recorders in class. Some instructors don't mind, while others don't allow students to use them.

Use a small, portable tape recorder. Sit near the front for the best possible recording.

Participate actively in class. Take notes just as you would if the tape recorder were not there.

Make study tapes. Questions on tape can be like audio flashcards. One way to do it is to record study questions, leaving 10–15 seconds between questions for you to answer out loud. Recording the correct answer after the pause will give you immediate feedback. For example, part of a recording for a writing class might say, "The three elements of effective writing are . . . (10–15 seconds) . . . topic, audience, and purpose."

Potential Positive Effects of Using Tape Recorders

- You can listen to an important portion of the lecture over and over again.
- You can supplement or clarify sections of the lecture that confused you or that you missed.
- You have additional study materials to listen to when you exercise or drive in your car.
- Your study groups can reconcile conflicting notes.
- If you miss class, you might be able to have a friend record the lecture for you.

Potential Negative Effects of Using Tape Recorders

- You may tend to listen less in class.
- You may take fewer notes, figuring that you will rely on your tape.
- It may be time-consuming. When you attend a lecture in order to record it and then listen to the entire recording, you have taken twice as much time out of your schedule.
- If your tape recorder malfunctions or the recording is hard to hear, you may end up with very little study material, especially if your notes are sparse.

Think critically about whether using a tape recorder is a good idea for you. If you choose to try it, let the tape recorder be an additional resource for you instead of a replacement for your active participation and skills. Tape-recorded lectures and study tapes are just one study resource you can use in preparation for the tests that will often come your way.

HOW CAN PREPARATION HELP IMPROVE TEST SCORES?

Many people don't look forward to taking tests. If you are one of those people, try thinking of exams as preparation for life. When you volunteer, get a job, or work on your family budget, you'll have to apply what you know. This is exactly what you do when you take a test.

Like a runner who prepares for a marathon by exercising, eating right, taking practice runs, and getting enough sleep, you can take steps to master your exams. Your first step is to study until you know the material that will be on the test. Your next step is to use the following strategies to become a successful test taker: Identify the test type, use specific study skills, prepare physically, and conquer test anxiety.

Identify the Test Type and Material Covered

Before you begin studying, try to determine the type of test and what it will cover:

- Will it be a short-answer test with true/false and multiple-choice questions, solving problems, an essay test, or a combination?
- Will the test cover everything you studied since the semester began or will it be limited to a few specific topics?
- Will the test be limited to what you learned in class or will it also cover information from lab and recitations?

Your professors may answer these questions for you. Even though they may not tell you the specific questions that will be on the test, they might let you know what blocks of information will be covered and the question format. Some professors may even drop hints throughout the semester about possible test questions. While some comments are direct ("I might ask a question on the subject of "x" on your next exam"), other clues are subtle. For example, when professors repeat an idea or when they express personal interest in a topic ("One of my favorite theories is . . . "), they are letting you know that the material may be on the test.

Here are a few other strategies for predicting what may be on a test:

Identify important concepts. Go through your class notes and write down the particular areas that your professor emphasized during class. If you are unclear about whether a particular area is important, examine how much time the professor spent on that concept during class. Some students take this exercise a step further and set up an appointment with the professor or TA to confirm areas.

Study your annotated chapters and class notes. Use annotations from book chapters or class notes to identify important ideas and supporting details. In addition, studying charts and diagrams is also a good idea.

Examine old tests. Go to your college's or university's test file and get copies of old tests or download old tests off the Web. Peruse the questions on the exams and write down how many questions per topic appear on previous tests. This process helps you to identify important ideas that the exam will probably focus on, since previous professors who taught the course thought them to be important.

Use Specific Study Strategies

Certain study strategies are especially useful for test preparation. They include choosing study materials, setting a study schedule, critical thinking, working problems, and taking a pretest.

Choose Study Materials

Once you have identified as much as you can about the subject matter of the test, choose the materials that contain the information you need to study. You can save yourself time by making sure that you aren't studying anything you don't need to. Go through your notes, your texts, any primary source materials that were assigned, and any handouts from your instructor. Set aside any materials you don't need so they don't take up your valuable time.

Set a Study Schedule

Use your time-management skills to set a schedule that will help you feel as prepared as you can be. Consider all the relevant factors—the materials you need to study, how many days or weeks until the test date, and how much time you can study each day. If you establish your schedule ahead of time and write it in your date book, you will be much more likely to follow it.

Schedules will vary widely according to the situation. For example, if you have only three days before the test and no other obligations during that time, you might set two 2-hour study sessions for yourself during each day. On the other hand, if you have two weeks before a test date, attend classes during the day, and work three nights a week, you might spread out your study sessions over the nights you have off work during those two weeks.

Prepare Through Critical Thinking

Using the techniques from Chapter 5, approach your test preparation critically, working to understand rather than just to pass the test by repeating facts. As you study, try to connect ideas to examples, analyze causes and effects, establish truth, and look at issues from different perspectives.

Create concept maps to organize course information and assess what information you don't know. When you initially create a map, use your notes for reference. Refer to Chapter 7 for more information on concept mapping.

Work Problems

Rework homework problems and problems from old exams. Many professors put challenging homework problems or problems they did in class on the test, although the numbers may change or you may be asked to solve for a different parameter. Take time to review and understand lecture examples. By taking old exams in their entirety, you will determine which parts of the material you have learned and which parts you need to spend more time studying.

Take a Pretest

Use questions from the ends of textbook chapters to create your own pretest. Choose questions that are likely to be covered on the test, then answer them under testlike conditions—in quiet, with no books or notes to help you, and with a clock telling you when time is up. Try to duplicate the conditions of the actual test. If your course doesn't have an assigned text, develop questions from your notes and from assigned outside readings.

In order to write good test questions, you have to have a good understanding of the material. You may be surprised—some of your test questions may be very similar to the professor's questions as they appear on your test.

Prepare Physically

When taking a test, you often need to work efficiently under time pressure. If your body is tired or under stress, you will probably not think as clearly or perform as well. Avoid pulling an all-nighter. Get some sleep so that you can wake up rested and alert. If you are one of the many who press the snooze button in their sleep, try setting two alarm clocks and placing them across the room from your bed. That way you'll be more likely to get to your test on time.

Eating right is also important. Sugar-laden snacks will bring your energy up only to send it crashing back down much too soon. Similarly, too much caffeine can add to your tension and make it difficult to focus. Eating nothing will leave you drained, but too much food can make you want to take a nap. The best advice is to eat a light, well-balanced meal before a test. When time is short, grab a quick-energy snack such as a banana, some orange juice, or a granola bar.

Conquer Test Anxiety

A certain amount of stress can be a good thing. Your body is on alert, and your energy motivates you to do your best. For many students, however, the time before and during an exam brings a feeling of near-panic known as *test anxiety*. Described as a bad case of nerves that makes it hard to think or remember, test anxiety can make your life miserable and affect how you do on tests. When anxiety blocks performance, here are some suggestions:

Prepare so you'll feel in control. The more you know about what to expect on the exam, the better you'll feel. Find out what material will be covered, the format of the questions, the length of the exam, and the percentage of points assigned to each question.

Put the test in perspective. No matter how important it may seem, a test is only a small part of your educational experience and an even smaller part of your life. Your test grade does not reflect the kind of person you are or your ability to succeed in life.

Make a study plan. Divide the plan into a series of small tasks. As you finish each one, you'll feel a sense of accomplishment and control.

Practice relaxation. When you feel test anxiety coming on, take some deep breaths, close your eyes, and visualize positive mental images related to the test, like getting a good grade and finishing confidently with time to spare.

Test Anxiety and the Returning Adult Student

If you're returning to school after a layoff of 5, 10, or even 20 years, you may wonder if you can compete with younger students or if your mind is still able to learn new material. To counteract these feelings of inadequacy, focus on how your life experiences have given you skills you can use. For example, managing work and a family requires strong time management, planning, and communication skills that can help you plan your study time, juggle school responsibilities, and interact with students and professors.

In addition, your life experiences give you examples with which you can understand ideas in your courses. For example, your relationship experiences may help you understand concepts in a psychology course; managing your finances may help you understand economics or accounting practices; and work experience may give you a context for learning teamwork. If you recognize and focus on your knowledge and skills, you may improve your ability to achieve your goals.

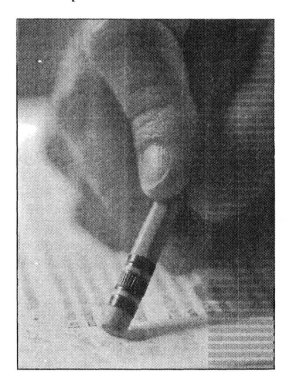

WHAT STRATEGIES CAN HELP YOU SUCCEED ON TESTS?

Even though every test is different, there are general strategies that will help you handle almost all tests, including short-answer and essay exams.

Write Down Key Facts

Before you even look at the test, write down any key information—including formulas, rules, and definitions—that you studied recently or even right before you entered the test room. Use the back of the question sheet. Recording this information right at the start will make forgetting less likely.

Begin with an Overview of the Exam

Even though exam time is precious, spend a few minutes at the start of the test to scan it and get a sense of the kinds of questions you'll be answering, what kind of thinking they require, the number of questions in each section, and the point value of each section. Use this information to schedule the time you spend on each section. For example, a $1\frac{1}{2}$ hour calculus exam may have 10 problems on it. As you plan your time, decide which problems are easier and which ones will take longer to solve. In addition, don't panic if you see problems that you think you can't solve. Skip them and come back to them later.

As you make your time calculations, think about the level of difficulty of each section. If you think you can handle the short-answer questions in less than an hour and that you'll need more time with the essays, rebudget your time in a way that works for you.

Know the Ground Rules

A few basic rules apply to any test. Following them will give you the advantage.

Read test directions. A calculus test made up of 10 problems may look straightforward, but the directions may tell you to answer 8 out of the 10 questions or explain which 5 problems you are required to do and which ones you can choose to do. Some questions or sections may be weighted more heavily than others. Try circling or underlining key words and numbers that remind you of the directions.

Begin with the problems or questions that seem easiest to you. Solving problems takes time. Do the easiest problems first, so you can have more time to complete the difficult ones. It will also help to build your self-confidence and reduce test anxiety.

Watch the clock. Keep track of how much time is left and how you are progressing. Wear a watch or bring a small clock with you to the test room. A wall clock may be broken, or there may be no clock at all! Also, take your time. Rushing is almost always a mistake, even if you feel you've done well. Stay till the end so you can refine and check your work.

Read the problems carefully. Make sure you underline important points and jot down a few facts about what the problem is asking. If you misinterpret the problem, chances are that you will receive little or no partial credit.

Draw a picture or diagram. When trying to solve engineering, chemistry, or physics problems, draw a picture or diagram to illustrate the information that has been given in the problem and what the problem is asking for. Many students need to see things visually before they start doing calculations.

Be sure to show all of your work. On calculus and physics exams it is imperative that you show *all of the steps* you did to obtain the solution to the problem. Professors can't give partial credit for a couple of steps and the answer. Professors are interested in the process you used to solve the problem, as well as the answer.

Qualifier
A word, such as *always*, *never*, or *often*, that changes the meaning of another word or word group.

Master the art of intelligent guessing. When you are unsure of an answer, you can leave it blank or you can guess. In most cases, guessing will benefit you. First eliminate all the answers you know—or believe—are wrong. Try to narrow your choices to two possible answers; then, choose the one that makes more sense to you. When you recheck your work, decide if you would make the same guesses again, making sure there isn't a **qualifier** or fact that you hadn't noticed before.

Follow directions on machine-scored tests. Machine-scored tests require that you use a special pencil to fill in a small box on a computerized answer sheet. Use the right pencil (usually a number 2) and mark your answer in the correct space. Neatness counts on these tests, because the computer can misread stray pencil marks or partially erased answers. Periodically, check the answer number against the question number to make sure they match. One question skipped can cause every answer following it to be marked incorrect.

Use Critical Thinking to Avoid Errors

When the pressure of a test makes you nervous, critical thinking can help you work through each question thoroughly and avoid errors. Following are some critical-thinking strategies to use during a test.

Recall facts, procedures, rules, and formulas. You base your answers on the information you recall. Think carefully to make sure you recall it accurately.

Think about similarities. If you don't know how to attack a question or problem, consider any similar questions or problems that you have worked on in class or while studying.

Notice differences. Especially with objective questions, items that seem different from what you have studied may indicate answers you can eliminate.

Think through causes and effects. For a numerical problem, think through how you plan to solve it and see if the answer—the effect of your plan—makes sense. For an essay question that asks you to analyze a condition or situation, consider both what caused it and what effects it has.

Find the best idea to match the example or examples given. For a numerical problem, decide what formula (idea) best applies to the example or examples (the data of the problem). For an essay question, decide what idea applies to, or links, the examples given.

Support ideas with examples. When you put forth an idea in an answer to an essay question, be sure to back up your idea with an adequate number of examples that fit.

Evaluate each test question. In your initial approach to any question, evaluate what kinds of thinking will best help you solve it. For example, essay questions often require cause-and-effect and idea-to-example thinking, while objective questions call for thinking through similarities and differences.

The general strategies you have just explored also can help you address specific types of test questions.

Master Different Types of Test Questions

Although the goal of all test questions is to discover how much you know about a subject, every question type has its own way of asking what you know.

Objective questions
Short-answer questions that test your ability to recall, compare, and contrast information and to choose the right answer from a limited number of choices.

Subjective questions
Essay questions that require you to express your answer in terms of your own personal knowledge and perspective.

Objective questions, such as multiple choice or true/false, test your ability to recall, compare, and contrast information and to choose the right answer from among several choices. **Subjective questions,** usually essay questions, demand the same information recall but ask that you analyze the mind actions and thinking processes required, then organize, draft, and refine a written response. The following guidelines will help you choose the best answers to both types of questions.

Multiple-Choice Questions

Multiple-choice questions are the most popular type on standardized tests. The following strategies can help you answer these questions:

Read the directions carefully. While most test items ask for a single correct answer, some give you the option of marking several choices that are correct.

First read each question thoroughly. Then look at the choices and try to answer the question.

Underline key words and phrases in the question. If the question is complicated, try to break it down into small sections that are easy to understand.

Pay special attention to qualifiers such as *only, except,* etc. For example, negative words in a question can confuse your understanding of what the question asks ("Which of the following is *not* . . .").

If you don't know the answer, eliminate those answers that you know or suspect are wrong. Your goal is to narrow down your choices. Here are some questions to ask:

- Is the choice accurate in its own terms? If there's an error in the choice—for example, a term that is incorrectly defined—the answer is wrong.
- Is the choice relevant? An answer may be accurate, but it may not relate to the essence of the question.
- Are there any qualifiers, such as *always, never, all, none,* or *every?* Qualifiers make it easy to find an exception that makes a choice incorrect. For example, the statement that "children *always* begin talking before the age of two" can be eliminated as an answer to the question, "When do children generally start to talk?"
- Do the choices give you any clues? Does a puzzling word remind you of a word you know? If you don't know a word, does any part of the word (prefix, suffix, or root) seem familiar to you?

> "A little knowledge that acts is worth infinitely more than much knowledge that is idle."
>
> **KAHLIL GIBRAN**

Look for patterns that may lead to the right answer, then use intelligent guessing. Test-taking experts have found patterns in multiple-choice questions that may help you get a better grade. Here is their advice:

- Consider the possibility that a choice that is more *general* than the others is the right answer.

- Look for a choice that has a middle value in a range (the range can be from small to large, from old to recent). This choice may be the right answer.
- Look for two choices with similar meanings. One of these answers is probably correct.

Make sure you read every word of every answer. Professors have been known to include answers that are right except for a single word.

When questions are keyed to a long reading passage, read the questions first. This will help you focus on the information you need to answer the questions.

Here are some examples of the kinds of multiple-choice questions you might encounter in an Introduction to Environmental Science course (the correct answer follows each question):

1. Significant increases in carbon dioxide levels have resulted from

   a. photosynthesis by land plants and algae

   b. deforestation and burning fossil fuels

   c. the evaporation of sweat

   d. the greenhouse effect

   (The correct answer is B.)

2. Human actions that might reasonably reduce the greenhouse effect include

   a. shifting to using more synthetic fuels

   b. maintaining food reserves

   c. building coastal dikes

   d. planting more trees

   (The correct answer is A.)

3. Which of the following would function as an output control device for motor vehicles?

   a. improving motor efficiency

   b. relying on mass transit and bicycles

   c. using emission control devices

   d. taxing new cars based on their efficiency

   (The correct answer is C.)

True/False Questions

True/false questions test your knowledge of facts and concepts. Read them carefully to evaluate what they truly say. Try to take these questions at face value without searching for hidden meaning. If you're truly stumped, guess (unless you're penalized for wrong answers).

Look for qualifiers in true/false questions—such as *all, only, always, because, generally, usually,* and *sometimes*—that can turn a statement that would otherwise be true into one that is false, or vice versa. For example, "The grammar rule, 'I before E except after C,' is *always* true" is *false*, whereas "The grammar rule, 'I before E except after C,' is *usually* true" is *true*. The qualifier makes the difference. Here are some examples of the kinds of true/false questions you might encounter in an Introduction to Psychology course.

Are the following questions true or false?

1. Alcohol use is always related to increases in hostility, aggression, violence, and abusive behavior. (False)

2. Marijuana is harmless. (False)

3. Simply expecting a drug to produce an effect is often enough to produce the effect. (True)

Essay Questions

An essay question allows you to use writing to demonstrate your knowledge and express your views on a topic. Start by reading the questions and deciding which to tackle if there is a choice. Then focus on what each question is asking, the mind actions you will have to use, and the writing directions. Read the question carefully and do everything you are asked to do. Some essay questions may contain more than one part.

Watch for certain action verbs that can help you figure out what to do. Figure 8.2, on the next page, explains some words commonly used in essay questions. Underline these words as you read any essay question and use them as a guide.

Next, budget your time and begin to plan. Create an informal outline or think link to map your ideas and indicate examples you plan to cite to support those ideas. Avoid spending too much time on introductions or flowery prose. Start with a thesis idea or statement that states in a broad way what your essay will say (see Chapter 7 for a discussion of thesis statements). As you continue to write your first paragraph, introduce the essay's points, which may be sub-ideas, causes and effects, or examples. End with a concise conclusion.

Use clear, simple language in your essay. Support your ideas with examples, and look back at your outline to make sure you are covering everything. Try to write legibly. If your professor can't read your ideas, it doesn't matter how good they are. If your handwriting is messy, try printing, skipping every other line, or writing on only one side of the paper.

Do your best to save time to reread and revise your essay after you finish getting your ideas down on paper. Look for ideas you left out and sentences that might confuse the reader. Check for mistakes in grammar, spelling, punctuation, and usage. No matter what subject you are writing about, having a command of these factors will make your work all the more complete and impressive.

Here are some examples of essay questions you might encounter in an Introduction to Psychology course. In each case, notice the action verbs from Figure 8-2.

1. Summarize the theories and research on the causes and effects of daydreaming. Discuss the possible uses for daydreaming in a healthy individual.

2. Describe the physical and psychological effects of alcohol and the problems associated with its use.

Analyze Break into parts and discuss each part separately.

Compare Explain similarities and differences.

Contrast Distinguish between items being compared by focusing on differences.

Criticize Evaluate the positive and negative effects of what is being discussed.

Define State the essential quality or meaning. Give the common idea.

Describe Visualize and give information that paints a complete picture.

Discuss Examine in a complete and detailed way, usually by connecting ideas to examples.

Enumerate/List/Identify Recall and specify items in the form of a list.

Explain Make the meaning of something clear, often by making analogies or giving examples.

Evaluate Give your opinion about the value or worth of something, usually by weighing positive and negative effects, and justify your conclusion.

Illustrate Supply examples.

Interpret Explain your personal view of facts and ideas and how they relate to one another.

Outline Organize and present the sub-ideas or main examples of an idea.

Prove Use evidence and argument to show that something is true, usually by showing cause and effect or giving examples that fit the idea to be proven.

Review Provide an overview of ideas, and establish their merits and features.

State Explain clearly, simply, and concisely, being sure that each word gives the image you want.

Summarize Give the important ideas in brief.

Trace Present a history of the way something developed, often by showing cause and effect.

FIGURE 8.2

Common action verbs on essay tests.

Types of Engineering Exam Questions

Engineering test questions are objective questions that test your ability to recall, compare and contrast, and analyze information. Types of test questions that appear on engineering exams include, but are not limited to, *multiple choice*, *short answer*, and *long answer*.

Multiple Choice

Distracter ◆━━━━━━━━━━
A choice that draws your attention away from other answers because it seems to be the right answer, but is not the correct answer.

The multiple-choice question is the most versatile type of test question. It can measure a variety of learning outcomes from simple to complex, and it is adaptable to most disciplines. Please keep in mind that most multiple-choice alternatives have one answer that is called a **distracter.** The purpose of a distracter is to keep the "unprepared" from selecting the correct answer. Students often refer to this answer as the one that "seems like the right answer," but has a minor flaw.

Multiple-choice questions on engineering exams generally are very different from arts and sciences or business questions. Arts and sciences or business multiple-choice test questions ask about general information from the lecture or the book: theories, principles, dates, facts, and people. Engineering multiple-choice questions ask you to decide whether information is true or false, to make a determination about a specific concept, or to solve a problem.

Helpful Hints for Doing Well on Multiple-Choice Tests

1. Look for clues in the alternatives (answers) before you work the problem.
2. Eliminate answers that are not plausible as the right answer.
3. Work the problem until you have enough information to select an answer.
4. If your answer is close to one of the alternatives, then select it as the right answer.
5. Check the units in the alternatives (answers). Distracters are often close to the right answer, but the units haven't been converted or the number is off by one or more orders of magnitude.

Short-Answer Questions

Most short-answer questions require calculation. Professors often include this type of test question on an exam to see if you know the process to solve the problem.

Sample Chemistry Short Answer Question

4. What is the energy in a mole of photons emitted at 365 nm?

SAMPLE CHEMISTRY TEST QUESTIONS

MULTIPLE CHOICE—TRUE/FALSE

1. Which of the following statements is false?

   a) Metallic solids generally have a loose hold on their electrons.

   b) Semi-conductors are materials in which the conductivity increases as temperature increases.

   c) Ionic solids are typically soft and have a luster.

   d) Covalent solids are strong materials with very high melting points.

   e) Molecular solids have low melting points and are soft.

   (Answer C is false.)

MULTIPLE CHOICE—DETERMINATION OF A SPECIFIC CONCEPT

2. Based on the Lewis dot structure and Valence Shell Electron Pair Repulsion (VSEPR) theory, what is the molecular shape of XeF_4?

   a) Seesaw

   b) Square planar

   c) Trigonal bipyramidal

   d) Square pyramidal

   e) Octahedral

   (The correct answer is A.)

MULTIPLE CHOICE—SOLVING A PROBLEM

3. When the initial concentration is (A) = 1.35m, the half-life of a reaction that is second-order is 3.3 minutes. What will the half-life be if the initial concentration of A is (A) = 4.05?

   a) 9.9 minutes

   b) 3.3 minutes

   c) 1.1 minutes

   d) 0.7 minutes

   e) 0.33 minutes

   (The correct answer is C.)

Long-Answer Questions

Long-answer problems may ask you to find the answer for three or four parts of the problem. These problems tend to have a lot of extra information. They generally take a long time to solve.

Sample Physics Long-Answer Question[4]

5. What downward force is exerted on the air by the blades of a 4300-kg helicopter when it is

   a) hovering at constant altitude

   b) dropping at 21 m/s with speed decreasing at 3.2 m/s^2

   c) rising at 17 m/s with speed increasing at 3.2 m/s^2

   d) rising at a steady 15 m/s

   e) rising at 15 m/s with speed decreasing at 3.2 m/s^2

Most of the problems that you will work during your engineering education, be they homework or test problems, will be math and science problems. The following five-step strategy will help you in your homework and in test taking.

Five-Step Strategy for Solving Math/Science Problems

Step 1: Scan the problem from beginning to end. Try to pick out the relevant parameters of the exercise. Determine the desired objective. There is no need to panic; you will break down the problem into components to solve it.

Step 2: Return to the beginning of the problem and proceed through again—however, this time label all possible relevant quantities with mathematical "symbol" names. Sketch any appropriate pictures or diagrams of objects that will help you solve the exercise.

Step 3: Return once again to the beginning of the problem and pass through it again, translating all given (or pertinent implied) relationships between the quantities labeled in Step 2 into *mathematical* form. Restate the desired goal of the problem (as determined in Step 1) in *mathematical* form.

Step 4: By this point, you should have reduced the problem to essentially a purely mathematical one, and now you can solve it as such. Don't expect to find the solution suddenly "in your head"—work through the process on paper.

Step 5: Evaluate your mathematical solution(s) as obtained in Step 4. In light of the original form of your problem, determine if all, just some, or none of your solutions make sense or are reasonable in that context (a so-called "reality check"). Only those solutions that pass this check should be considered for your final answer. If none of your solutions make sense, you may need to reexamine not just your calculations, but also your mathematical translation of the problem.

⚓ HOW CAN YOU LEARN FROM TEST MISTAKES? ⬤━━━━━━━━

The purpose of taking a test is to see how much you know, not merely to achieve a grade. The knowledge that comes from attending class and studying should allow you to correctly answer test questions. Knowledge also comes when you learn from your mistakes. If you don't learn from what you get wrong on a test, you are likely to repeat the same mistake again on another test and in life. Learn from test mistakes just as you learn from mistakes in your personal and business life.

Try to identify patterns in your mistakes by looking for:

- Careless errors—In your rush to complete the exam, did you misread the question or directions, blacken the wrong box, skip a question, or write illegibly?
- Conceptual or factual errors—Did you misunderstand a concept or never learn it in the first place? Did you fail to master certain facts? Did you skip part of the assigned text or miss classes in which important ideas were covered?

You may want to rework the questions you got wrong. Based on the feedback from your professor, try rewriting an essay, recalculating a math problem, or redoing the questions that follow a reading selection. As frustrating as they are, remember that mistakes show that you are human, and that they can help you learn. If you see patterns of careless errors, promise yourself that next time you'll budget enough time to double-check your work. If you pick up conceptual and factual errors, rededicate yourself to better preparation.

When you fail a test, don't throw it away. First, take comfort in the fact that a lot of students have been in your shoes and that you can (with effort) improve your performance. Then recommit to the process by reviewing and analyzing your errors. Be sure you understand why you failed. You may want to ask for an explanation from your professor. Finally, develop a plan to really learn the material if you didn't understand it in the first place.

ENDNOTES

1. Ralph G. Nichols, "Do We Know How to Listen? Practical Helps in a Modern Age," *Speech Teacher* (March 1961): 118–124.

2. Ibid.

3. Herman Ebbinghaus, *Memory: A Contribution to Experimental Psychology*, trans. H. A. Ruger and C. E. Bussenius (New York: New York Teacher's College, Columbia University, 1885).

4. Richard Wolfson and Jay M. Pasachoff, *Physics*, vol. 1 (Boston: Little, Brown & Co., 1987), 96.

Name   Date

CHAPTER 8 Applications

KEY INTO YOUR LIFE *Opportunities to Apply What You Learn*

EXERCISE 8.1 **Optimum Listening Conditions**

a. Describe a recent classroom situation in which you had an easy time listening to the professor.

Where are you?

_____

What is the professor discussing?

_____

Is it a straight lecture or is there give-and-take between professor and students?

_____

_____

What is your state of mind? (List factors that might affect your ability to listen.)

_____

_____

Are there any external barriers to communication? If yes, what are they, and how do they affect your concentration?

_____

_____

b. Now describe a situation where you have found it more difficult to listen.

Where are you?

_____

What is the professor discussing?

_____

Is it a straight lecture or is there give-and-take between professor and students?

_____

_____

What is your state of mind? (List factors that might affect your ability to listen.)

_____

_____

Are there any external barriers to communication? If yes, what are they, and how do they affect your concentration?

_____

_____

c. Examine the two situations. Based on your descriptions, name three conditions that are crucial for you to listen effectively.

1. _____

2. _____

3. _____

What steps can you take to recreate these conditions in more difficult situations, such as the second one you described?

_____

_____

Learning From Your Mistakes

EXERCISE   8.2

For this exercise, use an exam on which you made one or more mistakes.

a. Why do you think you answered the question(s) incorrectly?

_____

_____

b. Did any qualifying terms, such as _always, sometimes, never, often, occasionally, only, no,_ or _not,_ make the question(s) more difficult or confusing? What steps could you have taken to clarify the meaning?

_____

_____

c. Did you try to guess the correct answer? If so, why do you think you made the wrong choice?

_____

_____

_____

_____

d. Did you feel rushed? If you had had more time, do you think you would have gotten the right answer(s)? What could you have done to budget your time more effectively?

_____

_____

_____

_____

e. If an essay question was a problem, what do you think went wrong? What will you do differently the next time you face an essay question on a test?

_____

_____

_____

_____

_____

_____

_____

Relating to Others

Appreciating Your Diverse World

The greater part of your waking life involves interaction with people—family and friends, peers, fellow students, co-workers, professors, and many more. When you put energy into your relationships and open the lines of communication, you can receive much in return. Having a strong network of relationships can help you grow and progress toward your goals.

This chapter will explore the issues of diversity that can hinder or help how you perceive others and relate to them. You will also explore communication styles, personal relationships, and the roles you can play in groups and on teams. Finally, you will read about various kinds of conflict and criticism, examining how to handle them so they benefit you instead of setting you back.

In this chapter, you will explore answers to the following questions:

- How can you understand and accept others?

- How can you express yourself effectively?

- How do your personal relationships define you?

- How can you handle conflict and criticism?

- What role do you play in groups?

HOW CAN YOU UNDERSTAND AND ACCEPT OTHERS?

Human interaction is an essential element of life. In a diverse world, many people are different from what you are familiar with and perceive as "normal." In this section you will explore diversity in your world, the positive effects of accepting diversity, and how to overcome barriers to understanding. The first requirements for dealing with differences are an open mind and a willingness to learn.

Diversity in Your World

For centuries, travel to different countries was seen as part of a complete education. Edith Wharton, a nineteenth-century author, wrote a story called "False Dawn" in which a character named Mr. Raycie recommends travel to his son: "A young man, in my opinion, before setting up for himself, must see the world; form his taste; fortify his judgment. He must study the most famous monuments, examine the organization of foreign societies, and the habits and customs of those older civilizations . . . I believe he will be able to learn much."[1] When cultures were so separated, learning about differences was best accomplished through travel.

Diversity
The variety that occurs in every aspect of humanity, involving both visible and invisible characteristics.

Today, although traveling is still a valuable way to learn, different places and people often come to you. More and more, **diversity** is part of your community, on your television, on your Internet browser, at your school, in your workplace, and in your family. It used to be that most people lived in societies with others who seemed very similar to them. Now, differences are often woven into everyday life.

You may encounter examples of diversity like these:

- Communities with people of various ages and from different stages of life
- Co-workers who represent a variety of ethnic origins
- Classmates who speak a number of different languages
- Social situations featuring people from various cultures, religions, and sexual orientations
- Individuals who marry a person or adopt a child from a different racial or religious background
- A broad range of restaurants, services, and businesses in the community

- Neighborhoods with immigrants from a variety of social-class backgrounds

- Different lifestyles as reflected in books, magazines and news-papers, television, movies, music, the Internet, and other forms of popular culture

- People in the workplace who have a variety of disabilities—some more obvious than others

THE FAR SIDE   By GARY LARSON

Each person has a choice about how to relate to others—or *whether* to relate to them at all. No one can force you to interact with any other person or to adopt a particular attitude as being "right." As you deal with other people, you should consider two important responsibilities: your responsibility to yourself and your responsibility to others.

- Your responsibility to yourself lies in being true to yourself, in taking time to think through your reactions to other people. When you evaluate your thoughts, try to also consider their source: Have you heard these ideas from other people or organizations or the media? Do you agree with them, or does a different approach feel better to you? Through critical thinking you can arrive at decisions about which you feel comfortable and confident.

- Your responsibility to others lies in treating people with tolerance and respect. No one will like everyone he or she meets, but acknowledging that others deserve respect and have a right to their opinions will build bridges of communication. The more people accept one another, the more successful relationships will be able to thrive.

The Positive Effects of Diversity

More than just "a nice thing to do," accepting diversity has very real benefits to people in all kinds of relationships. Acceptance and respect form the basis for any successful interaction. As more situations bring diverse people into relationships, communication will become more and more dependent upon acceptance and mutual understanding.

Consider how positive relationships with diverse people may contribute to success. Relationships among family, friends, and neighbors affect personal life. Relationships among students, instructors, and other school personnel affect student life. Relationships among co-workers, supervisors, and customers/clients affect work life. Understanding and communication in these relationships can bring positive effects such as satisfying relationships, achievement, and progress. Failure to understand and communicate well can have negative effects.

For example, examine the potential effects of reactions to diversity in the following situations. Although each of these situations focuses on the reaction of only one person, it's important to note that both parties need to work together to establish mutual trust and openness.

"Minds are like parachutes. They only function when they are open."

SIR JAMES DEWAR

A male Hispanic employee has a female African-American supervisor. If the employee believes negative stereotypes about women or African-American people and resists taking directions from the supervisor, he may lose his job or be viewed as a liability. On the other hand, if the employee can respect the supervisor's authority and consider any different methods or ideas she has, their relationship is more likely to become supportive and productive. He may then be more likely to feel comfortable, perform well, and get promoted.

A learning-disabled student has an Asian professor. If the student assumes that Asian people are superior and intimidating, letting that opinion lead him to resist the advice and directions his professor gives him, he may do poorly in the class or drop the course. On the other hand, if the student stays open to what the professor has to offer, the professor may feel respected and may be more encouraging. The student may then be more likely to pay attention in class, work hard, and advance in his education.

A Caucasian man has a sister who adopts a biracial child. If the man cuts off contact with his sister because he fears racial differences and doesn't approve of racial mixing, he may create a rift in the family. On the other hand, if the man can accept the new family member and respect his sister's choice, the situation may help to build a close and rewarding family relationship.

Accepting others isn't always easy, and people often let perceptions about others block their ability to communicate. Following are some barriers that can hinder your ability to accept and understand others, and suggestions for how to overcome them.

Barriers to Understanding

You deserve to feel positive about who you are, where you come from, what you believe, and the others with whom you identify. However, problems arise when people use the power of group identity to put others down or cut themselves off from others and act in a closed-minded fashion. Table 9.1 shows how an open-minded approach can differ from an approach that is characterized by barriers.

Stereotypes, prejudice, discrimination, and fear of differences all can form barriers to communication.

Stereotypes

Stereotypes
A standardized mental picture that represents an oversimplified opinion or uncritical judgment.

As you learned in Chapter 5, an assumption is an idea that you accept without looking for proof. A **stereotype** occurs when someone makes an assumption about a person or group of people, based on one or more characteristics. You may have heard stereotypical assumptions such as these: "Women are too emotional for business." "African-Americans can run fast and sing well." "Hispanics are Catholic and have tons of kids." "White people are cold and power-hungry." "Gay people sleep around." "Learning-disabled people can't hold down jobs." "Older people can't learn new things." "Engineers are boring." Stereotypes are as common as they are destructive.

Why might people stereotype? Here are a few reasons:

A closed-minded approach vs. an open-minded approach.   **TABLE 9.1**

YOUR ROLE	SITUATION	CLOSED-MINDED APPROACH	OPEN-MINDED APPROACH
Team member on the job	A co-worker from India observes a Hindu religious ritual at lunchtime.	You stare at the religious ritual, thinking it weird. You feel that this co-worker should just blend in and act like everyone else.	Your observe the ritual, respecting how the person expresses religious beliefs. You look up Hindu religion in your spare time to learn more.
Fellow student	For an assignment, you are paired up with a student old enough to be your mother.	You figure that the student will be closed off to the modern world. You think that she might also act like a parent and preach to you about how to do the assignment.	You avoid thinking that this student will act like your parents and get to know her as an individual. You stay open to what you can learn from her experiences and knowledge.
Friend	You are invited to dinner at a friend's house for the first time. When he introduces you to his partner, you realize that he is gay.	You are turned off by the idea of two men in a relationship and by gay culture in general. You are uncomfortable and make an excuse to leave early. You avoid your friend from then on.	You have dinner with your friend and his partner. You learn that they have a committed, supportive relationship. You take the opportunity to learn more about who they are and what their lives are like.
Employee	Your new boss is Japanese-American, hired from a competing company.	You assume that your new boss is very hard-working, expecting unrealistic things from you and your co-workers. You assume he doesn't take time to socialize.	Your rein in your assumptions, knowing they are based on stereotypes, and approach your new boss without preconceived ideas.

People seek patterns and logic. Trying to make sense of a complex world is part of human nature. People often try to find order by using the labels and categories that stereotypes provide.

Stereotyping is quick and easy. Making an assumption about a person from observing an external characteristic is easier than working to know a person as a unique individual. Labeling a group of people based on a characteristic they seem to have in common takes less time and energy than exploring the differences and unique qualities within the group.

Movies, magazines, and other media encourage stereotyping. The more people see stereotypical images—the unintelligent blonde, the funny overweight person, the evil white businessman—the easier it is to believe that such stereotypes are universal.

The use of stereotypes comes at a high price. First and foremost, stereotypes can perpetuate harmful generalizations and falsehoods about others. These false ideas can promote discrimination. For example, if an employer believes that Vietnamese people cannot speak English well, he might not even bother to interview them. Second, stereotypes also communicate the message that you don't care about or respect others enough to discover who they really are. This may encourage others to stereotype you in return. Others may not give you a chance if they feel that you haven't given them a chance.

Addressing stereotypes. Recall from the critical-thinking material in Chapter 5 the questions you can ask about an assumption in order to examine its validity. Apply these questions to stereotypes:

1. In what cases is this stereotype true, if ever? In what cases is it not true?
2. Has stereotyping others benefited me? Has it hurt me? In what ways?
3. If someone taught me this stereotype, why? Did that person think it over or just accept it?
4. What harm could be done by always accepting this stereotype as true?

Using these steps, think through the stereotypes you assume are true. When you hear someone else use a stereotype and you know some information that contradicts it, volunteer that information. Encourage others to think through stereotypes and to reject them if they don't hold up under examination.

Give others the benefit of the doubt. Thinking beyond stereotypes is an important step toward more open lines of communication.

Prejudice

Prejudice
A preconceived judgment or opinion, formed without just grounds or sufficient knowledge.

Prejudice occurs when people "prejudge," meaning that they make a judgment before they have sufficient knowledge upon which to base that judgment. People often form prejudiced opinions on the basis of a particular characteristic—gender, race, culture, abilities, sexual orientation, religion, and so on. You may be familiar with the labels for particular kinds of prejudice, such as *racism* (prejudice based on race) or *ageism* (prejudice based on age). Any group can be subjected to prejudice, although certain groups have more often been on the receiving end of such closed-minded attitudes. Prejudice can lead people to disrespect, harass, and put down others. In some cases, prejudice may lead to unrealistic expectations of others that aren't necessarily negative, such as if someone were to judge all Jewish people as excelling in business.

Prejudice can have one or more causes. Some common causes are presented in the following paragraphs.

People experience the world through the lens of their own particular identity. You grow up in a particular culture and family and learn their attitudes. When you encounter different ideas and ways of life, you may react by categorizing them. You may also react with *ethnocentrism*—the idea that your group is better than anyone else's.

When people get hurt, they may dislike or blame anyone who seems similar to the person who hurt them. Judging others based on a bad experience is human, especially when a particular characteristic raises strong emotions.

Jealousy and fear of personal failure can lead a person to want to put others down. When people are feeling insecure about their own abilities, they might find it easier to devalue the abilities of others rather than to take risks and try harder themselves.

The many faces of prejudice are often visible on college campuses. A student may not want to work with an in-class group that contains people of another race. Campus clubs may tend to limit their membership to a particular group and exclude others. Religious groups may devalue the beliefs of other religions. Groups that gather based on a common characteristic might be harassed by others. Women or men may find that instructors or fellow students judge their abilities and attitudes based on their gender. All of these attitudes severely block attempts at mutual understanding.

Addressing prejudice. Being critical of people who are different cuts you off from all kinds of perspectives and people that can enhance the quality of your life. Critical thinking is your key to changing prejudicial attitudes. For example, suppose you find yourself thinking that a certain student in your class isn't the type of person you want to get to know. Ask yourself: Where did I get this attitude? Am I accepting someone else's judgment? Am I making judgments based on how this person looks or speaks or behaves? How does having this attitude affect me or others? If you see that your attitude needs to change, have the courage to activate that change by considering the person with an open, accepting mind.

At times in your job and in your personal life, you may come into contact with people who display prejudiced attitudes toward you, your co-workers, or members of your family. You may decide that this prejudice is unacceptable and choose to address it by confronting those people when they display a prejudiced attitude. It can be hard to stand up to someone and risk a relationship or, if the person is your employer, even a job. On the other hand, your silence may imply that you agree. Evaluate the situation and decide what choice is most suitable and true to your values. Ask yourself if you can associate with a person if he or she thinks or behaves in a way that you do not respect.

You have a range of choices when deciding whether to reveal your feelings about someone's behavior. You can decide not to address it at all. You may drop a humorous hint and hope that you make your point. You may make a small comment to "test the waters" and see how the person reacts, hoping that later you can have a more complete discussion about it. Whatever you do, express your opinion respectfully. Perhaps the other person will take that chance to rethink the attitude; perhaps he or she will not. Either way, you have taken an important stand.

Discrimination

Discrimination occurs when people deny others opportunities because of their perceived differences. Prejudice often accompanies discrimination. Discrimination can involve the denial of jobs or advancement, equal educational opportunities, equal housing opportunities, services, or access to events, people, rights, privileges, or commodities to someone who deserves them.

Discrimination happens in all kinds of situations, revolving around gender, language, race, culture, and other factors. A 32-year-old married woman may not win a job because the interviewer assumes that she will become pregnant. A Russian person may be fired from a restaurant job because his English is heavily accented. Sheryl McCarthy, an African-American columnist for *New York Newsday*, sees it on the street. "Nothing is quite so basic and clear as

having a cab go right past your furiously waving body and pick up the white person next to you," she says in her book, *Why Are the Heroes Always White?*[2] "Sometimes you can debate whether racism was the motivating factor in an act; here there is no doubt whatsoever." Even so-called majority populations may now experience discrimination.

The disabled are often targets of discrimination because people may believe that they are depressed and incapacitated. John Hockenberry, a wheelchair-using paraplegic who travels the world in his work as an award-winning journalist, challenges the idea that disabled people lead lives of unproductive misery. "My body may have been capable of less, but virtually all of what it could do was suddenly charged with meaning. This feeling was the hardest to translate to the outside, where people wanted to believe that I must have to paint things in this way to keep from killing myself," he says in his memoir *Moving Violations.*[3]

Obesity can invite discrimination as well. People who are overweight may have trouble winning jobs or being promoted at work. Even shopping for clothing can present limited options. Only recently have certain brand-name designers begun to create clothing in women's sizes above 12, while many designers still discriminate.

Addressing discrimination. U.S. federal law states that it is unlawful for you to be denied an education, work (or the chance to apply for work), housing, or basic rights based on your race, creed, color, age, gender, national or ethnic origin, religion, marital status, potential or actual pregnancy, or potential or actual illness or disability (unless the illness or disability prevents you from performing required tasks, and unless accommodations for the disability are not possible). Unfortunately, the law is frequently broken, and the incidents often go unreported. Many times people don't report incidents, fearing trouble from those they accuse. Sometimes people don't even notice their attitudes seeping through, such as in an interview situation. So what can you do?

First and foremost, be responsible for your own behavior. Never knowingly participate in or encourage discrimination. When you act on prejudicial attitudes by discriminating against someone, the barrier to communication this discrimination causes hurts you as well as anyone else involved. A person who feels denied and shut out may be likely to do the same to you, and may even encourage others to do so.

Second, if you witness a discriminatory act or feel that you have been discriminated against, decide whether you want to approach an authority about it. You may want to begin by talking to the person who can most directly affect the situation—an instructor, your supervisor, a housing authority. Don't assume that people know when they hurt or offend someone. For example, if you have a disability and you find that accommodations haven't been made for

Success in the Real World

T. Meredith Ross, P. E.

Business Process Manager, Applied Materials

I specifically chose my career in junior high school in the late 50s. I wanted to spend my career playing golf. After I graduated from college with an M.A.T. in math, I turned pro. I spent two and a half wonderful years traveling the country, playing golf courses. However, I also spent lots of that time on the injured and disabled list. Torn muscles, torn ligaments, heat strokes, you name it, this math major had the strangest set of golf-course injuries ever strung together. Eventually, if I wanted to eat consistently, I had to go back to work for a living. I joined a preeminent architectural, engineering, and construction firm as a financial systems analyst. After two years, I realized this firm had no career path established for an ex-professional golfer turned systems analyst. I had several choices: one was to move to a more computer-oriented company; another was to stay.

Surely this was a diverse enough company to have something else for me to do! But what? I looked to the top of the company organization—almost every one in the top several rows of this architectural, engineering, and construction firm were male engineers! That caused me to wonder what engineers did for a living. Obviously there were career paths for engineers. Since I liked the people I worked with, the personality of the company, and the corporate stance of the company, my preference was to stay rather than change and have to relearn all those things one has to learn in a new situation.

I noticed on the bulletin board one day that a review class for engineers in training was being given at the local university in the evenings. I was most surprised that the first several weeks were taken up with chemistry, physics, mathematics, computers,

thermodynamics, numerical analysis, and economics. Some of these were areas in which I had developed strengths during college. Then finally we started with the engineering. We talked about some guy by the name of Ohm and then about how a material's shear strength is related to its tensile strength. (I'd always thought that tensile was something you put on the Christmas tree!) I didn't really find out what engineers do for a living, but I did gain confidence that it was not beyond the wit of this ex-professional golfer.

I made an appointment with the Chief Engineer. *She* was significantly less surprised to find that a person from finance and accounting was applying for her engineering job than I was to be sitting across the desk from a woman. We made a deal: I would complete a file-conversion project, and by then maybe I would know what engineers did for a living and they would know if I had the skill set to become an engineer. The rest is history. That particular chief engineer and a couple of others have always said they hired me so I could help them with their golf game. But somehow, in the 20 years I worked at that firm, I never played golf with any one of them!

you at school, speak up. Meet with an advisor to discuss your needs for transport, equipment, or a particular schedule.

If you don't find satisfaction at that level, try the next level of authority (an administrator, your supervisor's boss, a government official). If that doesn't produce results, you can take legal action, although legal struggles require a large investment of your time and energy, erode personal relationships, and drain a great deal of money out of your pocket. At each decision stage, weigh all the positive and negative effects and evaluate whether the action is feasible for you. Although keeping quiet does not bring change, you may not be able to act right away. In the long run, if you are able to stand up for what you believe, your actions may be worthwhile.

Fear of Differences

It's human instinct to fear the unknown. Many people stop long before they actually explore anything unfamiliar. They allow their fear to prevent them from finding out anything about what's outside their known world. As cozy as that world can be, it also can be limiting, cutting off communication from people who could enrich that world in many different ways.

The fear of differences has many effects. A young person who fears the elderly may avoid visiting a grandparent in a nursing home. A person of one religion might reject friendships with those of other religions out of a fear of different religious beliefs. Someone in a relationship may fear the commitment of marriage. A person might turn down an offer to buy a house in a neighborhood that is populated with people from a different ethnic group. In each case, the person may forgo a chance to learn a new perspective, communicate with new individuals, and grow from new experiences.

Address fear of differences. Diversity doesn't mean that you have to feel comfortable with everyone or agree with what everyone else believes. The fear of differences, though, can keep you from discovering anything outside your own world. Challenge yourself by looking for opportunities to expose yourself to differences. Today's world increasingly presents such opportunities. You can choose a study partner in class who has a different ethnic background. You can expand your knowledge with books or magazines. You can visit a museum or part of town that introduces a culture new to you. You can attend an unfamiliar religious service with a friend. Gradually broaden your horizons and consider new ideas.

If you think others are uncomfortable with differences, encourage them to work through their discomfort. Explain the difference so that it doesn't seem so mysterious. Offer to help them learn more in a setting that isn't threatening. Bring your message of the positive effects of diversity to others.

Accepting and Dealing with Diversity

Successful interaction with the people around you benefits everyone. The success of any exchange depends on your ability to accept differences. How open can you be? Your choices range from rejecting all differences to freely celebrating them, with a range of possibilities in between. Ask yourself important questions about what course of action you want to take. Realize that the

> "I have a dream that one day on the red hills of Georgia the sons of former slaves and the sons of former slave owners will be able to sit down together at the table of brotherhood."
>
> **MARTIN LUTHER KING, JR.**

opinions of family, friends, the media, and any group with which you identify may sometimes lead you into perspectives and actions that you haven't thought through completely. Do your best to sort through outside opinions and make a choice that feels right.

At the top of the list of ways to deal with differences is mutual respect. Respect for yourself and others is essential. Admitting that other people's cultures, behaviors, races, religions, appearances, and ideas deserve as much respect as your own promotes communication and learning.

What else can you do to accept and deal with differences?

Avoid judgments based on external characteristics. These include skin color, weight, facial features, and gender.

Cultivate relationships with people of different cultures, races, perspectives, and ages. Find out how other people live and think, and see what you can learn from them.

Educate yourself and others. "We can empower ourselves to end racism through massive education," say Tamara Trotter and Joycelyn Allen in *Talking Justice: 602 Ways to Build and Promote Racial Harmony.*[4] "Take advantage of books and people to teach you about other cultures. Empowerment comes through education. If you remain ignorant and blind to the critical issues of race and humanity, you will have no power to influence positive change." Read about other cultures and people.

Be sensitive to the particular needs of others at school and on the job. Think critically about their situations. Try to put yourself in their place by asking yourself questions about what you would feel and do if you were in a similar situation.

Work to listen to people whose perspectives clash with or challenge your own. Acknowledge that everyone has a right to an opinion, whether or not you agree with it.

Look for common ground—classes, personal challenges, interests.

Help other people, no matter how different they may be. Sheryl McCarthy writes about an African-American man who, in the midst of the 1992 Los Angeles riots, saw a man being beaten and helped him to safety. "When asked why he risked grievous harm to save an Asian man he didn't even know, Williams said, 'Because if I'm not there to help someone else, when the mob comes for me, will there be someone there to save me?'"[5] Continue the cycle of kindness.

Explore your own background, beliefs, and identity. Share what you learn with others.

Success in the Real World

Katherine Osborne

Graduate Student, Joint Degree Program—Business and Engineering, University of Texas

It was the best day of my Peace Corps service. As I walked house to house, I realized that I was no longer the only water expert in La Horma. Together, the community and I had achieved our goal of constructing two gravity-fed aqueducts, providing the community with reliable access to potable water. And, more important to me, community members now possessed the skills to maintain the system in the years to come.

Constructing these aqueducts in the Dominican Republic was the most challenging undertaking of my life. Strictly speaking, it presented an engineering problem that I was eager to confront. However, my Peace Corps experience showed me that there was more to engineering than the technical application of science and math. Not only did I face the hurdle of Dominican language and culture, but also I was forced to come to grips with the complex roles that government, economics, and society play in the success of a community endeavor.

For two years, I worked as an environmental sanitation engineer with the Peace Corps in La Horma, a rural community of 700 located in the central mountains of the Dominican Republic. The community water committee and I began a feasibility study for construction of an aqueduct within my first few months in La Horma. The study consisted of predictable engineering factors: a community census, topographic study, and evaluation of the possible water sources. Our first obstacle arose almost immediately: conflicting water rights between a farmer who claimed the water for irrigation and the community that wanted it for drinking water. We were able to reach an agreement only after much smoothing of feathers and the help of an outside mediator.

Upon securing this agreement and funds, we began construction. For over a year, Monday through Saturday, 120 farmers and I worked cooperatively to construct the two aqueducts: gravity-fed potable water systems consisting of cement block tanks, break pressure boxes, and over six miles of PVC piping. The farmers worked in brigades: 20 men in each brigade, and one brigade for each day of the week. As a North American woman, I had to gain the trust and respect of the men that worked on these brigades—a journey in itself. As the construction phase ended, I took pride not only in having learned to work with and manage the brigades, but also in the tangible result of that relationship: two functioning aqueducts and the infrastructure to maintain them.

On a college application, answering the question, "Which academic subject is most meaningful to you and why?" I responded: "It is science. No, math. No, science *and* math. For me, it's a blend.  I want to study, discover, and add something significant to the world in which we live." In engineering, I found a career that combines my interests in multiple academic subjects and fosters development and discovery. As I finish my graduate work, where I have focused on water resources, I am even more confident of my decision to pursue engineering. My work has the potential to affect people and the environment positively, both in the United States and abroad, while utilizing and challenging my technical ability.

Cultivate your own personal diversity. You may be part of the growing population of people who have two, three, or ten different cultures in your background. Perhaps your father is Native American and Filipino and Scottish, and your mother is Creole (French, Spanish, and African-American). Respect and explore your heritage. Even if you identify only with one group or culture, there are many different sides of you.

Take responsibility for making changes instead of pointing the finger at someone else. Avoid blaming problems in your life on certain groups of people.

Learn from the atrocities of history, such as slavery and the Holocaust. Consider the ethical implications of chemical warfare research or exporting banned or unsafe materials to third-world countries. Cherish the level of freedom you have and seek continual improvement at home and elsewhere in the world.

Recognize that people everywhere have the same basic needs. Everyone loves, thinks, hurts, hopes, fears, and plans. People are united through their essential humanity.

Expressing your ideas clearly and interpreting what others believe are crucial keys to communicating within a diverse world. The following section examines how you can communicate most effectively with the people around you.

HOW CAN YOU EXPRESS YOURSELF EFFECTIVELY?

One of the best ways for people to know each other's needs is to communicate as clearly and directly as possible. Successful communication promotes successful school, work, and personal relationships. However, people can communicate very differently as a result of their culture, thinking style, life approach, and upbringing. Exploring communication styles, addressing communication problems, and using specific success strategies will help you express yourself effectively.

Adjusting to Communication Styles

Communication is an exchange between two or more people. The speaker's goal is for the listener (or listeners) to receive the message exactly as the speaker intended. Different people, however, have different styles of communicating. Problems arise when one person has trouble "translating" a message that comes from someone who uses a different style. There are four general communication styles into which people tend to fit: the Intuitor, the Senser, the Thinker, and the Feeler. Of course, people may shift around or possess characteristics from more than one category, but for most people one or two styles are dominant. Recognizing specific styles in others will help you communicate more clearly.[6]

The Styles

The following are characteristics of each communication style.

An Intuitor is interested in ideas more than details, often moves from one concept or generalization to another without referring to examples, values insight and revelations, talks about having a vision, looks toward the future, and can be oriented toward the spiritual.

A Senser prefers details or concrete examples to ideas and generalizations, is often interested in the parts rather than the whole, prefers the here-and-now to the past or future, is suspicious of sudden insights or revelations, and feels that "seeing is believing."

A Thinker prefers to analyze situations, likes to solve problems logically, sees ideas and examples as useful if they help to figure something out, and becomes impatient with emotions or personal stories unless they have a practical purpose.

A Feeler is concerned with ideas and examples that relate to people, often reacts emotionally, is concerned with values and their effects on people and other living things, and doesn't like "cold logic" or too much detail.

You can benefit from shifting your communication style according to the situation, particularly when trying to communicate with someone who prefers a style different from yours. Shifting, however, is not always easy or possible. The most important task is to try to understand the different styles others use and help others understand the style you use. In general, no one style is any better than another. Each has its own positive effects that enhance communication and negative effects that can hinder it, depending on the situation.

Identifying Your Styles

These four styles are derived from the Myers-Briggs Type Indicator (MBTI). Because the learning style assessments are also in part derived from the MBTI, you will notice similarities between those assessments and these communication styles. Table 9.2 shows how some learning styles may correspond loosely to the communication styles. Not all individual learning styles within the assessments are mentioned, and the styles that are noted may correspond with different styles in different situations, but these matchups depict the most common associations. Finding where your learning styles fit may help you to determine your dominant communication style or styles.

Adjusting to the Listener's Style

When you are the speaker, you will benefit from an understanding of both your own style and the styles of your listeners. It doesn't matter how clear you

TABLE 9.2 Learning styles and communication styles.	COMMUNICATION STYLE	LEARNING STYLES INVENTORY	PATHWAYS TO LEARNING (MULTIPLE INTELLIGENCES)	PERSONALITY SPECTRUM
	Intuitor	Theoretical, Holistic	Intrapersonal	Adventurer
	Senser	Factual	Bodily-Kinesthetic	Organizer
	Thinker	Linear	Logical-Mathematical	Thinker
	Feeler	Reflective	Interpersonal	Giver

think you are being if the person you are speaking to can't "translate" your message by understanding your style. Try to take your listener's style into consideration when you communicate.

Following is an example of how adjusting to the listener can aid communication.

An intuitor-dominant professor to a senser-dominant student: "Your writing isn't clear." The student's reply: "What do you mean?"

- Without adjustment: If the intuitor doesn't take note of the senser's need for detail and examples, he or she may continue with a string of big-picture ideas that might further confuse and turn off the senser. "You need to elaborate more. Try writing with your vision in mind. You're not considering your audience."

- With adjustment: If the intuitor shifts toward a focus on detail and away from his or her natural focus on ideas, the senser may begin to understand, and the lines of communication can open. "You introduced your central idea at the beginning but then didn't really support it until the fourth paragraph. You need to connect each paragraph's idea to the central idea. Also, not using a lot of examples for support makes it seem as though you are writing to a very experienced audience."

Adjusting to the Communicator's Style

As a facet of communication, listening is just as important as speaking. When you are the listener, try to stay aware of the communication style of the person who is speaking to you. Observe how that style satisfies, or doesn't satisfy, what a person of your particular style prefers to hear. Work to understand the speaker in the context of his or her style and translate the message into one that makes sense to you.

Following is an example of how adjusting to the communicator can boost understanding.

A feeler-dominant employee to a thinker-dominant supervisor: "I'm really upset about how you've talked down to me. I don't think you've been fair. I haven't been able to concentrate since our discussion and it's hurting my performance."

- Without adjustment. If the thinker becomes annoyed with the feeler's focus on emotions, he or she may ignore them, putting up an even stronger barrier between the two people. "There's no reason to be upset. I told you clearly and specifically what needs to be done. There's nothing else to discuss."

- With adjustment. If the thinker considers that emotions are dominant in the feeler's perspective, he or she could respond to those emotions in a way that still searches for the explanations and logic the thinker understands best: "Let's talk about how you feel. Please explain to me what has caused you to become upset, and we'll discuss how we can improve the situation."

Overcoming Communication Problems

Communication problems may occur when information is not clearly presented, or when those who receive information filter it through their own perspectives and interpret it in different ways than intended. A few of the most common communication problems follow, along with strategies to help you solve them.

Problem: Unclear or incomplete explanation

Solution: Support ideas with examples

When you clarify a general idea with supporting examples that illustrate how it works and what effects it causes, you will help your receiver understand what you mean and therefore have a better chance to hold his or her attention.

For example, if you tell a friend to take a certain class, that friend might not take you seriously until you explain why. If you then communicate the positive effects of taking that class (progress toward a major, an excellent professor, friendly study sessions), you may get your message across. The same principle applies to your attitude toward this course. If others communicate to you specific examples of how your work in the course will benefit your education, career, and personal life, you may be more likely to apply yourself.

Work situations benefit from explanation as well. As a supervisor, if you assign a task without explanation, you might get a delayed response or find mistakes in your employee's work. If, however, you explain the possible positive effects of the task, you'll have better results.

Problem: Attacking the receiver

Solution: Send "I" messages

When a conflict arises, often the first instinct is to pinpoint what someone else did wrong. "You didn't lock the door!" "You never called last night!" "You left me out!" Making an accusation, especially without proof, puts the other person on the defensive and shuts down the lines of communication.

Using "I" messages will help you communicate your own needs rather than focusing on what you think someone else did wrong or should do differently. "I felt uneasy when I came to work and the door was unlocked." "I became worried about you when I didn't hear from you last night." "I felt disappointed when I realized that I couldn't join the party." "I" statements soften the conflict by highlighting the *effects* that the other person's actions have had on you, rather than the person or the actions themselves. When you focus on your own response and needs, your receiver may feel more free to respond, perhaps offering help and even acknowledging mistakes.

If you often feel dissatisfied and tense after an exchange, you may benefit from focusing more on your own needs when you communicate. Translate your anger into an "I" statement before speaking. Ask the other person, "Can we decide together how to improve this situation? Here's how I feel about what has happened." Using "I" statements will bring better results.

Problem: Passive or aggressive communication behaviors

Solution: Become assertive

Among the three major communication behaviors—aggressive, passive, assertive—the one that conveys a message in the clearest, most productive way is the **assertive** behavior. The other two, while commonly used, throw the communication out of balance. An aggressive communicator often denies the receiver a chance to respond, while a passive communicator may have trouble getting the message out. Assertive behavior strikes a balance between aggression and passivity. If you can be an assertive communicator, you will be more likely to get your message across while assuring that others have a chance to speak as well. Table 9.3 compares some characteristics of each kind of communicator.

> **Assertive**
> Able to declare and affirm one's own opinions while respecting the rights of others to do the same.

Aggressive communicators focus on power and relative advantage, and try to express their opinions to the detriment of others. They can become angry and impatient when their needs are not immediately satisfied. In order to become more effective, aggressive communicators might try to take time to think before speaking, avoid ordering people around, use "I" statements, focus on listening to what the other person has to say, and becoming more accommodating and considerate.

Passive communicators deny themselves the power that aggressive people grab. They focus almost exclusively on the needs of others instead of on their own needs, experiencing frustration and tension that remains unexpressed. In order to become more assertive, passive communicators might try to acknowledge anger or hurt more often, speak up when they feel strongly about something, realize that they have a right to make requests, and know that their ideas and feelings are as important as anyone else's.

AGGRESSIVE	PASSIVE	ASSERTIVE
Loud, heated arguing	Concealing one's own feelings	Expressing feelings without being nasty or overbearing
Physically violent encounters	Denying one's own anger	Acknowledging emotions but staying open to discussion
Blaming, name-calling, and verbal insults	Feeling that one has no right to express anger	Expressing self and giving others the chance to express themselves equally
Walking out of arguments before they are resolved	Avoiding arguments	Using "I" statements to defuse arguments
Being demanding: "Do this"	Being noncommittal: "You don't have to do this unless you really want to . . ."	Asking and giving reasons: "I would appreciate it if you would do this, and here's why . . ."

> **TABLE 9.3**
> Aggressive, passive, and assertive styles.

Communication Success Strategies

These additional strategies can help improve your communication.

Think before you speak. Spoken too soon, ideas can come out sounding nothing like you intended them to. Taking time to think, or even rehearsing mentally, can help you choose the best combination of words. Think it through and get it right the first time.

Don't withhold your message for too long. One danger of holding back is that a problem or negative feeling may become worse. In the predominant U. S. culture, speaking promptly has two benefits: (1) you solve the problem sooner, and (2) you are more likely to focus on the problem at hand than to spill over into other issues.

Communicate in a variety of ways, and be sensitive to cultural differences. Remember that words, gestures, and tones mean different things to different people.

Be clear, precise, and to the point. Say exactly what you need to say. Link your ideas to clear examples, avoiding any extra information that can distract.

Communication is extremely important for building and maintaining personal relationships. Explore how those relationships define who you are.

HOW DO YOUR PERSONAL RELATIONSHIPS DEFINE YOU?

The relationships you have with friends, family members, and significant others often take center stage. Jobs and schooling can come and go, but you rely on the people with whom you share your life.

In addition to being part of your life, the people around you help to define who you are. Since birth, you have learned by taking in information from verbal and nonverbal language. The chain of learning stretches back through time, each link formed by an exchange of information between people. Those with whom you live, play, study, and work are primary sources of ideas, beliefs, and ways of living. You grow and change as you have new experiences, evaluate them, and decide what to learn from them.

These influential relationships can affect other areas of your life. You have probably experienced conflict that caused you to be unable to sleep, eat, or get any work done. On the other hand, a successful relationship can have positive effects on your life, increasing your success at work or at school. Following are some strategies for improving your personal relationships.

Relationship Strategies

If you can be comfortable with your personal relationships, other areas of your life will benefit. Here are some suggestions.

Make personal relationships a high priority. Nurture the ones you have and be open to developing new ones. Life is meant to be shared. In some marriage ceremonies, the bride and groom share a cup of wine that symbolizes life. One of the reasons for this tradition is to double the sweetness of life by tasting it together, and to cut the bitterness in half by sharing it. Any personal relationship can benefit from the experience of this kind of sharing.

Invest time. You devote time to education, work, and the other priorities in your life. Relationships need the same investment. They are like plants in a garden, needing nourishment to grow and thrive. Your attention provides that nourishment. In addition, spending time with people you like can relieve everyday stress and strain. When you make time for others, everyone benefits.

Spend time with people you respect and admire. Life is too short to hang out with people who bring you down, encourage you to participate in activities you don't approve of, or behave in ways that upset you. Develop relationships with people whom you respect, whose choices you admire, and who inspire you to be all that you can be. This doesn't mean that you have to agree with everything that others do. For example, you may disagree with a friend who drinks heavily every weekend. However, you may severely disapprove of someone who is physically abusive, and you may choose to end your association with that person.

Work through tensions. Negative feelings can multiply when left unspoken. Unexpressed feelings about other issues may cause you to become disproportionately angry over a small issue. A small annoyance over clothes left on the floor in your dorm room can turn into a gigantic fight about everything under the sun. Discuss it, deal with it, and move on.

Refuse to tolerate violence. It isn't easy to face the problem of violence or to leave a violent relationship. People may tolerate violence out of a belief that it will end, a desire to keep their families together, a self-esteem so low that they believe they deserve what they get, or a fear that trying to leave may lead to greater violence. No level of violence is acceptable. Someone who behaves violently toward you cannot possibly have your best interests at heart. If you find that you are either an aggressor or a victim, do your best to get help.

Show appreciation. In this fast-moving world, people don't thank each other often enough. If you think of something positive, say it. Thank someone for a service, express your affection with a smile. A little positive reinforcement goes a long way toward nurturing a relationship.

If you want a friend, be a friend. The Golden Rule, "Do unto others as you would have them do unto you," never goes out of style. If you treat a friend with the kind of loyalty and support that you appreciate yourself, you are more likely to receive the same in return.

Take risks. It can be frightening to reveal your deepest dreams and frustrations, to devote yourself to a friend, or to fall in love. You can choose not to reveal yourself or give yourself to a friendship at all. However, giving is what feeds a relationship, bringing satisfaction and growth. If you take the plunge, you risk disappointment and heartbreak, but you stand to gain the incredible benefits of companionship, which for most people outweigh the risks.

Keep personal problems in their place. Solve personal problems with the people directly involved and no one else. If at all possible, try not to bring your emotions into class or work. Doing so may hurt your performance while doing nothing to help your problem. If you are overwhelmed by a personal problem, try to address it before you go to class or work. If it's impossible to address it at that time, at least make a plan that you can carry out later. Making some step toward resolving the problem will help you concentrate on other things.

If it doesn't work out, find ways to cope. Everyone experiences strain and breakups in intimate relationships, friendships, and family ties. Be kind to yourself and use coping strategies that help you move on. Some people need lots of time alone; others need to spend time with their friends and family. Some seek more formal counseling. Some people throw their energy into a project, a job, a class, a new workout regimen, or anything else that will take their mind off what hurts. Some just need to cry it out and be miserable for a while. Some write in a journal or write letters to the person that they never mail. Do what's right for you, and believe that sooner or later you can emerge from the experience stronger and with new perspective.

Now and again, you will experience conflict in your personal relationships. Following are ideas for how to deal with conflict and criticism in a productive and positive way.

HOW CAN YOU HANDLE CONFLICT AND CRITICISM?

Conflict and criticism, as unpleasant as they can often be, are natural elements in the dynamics of getting along with others. It's normal to want to avoid people or situations that cause distress. However, if you can face your fears and think through them critically, you can gain valuable insight into human nature—your own and that of others. You may be able to make important changes in your life based on what you learn.

Conflict Strategies

Conflicts both large and small arise when there is a clash of ideas or interests. You may have small conflicts with a housemate over food left out overnight, a door left unlocked, or a bill that needs paying. On the other end of the spectrum, you might encounter major conflicts with your partner about finances, with a professor about a failing grade, or with a person who treats you unfairly because of your race, gender, age, or ethnic origin.

Conflict can create anger and frustration, shutting down communication. The two most destructive tendencies are to avoid the conflict altogether (a passive tactic) or to prod it until it escalates (an aggressive tendency). Avoidance doesn't make the problem go away—in fact, it will probably worsen. If you tend to be passive, assert yourself by acknowledging and expressing your feelings as soon as you can put them into words. On the other hand, a shouting match gives no one an opportunity or desire to listen. If you tend to be aggressive, give yourself time to cool down before you address a conflict. Try to express what you feel without letting your emotions explode.

If calmly and intelligently handled, conflict can shed light on new ideas and help to strengthen bonds between those involved. The primary keys to conflict resolution are calm communication and critical-thinking skills. Think through any conflict using what you know about problem solving.

Identify and analyze the problem. Determine the severity of the problem by looking at its effects on everyone involved. Then, find and analyze the causes of the problem.

Brainstorm possible solutions. Consider as many angles as you can, without judgment. Explore what ideas you can come up with from what you or others have done in a similar situation.

Explore each solution. Evaluate the positive and negative effects of each solution. Why might each work, or not work, or work partially? What would take into account everyone's needs? What would cause the least stress? Make sure everyone has a chance to express an opinion.

Choose, carry out, and evaluate the solution you decide is best. When you have implemented your choice, evaluate its effects. Decide whether you feel it was a good choice.

One more hint: Use "I" statements. Focus on the effects the problem has had on you rather than focusing on someone who caused it. Show that you are taking responsibility for your role in the exchange.

Dealing With Criticism and Feedback

No one gets everything right all the time. People use constructive criticism and **feedback** to communicate what went wrong and to suggest improvements. Consider any criticism carefully. If you always interpret criticism as a threat, you will close yourself off from learning. Even if you eventually decide that you disagree, you can still learn from exploring the possibility. Know that you are strong enough to embrace criticism and become a better person because of it.

Criticism can be either constructive or unconstructive. Criticism is considered *constructive* when it is offered supportively and contains useful suggestions for improvement. On the other hand, *unconstructive* criticism focuses on what went wrong, doesn't offer alternatives or help, and is often delivered in a negative or harsh manner. Whereas constructive criticism can promote a sense of hope for improvement in the future, unconstructive criticism can create tension, bad feelings, and defensiveness.

Feedback
Evaluative or corrective information about an action or process.

Constructive
Promoting improvement or development.

Any criticism can be offered constructively or unconstructively. Consider a case where someone has continually been late to work. A supervisor can offer criticism in either of these ways:

Constructive: The supervisor talks privately with the employee. "I've noticed that you have been late to work a lot. Other people have had to do some of your work. Is there a problem that is keeping you from being on time? Is it something that I or someone else can help you with?"

Unconstructive: The supervisor watches the employee slip into work late. The supervisor says, in front of other employees, "Nice to see you could make it. If you can't start getting here on time, I might look for someone else who can."

> "Do not use a hatchet to remove a fly from your friend's forehead."
>
> CHINESE PROVERB

If you can learn to give constructive criticism and deal with whatever criticism comes your way from others, you will improve your relationships and your productivity. When offered constructively and carefully considered, criticism can bring about important positive changes.

Giving Constructive Criticism

When you offer criticism, use the following steps to communicate clearly and effectively:

1. Criticize the behavior rather than the person. In addition, make sure the behavior you intend to criticize is changeable. Chronic lateness can be changed; a physical inability to perform a task cannot.

2. Specifically define the behavior you want to change. Try not to drag any side issues into the conversation.

3. Balance criticism with positive words. Alternate critical comments with praise in other areas.

4. Stay calm and be brief. Avoid threats, ultimatums, or accusations. Use "I" messages; choose positive, nonthreatening words, so the person knows that your intentions are positive.

5. Explain the effects caused by the behavior that warrants the criticism. Help the person understand why a change needs to happen, and talk about options in detail. Compare and contrast the effects of the current behavior with the effects of a potential change.

6. Offer help in changing the behavior. Lead by example.

Receiving Criticism

When you find yourself on the receiving end of criticism, use these coping techniques:

1. Listen to the criticism before you speak up. Resist the desire to defend yourself until you've heard all the details. Decide if the criticism is offered in a constructive or unconstructive manner.

2. Think the criticism through critically. Evaluate it carefully. While some criticism may come from a desire to help, other comments may have less honorable origins. People often criticize others out of jealousy, anger, frustration, or displaced feelings. In cases like those, it is best (though not always easy) to let the criticism wash right over you.

3. If it is unconstructive, you may not want to respond at that moment. Unconstructive criticism can inspire anger that might be destructive to express. Wait until you cool down and think about the criticism to see if there is anything important hiding under how it was presented. Then, tell the person that you see the value of the criticism, but also communicate to him or her how the delivery of the criticism made you feel. If he or she is willing to talk in a more constructive manner, continue with the following steps below. If not, your best bet may be to consider the case closed and move on.

4. If it is constructive, ask for suggestions for how to change the criticized behavior. You could ask, "How would you handle this if you were in my place?"

5. Before the conversation ends, summarize the criticism and your response to it. Repeat it back to the person who offered it. Make sure both of you understand the situation in the same way.

6. If you feel that the criticism is valid, plan a specific strategy for correcting the behavior. Think over what you might learn from changing your behavior. If you don't agree with the criticism even after the whole conversation, explain your behavior from your point of view.

Remember that the most important feedback you will receive in school is from your professors, and the most important on-the-job feedback will come from your supervisors, more experienced peers, and, occasionally, clients. Making a special effort to take in this feedback and consider it carefully will help you learn many important lessons. Even when the criticism is not warranted, the way you respond is important. Furthermore, knowing how to handle conflict and criticism will help you define your role and communicate with others when you work in groups.

WHAT ROLE DO YOU PLAY IN GROUPS?

Group interaction is an important part of your educational, personal, and working life. With a team project at work or a cooperative learning exercise in school, for example, being able to work well together is necessary in order to accomplish a goal. Study groups may be a very important part of your engineering educational experience. Ways to ensure you benefit from and avoid the pitfalls associated with study groups are described in Figure 9.1.

The four roles in the group experience are those of *task leader, group maintenance (socioemotional) leader, active participant,* and *passive participant.* Any group needs leaders and participants in order to function successfully. Become aware of the role you tend to play when relating to others. Try dif-

FIGURE 9.1   Study group techniques.

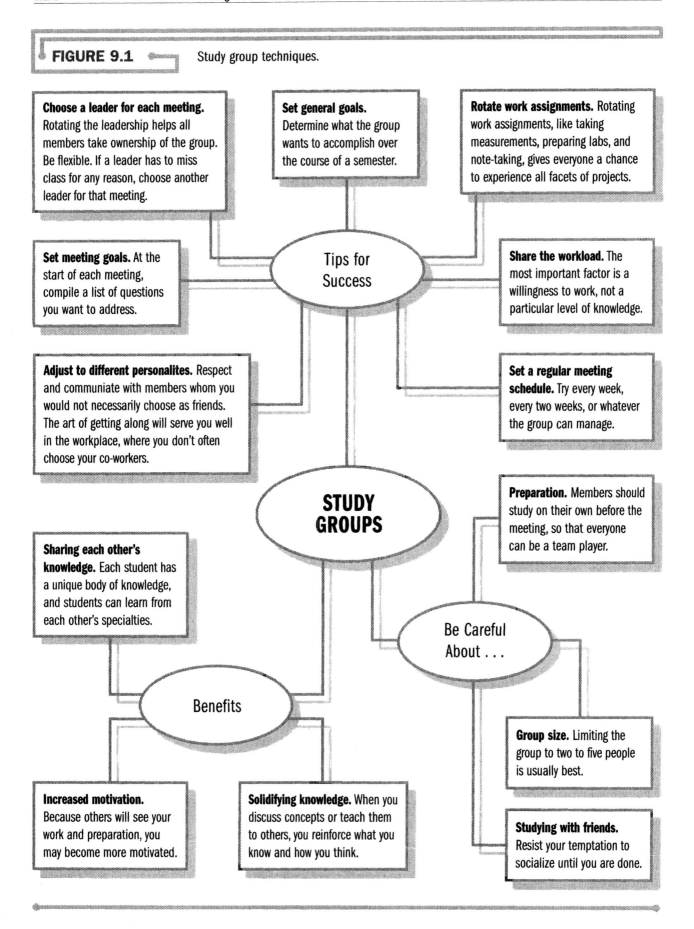

Choose a leader for each meeting. Rotating the leadership helps all members take ownership of the group. Be flexible. If a leader has to miss class for any reason, choose another leader for that meeting.

Set general goals. Determine what the group wants to accomplish over the course of a semester.

Rotate work assignments. Rotating work assignments, like taking measurements, preparing labs, and note-taking, gives everyone a chance to experience all facets of projects.

Set meeting goals. At the start of each meeting, compile a list of questions you want to address.

Tips for Success

Share the workload. The most important factor is a willingness to work, not a particular level of knowledge.

Adjust to different personalites. Respect and communiate with members whom you would not necessarily choose as friends. The art of getting along will serve you well in the workplace, where you don't often choose your co-workers.

Set a regular meeting schedule. Try every week, every two weeks, or whatever the group can manage.

STUDY GROUPS

Preparation. Members should study on their own before the meeting, so that everyone can be a team player.

Sharing each other's knowledge. Each student has a unique body of knowledge, and students can learn from each other's specialties.

Be Careful About . . .

Benefits

Group size. Limiting the group to two to five people is usually best.

Increased motivation. Because others will see your work and preparation, you may become more motivated.

Solidifying knowledge. When you discuss concepts or teach them to others, you reinforce what you know and how you think.

Studying with friends. Resist your temptation to socialize until you are done.

ferent roles to help you decide where you can be most effective. The following strategies (from *Contemporary Business Communication*, by Louis E. Boone, David L. Kurtz, and Judy R. Block) are linked to either participating or leading.[6]

Being an Effective Participant

Some people are happiest when participating in group activities that someone else leads and designs. They don't feel comfortable in a position of control or having the power to set the tone for the group as a whole. They trust others to make those decisions, preferring to help things run smoothly by taking on an assigned role in the project and seeing it through. Participators need to remember that they are "part owners" of the process. Each team member has a responsibility for and a stake in the outcome. The following strategies will help a participant to be effective.

Participation Strategies

Get involved. If a decision you don't like is made by a group of which you are a member, and you stayed uninvolved in the decision, you have no one to blame but yourself for not speaking up. Put some energy into your participation and let people know your views. You are as important a team member as anyone else, and your views are likewise valuable.

Be organized. When you participate with the group as a whole, or with any of the team members, stay focused and organized. The more organized your ideas are, the more people will listen, take them into consideration, and be willing to try them.

Be willing to discuss. Everyone has an equal right to express ideas. Even as you enthusiastically present your opinions, be willing to consider those of others. Keep an open mind and think critically about other ideas before you assume they won't work. If a discussion heats up, take a break or let a more neutral group member mediate.

Keep your word. Make a difference by doing what you say you're going to do. Let people know what you have accomplished. If you bring little or nothing to the process, your team may feel as if you weigh them down.

Focus on ideas. One of the easiest ways to start an argument is for participants to attack group members themselves instead of discussing their ideas. Separate the person from the idea, and keep the idea in focus.

Play fairly. Give everyone a chance to participate. Be respectful of other people's ideas. Don't dominate the discussion or try to control or manipulate others.

Adjust to personalities. Remember to be aware of the diversity of the people in your group. Be cognizant of people's styles, feelings, safety, and confidence.

Being an Effective Leader

Some people prefer to initiate the action, make decisions, and control how things proceed. They have ideas they want to put into practice and enjoy explaining them to others. They are comfortable giving direction to people and guiding group outcomes. Leaders often have a big-picture perspective; it allows them to see how all of the different aspects of a group project can come together. In any group setting the following strategies will help a leader succeed.

Leadership Strategies

Define and limit projects. One of the biggest ways to waste time and energy is to assume that a group will know its purpose and will limit tasks on its own. A group needs a leader who can define the purpose of the gathering and limit tasks so the group doesn't take on too much. Some common purposes are giving/exchanging information, brainstorming, making a decision, delegating tasks, or collaborating on a project.

Map out who will perform which tasks. A group functions best when everyone has a particular contribution to make. You don't often choose who you work with—in school, at work, or in your family—but you can help different personalities work together by exploring who can do what best. Give people specific responsibilities and trust that they will do their jobs.

Set the agenda. The leader is responsible for establishing and communicating the goal of the project and how it will proceed. Without a plan, it's easy to get off track. Having a written agenda to which group members can refer is helpful. A good leader invites advice from others when determining group direction.

Focus progress. Even when everyone knows the plan, it's still easy to wander off the topic. The leader should try to rein in the discussion when necessary, doing his or her best to keep everyone to the topic at hand. When challenges arise midstream, the leader may need to help the team change direction.

Set the tone. Different group members bring different attitudes and mental states to a gathering. Setting a positive tone helps to bring the group together and motivate people to peak performance. When a leader values diversity in ideas and backgrounds and sets a tone of fairness, respect, and encouragement, group members may feel more comfortable contributing their ideas.

Evaluate results. The leader should determine whether the team is accomplishing its goals. If the team is not moving ahead, the leader needs to make changes and decisions.

If you don't believe you fit into the traditional definition of a leader, remember that there are other ways to lead that don't involve taking charge of a group. You can lead others by setting an honorable example in your actions, choices, or words. You can lead by putting forth an idea that takes a group in a new direction. You can lead by being the kind of person whom others would like to be.

It takes the equal participation of all group members to achieve a goal. Whatever role works best for you, know that your contribution is essential. You may even play different roles with different groups, such as if you were a participator at school and a leader in a self-help group. Finally, stay aware of group dynamics; they can shift quickly and move you into a new position you may or may not like. If you don't feel comfortable, speak up. The happier each group member is, the more effectively the group as a whole will function.

ENDNOTES

1. Edith Wharton. "False Dawn," In *Old New York* (New York: Simon & Schuster, 1951), 18–19.

2. Sheryl McCarthy, *Why Are the Heroes Always White?* (Kansas City: Andrews and McMeel, 1995), 188.

3. John Hockenberry, *Moving Violations* (New York: Hyperion, 1995), 78.

4. Tamera Trotter and Joycelyn Allen, *Talking Justice: 602 Ways to Build and Promote Racial Harmony* (Saratoga, CA: R & E Publishers, 1993), 51.

5. Sheryl McCarthy, *Why Are the Heroes . . . ?*, 137.

6. Louis E. Boone, David L. Kurtz, and Judy R. Block, *Contemporary Business Communication* (Upper Saddle River, NJ: Prentice Hall, 1994), 49–54.

Name _____   Date _____

CHAPTER 9   Applications

KEY INTO YOUR LIFE   *Opportunities to Apply What You Learn*

EXERCISE   9.1   Diversity Discovery

Discover your own personal characteristics. Describe yourself in response to the following questions.

What ethnic background(s) do you have? Where were you brought up—a small town or a large city?

_____

_____

_____

Name one or more facts about you that someone wouldn't know from simply looking at you.

_____

_____

_____

Name two values or beliefs that govern how you live, what you pursue, and/or with whom you associate.

_____

_____

_____

What other characteristics or choices define your uniqueness?

_____

_____

_____

Now, join with a partner in your class. Try to choose someone you don't know well. Your goal is to communicate what you have written to your partner, and for your partner to communicate to you in the same way. Spend ten minutes talking together and take notes on what the other person says. At the end of that period, join together as a class. Describe your partner to the class.

What did you learn about your partner that surprised you?

_____

_____

_____

What did you learn that went against any assumptions you may have made about that person based on his or her appearance, background, or behavior?

_____

_____

_____

Has this exercise changed the way you see this person or other people? Why or why not?

_____

_____

_____

Your Communication Style

EXERCISE | 9.2

Look back at the four styles: Intuitor, Thinker, Feeler, and Senser. Which describes you the best? Rank the four styles, listing first the one that fits most, and listing last the one that fits least.

1. _____

2. _____

3. _____

4. _____

Of the two styles that best fit you, which one has more positive effects on your ability to communicate? What are those effects?

_____

_____

_____

Which style has more negative effects? What are they?

_____

_____

_____

To determine whether you are primarily passive, aggressive, or assertive, read the following sentences and circle the ones that sound like something you would say to a peer.

1. Get me the keys.
2. Would you mind if I stepped out just for a second?
3. Don't slam the door.
4. I'd appreciate it if you would have this done by two o'clock.
5. I think maybe it needs a little work just at the end, but I'm not sure.
6. Please take this back to the library.
7. You will have a good time if you join us.
8. Your loss.
9. I don't know—if you think so. I'll try it.
10. Let me know what you want me to do.
11. Turn it this way and see what happens.
12. We'll try both our ideas and see what works best.
13. I want it on my desk by the end of the day.
14. Just do what I told you.
15. If this isn't how you wanted it to look, I can change it. Just tell me and I'll do it.

Aggressive communicators would be likely to use sentences 1, 3, 8, 13, and 14.

Passive communicators would probably opt for sentences 2, 5, 9, 10, and 15.

Assertive communicators would probably choose sentences 4, 6, 7, 11, and 12.

In which category did you choose the most sentences?

_____

If you scored as an assertive communicator, you are on the right track. If you scored in the aggressive or passive categories, analyze your behavior. What are the effects? Give an example in your own life of the effects of your behavior.

_____

_____

_____

Review the suggestions for aggressive or passive communicators. What can you do to improve your skills?

_____

_____

_____

Problem Solving Close to Home

Divide into small groups of two to five. Assign one group member to take notes. Discuss the following questions, one by one:

1. What are common stereotypes of engineers?
2. What could your group do about this stereotype?
3. What could each individual group member do? (Talk about what you specifically think that you can do.)

When you are finished, gather as a class. Each group should share its responses with the class. Observe the variety of stereotypes and solutions. Notice whether more than one group came up with one or more of the same stereotypes.

10

Managing Career and Money

Reality Resources

Many people either love their jobs but don't make much money, or dislike their jobs but are paid well. Still other people have neither job satisfaction nor a good paycheck to show for their work. The most ideal career interests and challenges you *and* pays you enough to live comfortably.

Career exploration, job-hunting strategy, and money management can work together to help you find that ideal career. In this chapter, you will first look at career exploration and how to balance work and school. Then you will explore how to manage the money you have. Managing your resources and investigating career options can help you develop skills and insights that will serve you throughout your life.

In this chapter, you will explore answers to the following questions:

- How can you plan your career?

- How can you juggle work and school?

- How can strategic planning help you manage money?

- How can you create a budget that works?

HOW CAN YOU PLAN YOUR CAREER?

By embarking on an undergraduate engineering education, you are keeping your career options extremely flexible. You will have the exciting opportunity to make a decision as to the direction of your career at a variety of times in your life, including your senior year in college. For example, do you want to pursue design, manufacturing, product development, sales and marketing, research, planning, or consulting within an engineering field? Or do you wish to pursue more education, such as in the form of an advanced engineering degree, or go to graduate business school, law school, or medical school? The wonderful fact is, these options are probably all open to you—because you have an engineering degree.

This book is geared to help you achieve workplace success. As you read the text, examine the vignettes of individuals with undergraduate engineering degrees, and work on the exercises, you will hone your critical thinking skills, improve your teamwork skills, and develop long-term planning skills, all of which will help in your career as well as in your studies.

Define a Career Path

Aiming for a job in a particular career area requires planning the steps that can get you there. Whether these steps take months or years, they help you focus your energies on your goal. Defining a career path involves investigating yourself, exploring potential careers, and building knowledge and experience.

Investigate Yourself

When you explored why you are embarking on an engineering education and what you might expect in an engineering career in Chapter 1, you began to build self-knowledge. Gather everything that you know about yourself, from this class or from any of your other life experiences, and investigate. What do you know or do best? Out of jobs you've had, what did you like and not like to do? How would you describe your personality? And finally, what kinds of careers would make the best use of everything you are?

Don't feel as though you should automatically know what you want to do. Most students who have not been in the workplace don't know which career they want to pursue. Students who have been working often return to school to explore other careers that they might prefer. More and more, people are changing careers many times in their lives instead of sticking with one choice. This discovery is a lifelong process.

The potential for change applies to majors as well. If you declare a major and decide later that you don't like it, feel glad that you were able to discover that fact about yourself.

Explore Potential Careers

Career possibilities extend far beyond what you can imagine. Brainstorm about career areas. Ask professors, relatives, and fellow students about their own careers and ones they know about. Check your library for books on careers or biographies of people who worked in fields that interest you. Explore careers you discover through reading the newspaper, novels, or nonfiction. If a character in your favorite movie has a job you think you'd like, see what you can find out about it.

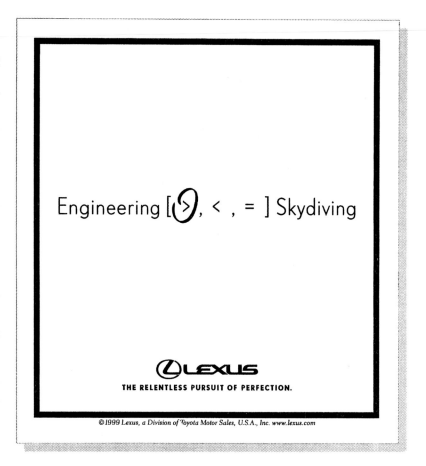

Created by: Team One Advertising

Your school's career center is an important resource in your investigation. The career center may offer job listings, occupation lists, assessments of skills and personality types, questionnaires to help you pinpoint career areas that may suit you, informational material about different career areas, and material about various companies. The people who work at the center can help you sort through the material.

Use your critical-thinking skills to broaden your investigation beyond just what tasks you perform for any given job. Many other factors will be important to you. Look at Table 10.1 for some of the questions you might ask as you talk to people or investigate options.

Within each job, there is also a variety of tasks and skills that often go beyond what you know. You may know that an engineering professor teaches, but you may not see that professors also often write, research, study, create course outlines, collaborate with other professors, give presentations, and counsel. Push past your first impression of any career and explore what else it entails. Expand your choices as much as you can through thorough investigation and an open mind.

Build Knowledge and Experience

Having knowledge and experience specific to the career area you want to pursue will be valuable on the job hunt. Courses, internships, jobs, and volunteering are four great ways to build both.

TABLE 10.1

Critical thinking questions for career investigation.

What can I do in this area that I like/am good at?	Do I respect the company and/or the industry?
What are the educational requirements (certificates or degrees, courses)?	Do companies in this industry generally accommodate special needs (child care, sick days, flex time, or working at home)?
What skills are necessary?	Can I belong to a union?
What wage or salary is normal for an entry-level position, and what benefits can I expect?	Are there opportunities in this industry within a reasonable distance of where I live?
What kinds of personalities are best suited to this kind of work?	What other expectations are there beyond the regular workday (travel, overtime, etc.)?
What are the prospects for moving up to higher-level positions?	Do I prefer a service or manufacturing industry?

Courses. When you narrow your career exploration to a couple of areas that interest you, look through your school course catalog and take a course or two in those fields. How you react to these courses will give you important clues as to how you feel about the area in general. Be careful to evaluate your experience based on how you feel about the subject matter and not other factors. Think critically. If you didn't like a course, what was the cause: a professor you didn't like, a time of day when you tend to lose energy, or truly a lack of interest in the material?

Internship

A temporary work program in which a student can gain supervised practical experience in a particular professional field.

Internships. An **internship** may or may not offer pay. While this may be a financial drawback, the experience you can gather and contacts you can make may be worth the work. Many internships take place during the summer, but some part-time internships are also available during the school year. Companies that offer internships are looking for people who will work hard in exchange for experience you can't get in the classroom.

Absorb all the knowledge you can while working as an intern. If you discover a career worth pursuing, you'll have the internship experience behind you when you go job hunting. Internships are one of the best ways to show a prospective employer some "real world" experience and initiative.

Jobs. No matter what you do for money while you are in college, whether it is in your area of interest or not, you may discover career opportunities that appeal to you.

Volunteering. Offering your services in the community or at your school can introduce you to career areas and increase your experience. Some schools have programs that can help you find opportunities to work as an aid on campus or volunteer off campus. Recently, certain schools have even begun listing volunteer activities on student transcripts. Find out what services your school offers. Volunteer activities are important to note on your resume. Many employers seek candidates who have shown commitment through volunteering.

Success in the Real World

George Sissel

Chairman and CEO, Ball Corporation

As a group, engineers are my kind of people. In the years since I graduated from the University of Colorado at Boulder in 1958 with a bachelor's degree in electrical engineering, I have worked with people from all over the world, from many walks of life, and in many professions.

On the occasions when I have been fortunate enough to spend time with engineers, it has been often refreshing and enlightening. There is something about the profession that allows, indeed even requires, that engineers be honest, candid, and exceptionally straightforward. An engineer does not and cannot depend on superficial persuasion or manipulation to make a point or achieve a goal. There is no need, because an engineer's solutions depend generally on some type of physical truth that is difficult to distort.

The great contribution of the profession is that engineers design and build things that have never been designed or built before. They create new solutions to old and new physical needs of humankind.

An engineering degree is the beginning of a promising journey. I think of it as a "career passport." Most higher-education degrees will open a door to the job market. An engineering degree will open *multiple* doors, which in turn may lead to a variety of careers, particularly when sprinkled along the way with influences of liberal arts and humanities.

The skills that make a good engineer are sought after in so many fields. During my career, I have been a Navy officer, an attorney, and a chief executive officer of a Fortune 500 company, among other things. In every case, the knowledge and experience I accumulated as an engineering major have served as a foundation for my success.

What sort of skills am I talking about?

- Discipline
- Logical thinking
- Immense ability to concentrate and cull the irrelevant
- Mathematical comprehension
- An understanding of engineering and scientific principles and methods
- A focus on the truth, be it physical truth or factual truth, or both

The level of respect many people assign to an engineering degree can be considerable. In fact, I

have labeled this the "halo effect." It flows from an engineer's skills, special knowledge, and hard work. It is often what others don't understand, and your help is appreciated. It is always with you, wherever you go and whatever your profession. Whether your choice is engineering practice—or teaching, or business, or music, or law, or medicine—your engineering background will serve you in good stead.

In my current role as CEO of a manufacturing and aerospace company, my engineering degree continues to be of benefit. There are people in Ball Corporation who would more proudly introduce me as an engineer than as a CEO or lawyer. When I visit on site with our packaging and aerospace engineers, we speak a common language and appreciate each other's skills and knowledge.

I suppose for many professionals, engineering isn't what they *do*, it is who they *are*. That can make all the difference in the world when it comes to selecting a fulfilling and prosperous career. An engineer's work speaks for itself. In today's complex business world, that simple fact can be a rare pleasure.

Map Out Your Strategy

After you've gathered enough information to narrow your career goals, plan strategically to achieve them. Make a career time line that illustrates the steps toward your goal, as shown in Figure 10.1. Mark years and half-year points (and months for the first year), and write in the steps where you think they should take place. If your plan is five years long, indicate what you plan to do by the fourth, third, and second years, and then the first year, including a six-month goal and a one-month goal for that first year. Set goals that establish whom you will talk to, what courses you will take, what skills you will work on, what jobs or internships you will investigate, and any other research you need to do. Your path may change, of course—use your time line as a guide rather than as a rigid plan. And be aware that people now commonly have as many as five careers over the course of their lives, and this number may continue to rise.

Seek Mentors

Mentor
A person of knowledge or authority who becomes a trusted counselor or guide.

You may go to many different people for career advice, but if you are lucky, you may find among them a true **mentor**. A mentor takes a special interest in helping you to reach your goals. People often seek a mentor who has excelled in a career area or specific skill in which they also wish to excel. You may also be drawn to a person who, no matter what his skills or specialty, has ideas and makes choices that you admire and want to emulate.

Because it requires depth and devotion on both sides, a mentoring relationship often evolves from a special personal relationship. A relative, professor, friend, supervisor, or anyone else whom you admire and respect may become your mentor. Think about whom you go to when you are confused or troubled, need guidance, or seek support. Also, consider who may know a lot about a skill

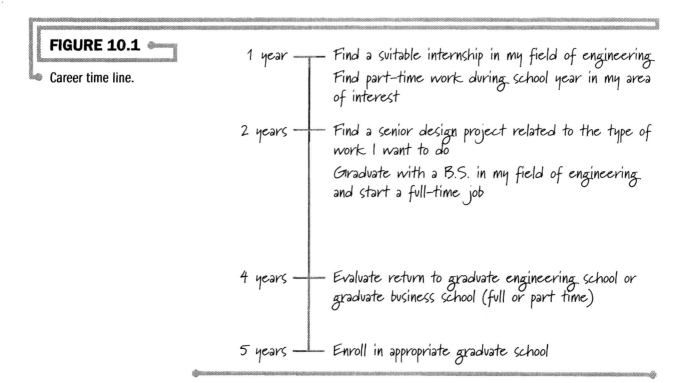

FIGURE 10.1

Career time line.

1 year — Find a suitable internship in my field of engineering
Find part-time work during school year in my area of interest

2 years — Find a senior design project related to the type of work I want to do
Graduate with a B.S. in my field of engineering and start a full-time job

4 years — Evaluate return to graduate engineering school or graduate business school (full or part time)

5 years — Enroll in appropriate graduate school

or career area you want to pursue. Some schools have faculty or peer mentoring programs to help match students with people who can help them. Check your student handbook or ask your advisor if this is offered at your school.

Mentoring relationships demand time and energy on both sides. A mentor can give you a private audience for questions and problems, advice tailored to your needs, a wealth of experience, support, guidance, and trust. A mentor cares about you deeply enough to be devoted to your success and growth, taking pleasure in your development. You owe it to your mentor to be open to his ideas and to take his advice respectfully into consideration. You and your mentor can learn from each other, receive positive energy from your relationship, and grow and develop together.

Know What Employers Want

Certain basic skills will make you an excellent job candidate no matter what career you decide to pursue. Employers look for particular skills and qualities that signify an efficient and effective employee. You can continue to develop these skills as you work in current and future jobs—and you will, if you always strive to improve.

Communication skills. Being able to listen well and express yourself in writing and speaking is a key to workplace success. Much can be accomplished through efficient, open communication. Being able to adjust to different communication styles is an important factor.

Problem solving. Any job will present problems that need to be solved. An employee who knows how to assess any situation and apply the problem-solving process to it will stand out.

Decision making. Decisions large and small are made in every workplace every day. Knowing how to think through and make decisions will help you in any job.

Teamwork. It is a rare workplace that has only one employee, and even then, that person will interact with different kinds of people on the phone or through a computer. The importance of being able to work well with others cannot be overemphasized. If there is a weak link in any team, the whole company suffers.

Multicultural communication. The workplace is becoming increasingly diverse. The more you can work well with people different from yourself and open your mind to their points of view, the more valuable an employee you will be.

Leadership. The ability to influence others in a positive way will earn you respect and keep you in line for promotions. Taking the lead will often command attention.

Creativity. When you can see the big picture as well as the details and can let your mind come up with unexpected new concepts and plans, you will bring valuable suggestions to your workplace.

"Whatever you think you can do or believe you can do, begin it. Action has magic, grace, and power in it."

JOHANN WOLFGANG VON GOETHE

Commitment. You will encounter many difficult situations at work. The ability to continue to work hard through such situations is extremely important. In addition, if you introduce a new and creative idea, you can gain support for it through having a strong commitment to it yourself.

Values and integrity. Your personal values and integrity will help guide everything you do. In your actions and decisions, consider what you value and what you believe is right.

These skills appear throughout this book, and they are as much a part of your school success as they are of your work success. The more you develop them now, the more employable and promotable you will prove yourself to be. You may already use them on the job if you are a student who works.

HOW CAN YOU JUGGLE WORK AND SCHOOL?

What you are studying today prepares you to find a job after you graduate that suits your abilities and brings in enough money to support your needs and lifestyle choices. In the meantime, though, you can make work a part of your student life in order to make money, explore a career, or increase your future employability through contacts or resume building.

As the cost of education continues to rise, more and more students are working and taking classes at the same time. However, being an employed student isn't for everyone. Adding a job to the list of demands on your time and energy may create problems if it sharply reduces study time or family time. However, many people want to work, and many need to work in order to pay for school. Ask yourself important questions about why or why not to work. Weigh the potential positive and negative effects of working. From those answers you can make a choice that you feel benefits you most.

Effects of Working While in School

Working while in school has many different positive and negative effects, depending on the situation. Evaluate any job opportunity by looking at these effects. Following are some that might come into play.

Potential Positive Effects

Money earned. A job can provide crucial income to pay for rent, transportation, food, and important bills. It may even help you put some savings away in order to create a financial cushion.

General and career-specific experience. Important learning comes from hands-on work. Your education "in the trenches" can complement your classroom experience. Even if you don't work in your chosen field, you can improve universal skills such as teamwork and communication.

Being able to keep a job you currently hold. If you leave a job temporarily, your company might not be able to hold your position open until you come back. Consider adjusting your responsibilities or hours while still holding down your job.

Keeping busy. Work can provide a stimulating break from studying. In fact, working up to 15 hours a week may actually enhance academic performance, because working students often manage their time more efficiently and may gain confidence from their successes in the workplace. Working on campus may help you manage your time and connect to your school experience.

Potential Negative Effects

Time commitment. A nonworking student splits time between academic and personal life, while a working student must add a third, time-consuming factor. More responsibilities with less time to fulfill them demand more efficient time management. Many schools recommend that students work a maximum of 20 hours a week while taking a full course load.

Adjusting priorities. The priority level of your job may vary. For a student who depends on the income, work may take priority over study time. Evaluate priorities carefully. Realize that you may have to reduce social activities, exercise at home, cut back on nonacademic activities, or lighten your course load in order to maintain a job and still get studying done. Your job is important, but if you are also committed to school, earning a good GPA may be just as crucial.

Shifting gears. Unless your job meshes with your classroom curriculum, it may take some effort to shift gears mentally as you move back and forth between academia and the workplace. Each environment has its own set of people, responsibilities, joys, and problems. Establish mental boundaries that can help you shake off academic stress while at work, and vice versa.

If you consider the positive and negative effects and decide that working will benefit you, you should establish what you need in a job. (See Table 10.2.)

Sources of Job Information

Many different routes can lead to satisfying jobs. Use your school's career planning and placement office, networking skills, classified ads, employment agencies, and on-line services to help you explore.

Your School's Career Planning and Placement Offices

Generally, the career planning and placement office deals with post-graduation job placements, while the student employment office, along with the financial aid office, has more information about working while in school. At

TABLE 10.2 What you may need in a job.

NEED	DESCRIPTION
Salary/wage level	Consider how much money you need to make month by month and yearly. You may need to make a certain amount for the year as a whole, but you may need to earn more of that total amount during the months when you are paying tuition. Consider also the amount that justifies taking the time to work. If a job pays well but takes extra hours that should go toward studying or classes, it might not be worth it. Take time to compare the positive effects with the negative effects of any job's pay structure.
Time of day	When you can work depends on your school schedule. For example, if you take classes Monday, Tuesday, and Thursday during the day, you could look for a job with weekend or evening hours. If you attend evening classes, a daytime job could work fine.
Hours per week (part-time vs. full-time)	If you take classes part-time, you may choose to work a full-time job. If you are a full-time student, it may be best to work part-time. Balance your priorities so that you can accomplish your schoolwork and still make the money you need.
Duties performed	If you want hands-on experience in your chosen field, narrow your search to jobs that can provide it. On the other hand, if a regular paycheck is your priority, you might not care as much about what you do. Consider if there is anything you absolutely hate to do. Working somewhere or doing something that makes you miserable may not be worth any amount of money.
Location	Weigh the effects of how long it takes to get to a job against what you are getting out of it, and decide whether it is worth your while. A job at or near your school may give unparalleled convenience. When you know you can get to work quickly, you can schedule your day more tightly and get more done.
Flexibility	Even if your classes are at regular times, you might have other projects and meetings at various times. Do you need a job that offers flexibility, allowing you to shift your working time when you have to attend to an academic or family responsibility that takes priority? Choose according to the flexibility you require.
Affiliation with school or financial aid program	Some financial aid packages, especially if they involve funds from your school, can require you to take work at the school or a federal organization. In that case you would have to choose among the opportunities offered.
Accommodation of special needs	If you have a hearing or vision impairment, reduced mobility, or other special needs, employers must accommodate them.

either location you might find general workplace information, listings of job opportunities, sign-ups for interviews, and contact information for companies. The career office may hold frequent informational sessions on different topics. Your school may also sponsor job or career fairs that give you a chance to explore job opportunities.

Many students, because they don't seek job information until they're about to graduate, miss out on much of what the career office can do. Don't wait until the last minute. Start exploring your school's career office early in your university life. The people and resources there can help you at every stage of your career and job exploration process.

Networking

Networking is one of the most important job-hunting strategies. With each person you get to know, you build your network and tap into someone else's. Imagine a giant think link connecting you to a web of people just a couple of phone calls away. Of course, not everyone with whom you network will come through for you. Keep in contact with as many people as possible in the hope that someone will. You never know who that person might be.

With whom can you network? Friends and family members may know of jobs or other people who can help you. At your school, professors, administrators, or counselors such as those in the school employment or career services office may give you job or **contact** information. Attending professional association meetings and conferences can help you locate work. Some schools even have opportunities for students to interact with alumni. Look to your present and past work experience for more leads. Employers or co-workers may know someone who needs new employees. A former employer might even hire you back with similar or adjusted hours, if you left on good terms.

The contacts with whom you network aren't just sources of job opportunities. They are people with whom you can develop lasting, valuable relationships. They may be willing to talk to you about how to get established, the challenges on the job, what they do each day, how much you can expect to make, or any other questions you have similar to those in Table 10.1. Thank your contacts for their help and don't forget them. Networking is a two-way street. Even as you receive help, be ready to extend yourself to others who may need help and advice from you.

> **Networking**
> The exchange of information or services among individuals, groups, or institutions.

> **Contact**
> A person who serves as a carrier or source of information.

Classified Ads

Some of the best job listings are in daily or periodic newspapers. Most papers print help-wanted sections in each issue, organized according to career field categories. At the beginning of most help-wanted sections you will find an index that tells you the categories and on what pages they begin in the listings. Individual ads describe the kind of position available and usually give a telephone number or post office box for you to contact. Some ads may include additional information such as job requirements, a contact person, and the salary or wages offered.

You can run your own classified ads if you have a skill you want to advertise. Many college students make extra cash by doing specific tasks for campus employees or other students, such as typing, editing, cleaning, tutoring, or baby sitting. You may want to advertise your particular job skills in your school or local paper.

On-Line Services

The Internet is growing as a source of job listings. Through it you can access job search databases such as the Career Placement Registry and U. S. Employment Opportunities. Web sites such as CareerPath.com and

CareerMosiac list all kinds of positions. Individual associations and companies may also post job listings and descriptions, often as part of their World Wide Web pages. For example, IBM includes job openings on its Web page.

Employment Agencies

Employment agencies are organizations that help people find work. Most employment agencies will put you through a screening process that consists of an interview and one or more tests in your area of expertise. For example, someone looking for secretarial work may take a word-processing test and a spelling test, while someone looking for accounting work may take accounting and math tests. If you pass the tests and interview well, the agency will try to place you in a job.

Most employment agencies specialize in particular career or skill areas, such as accounting, medicine, legal, computer operation, and technical areas. Agencies may place job seekers in either part-time or full-time employment. Many agencies also place people in temporary jobs, which can work well for students who are available from time to time. Such agencies may have you call in whenever you are free and will see if anything is available that day or week.

Employment agencies are a great way to hook into job networks. However, they usually require a fee that either you or the employer has to pay. Investigate any agency before signing on. See if your school's career counselors know anything about the agency, or if any fellow students have used it successfully. Ask questions so that you know as much as possible about how the agency operates.

Making a Strategic Job Search Plan

When you have gathered information on the jobs you want, formulate a plan for pursuing them. Organize your approach according to what you need to do and how much time you have to devote to your search. Do you plan to make three phone calls per day? Will you fill out three job applications a week for a month? Keep a record—on 3-by-5-inch cards, in a computer file, or in a notebook—of the following:

- People you contact
- Companies to which you apply
- Jobs you rule out (for example, jobs that become unavailable or that you find out don't suit your needs)
- Response from your communications (phone calls to you, interviews, written communications) and the information on whoever contacted you (names, titles, times, and dates)

Keeping accurate records will enable you to both chart your progress and maintain a clear picture of the process. You never know when information might come in handy again. If you don't get a job now, another one could open up at the same company in a couple of months. In that case, well-kept records would enable you to contact key personnel quickly and efficiently. See Figure 10.2 for a sample file card.

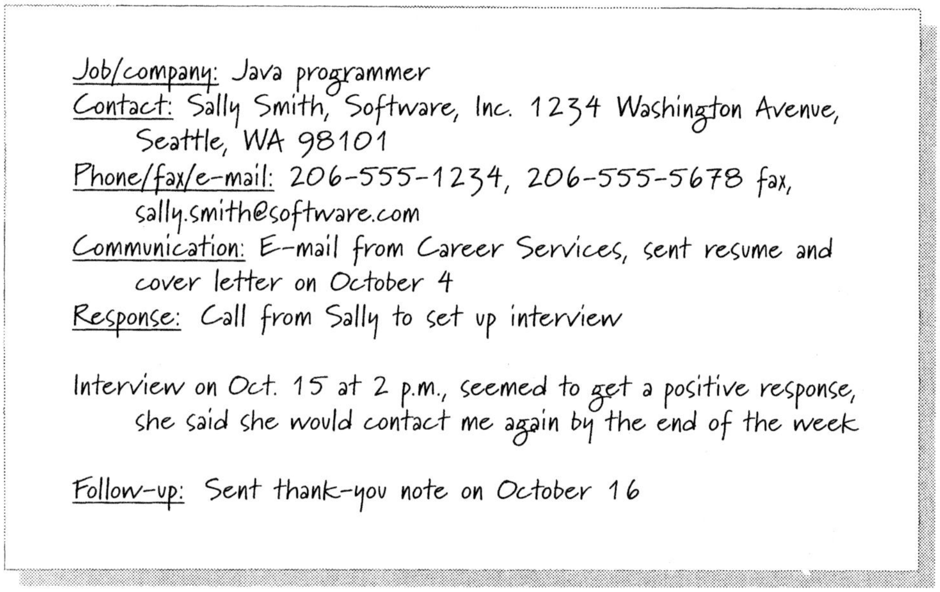

FIGURE 10.2

Sample file card.

Job/company: Java programmer
Contact: Sally Smith, Software, Inc. 1234 Washington Avenue,
    Seattle, WA 98101
Phone/fax/e-mail: 206-555-1234, 206-555-5678 fax,
    sally.smith@software.com
Communication: E-mail from Career Services, sent resume and
    cover letter on October 4
Response: Call from Sally to set up interview

Interview on Oct. 15 at 2 p.m., seemed to get a positive response,
    she said she would contact me again by the end of the week

Follow-up: Sent thank-you note on October 16

Your Resume and Interview

Information on resumes and interviews fills many books. Therefore, your best bet is to consult some that will go into more detail, such as *The Resume Kit*, by Richard Beatty, or *Job Interviews for Dummies*, by Joyce Lain Kennedy (don't be insulted by the title; it contains valuable information).

The following basic tips can get you started on giving yourself the best possible chance at a job.

Resume. Your resume should always be typed or printed on a computer. Design your resume neatly, using an acceptable format (books or your career office can show you some standard formats). Proofread it for errors, especially spelling errors, and have someone else proofread it as well. Type or print it on a heavier bond paper than is used for ordinary copies. Use white or off-white paper and black ink.

Interview. Pay attention to your appearance. Be clean, neat, and appropriately dressed. Don't forget to choose a nice pair of shoes—people notice. Bring an extra copy of your resume with you, and any other materials that you want to show the interviewer, even if you have already sent a copy ahead of time. Avoid chewing gum or smoking. Offer a confident handshake. Make eye contact. Show your integrity by speaking honestly about yourself. After the interview is over, no matter what the outcome, send a formal but pleasant thank-you note right away as a follow-up.

Earning the money you need is difficult, especially if you work part-time in order to have time for school. Financial aid (see Chapter 2) can take some of the burden off your shoulders. If you can gather one or more loans, grants, or scholarships, they may help make up for what you don't have time to earn.

HOW CAN STRATEGIC PLANNING HELP YOU MANAGE MONEY?

"It is thrifty to prepare today for the wants of tomorrow."

AESOP

So you work hard to earn your wages and study hard to hold on to your grants and loans. What do you do with that money? Popular culture tells you to buy. You are surrounded by commercials, magazine ads, and notices in the mail that tell you how wonderful you'll feel if you indulge in some serious spending. On the other hand, there are some definite advantages to not taking that advice. Making some short-term sacrifices in order to save money can help you a great deal in the long run.

Short-Term Sacrifices Can Create Long-Term Gain

When you think about your money, take your values and your ability to plan strategically into account. Ask yourself what goals you value most and what steps you will have to take over time to achieve those goals. You are already planning ahead by being in school and committing to paying for tuition. You may be scrimping now, but you are planning for a career that should reward you with job security and financial stability. Sometimes the most important goals are also the ones that require a long-term commitment. If you can make that commitment, the reward will be worth the short-term sacrifices.

Table 10.3 shows some potential effects of spending. Some effects are negative, some positive, and some more positive than others. Evaluate which you

would prefer in the long run. You may find that the pleasure luxuries provide isn't worth the stress created by debt.

Critical thinking is the key to smart money planning. Impulsive spending usually happens when you don't take time to think through your decision before you buy. To use your hard-earned money to your greatest benefit, take time to think critically about your finances. First, establish your needs, and be honest about what you truly need and what you just want. Second, brainstorm available options of what to do with your money; evaluate the positive and negative effects of each. Third, choose an option and carry it out. Finally, evaluate the result.

Develop a Financial Philosophy

You can develop your own personal philosophy about spending, saving, and planning. Following are a couple of strategies that you might want to incorporate into that philosophy.

Live beneath your means. Spend less than you make. This strategy helps you create savings. No matter how much or how little, any amount of savings will give you a buffer zone that can help with emergencies or bigger expenditures.

Potential effects of spending.   **TABLE 10.3**

OPTION	POTENTIAL SHORT-TERM EFFECTS	POTENTIAL LONG-TERM EFFECTS
Purchase new sound system	High-quality sound	If paid on credit, a credit card debt, with finance charges, that requires monthly payment; if paid in cash, a loss of benefits that could have come from saving that money
Reduce or pay off credit card debt	Less money for day-to-day expenses; reduction of monthly bills	Improved credit rating and credit history; increased ability to be approved for loans and mortgages; less money charged in interest and fees
Take a week's vacation	Fun and relaxation; stress reduction	Credit card debt or less money saved for future needs
Invest in mutual fund	Less money on hand; more money earning interest	More money earned, due to an interest rate higher than banks can offer
Buy a car	Transportation and independence; gas, maintenance, parking charges	Debt in the form of a car loan; monthly payments for a few years; gradual decrease in car value
Pay health insurance bills	Health insurance coverage; a tighter monthly budget	The safety and security of knowing that your health and the health of your family are protected
Put money toward tuition	Having to scrimp while in school due to less money on hand; fewer loans and debts	Less money to pay off later in student loans, which means less money charged in interest; more freedom to spend your money on getting settled after you graduate; shorter period of debt

Sometimes your basic needs will cost more than you make, in which case living beneath your means becomes very difficult. If you find, however, that extras are putting your spending over your earnings, cut back.

Pay yourself. After you pay your monthly bills, put whatever you can save from your monthly earnings in a savings account. Paying yourself helps you store money in your savings, where it can grow.

HOW CAN YOU CREATE A BUDGET THAT WORKS?

Every time you have some money in your pocket and have to figure out whether it will pay for what you want at that moment, you are **budgeting** your money. It takes some thought and energy to budget efficiently. The more money you can save each month, the more you will thank yourself later when you need it. Consider your resources (money coming in) and expenditures (money going out). A smart budget adjusts the money flow for the best possible chance that what comes in will be more than what goes out. Smart budgeting is a worthwhile investment in your future.

> **Budgeting**
> Making a plan for the coordination of resources and expenditures; setting goals with regard to money.

The Art of Budgeting

Budgeting involves following a few basic steps in order. These steps are: determining how much money you make, determining how much money you spend, subtracting the second number (what you spend) from the first number (what you make), evaluating the result, and making decisions about how to adjust your spending or earning based on that result. Budgeting regularly is easy. Use a specified time frame, such as a week or month. Most people budget on a month-by-month basis.

Determine How Much You Will Make

Do this by adding up all your money receipts from the month. If you currently have a regular full-time or part-time job, add your pay stubs. If you have received any financial aid, loan funding, or scholarship money, determine how much of that you can allow for each month's income and add it to your total. For example, if you received a $1200 grant for the year, each month would have an income of $100. Be sure, when you are estimating your income, to use the amounts that remain *after* taxes have been taken out.

Figure Out How Much You Spend

You may or may not have a handle on your spending. Many people don't take the time to keep track. If you have never before paid much attention to how you spend money, examine your spending patterns. Over a month's time, record expenditures in a small notebook or on a piece of paper on a home bulletin board. You don't have to list everything down to the penny. Just indicate expenditures over five dollars, making sure to count smaller expenditures if they are frequent (a bus pass for a month, soda or newspaper purchases per week). In your list, include an estimate of the following:

- Rent/mortgage/school room fees
- Tuition or educational loan payments (divide your annual total by 12 to arrive at a monthly figure)
- Books, lab fees, and other educational expenses
- Regular bills (heat, gas, electric, phone, car payment, water)
- Credit card or other payments on credit
- Food, clothing, toiletries, and household supplies
- Child care
- Entertainment and related items (eating out, books and publications, movies)
- Health, auto, and home/renter's insurance
- Transportation and auto expenses

Subtract what you spend from what you make. Ideally, you will have a positive number. You may end up with a negative number, however, especially if you haven't made a habit of keeping track of your spending. This indicates that you are spending more than you make, which over a long period of time can create a nasty debt.

Evaluate the Result

After you arrive at your number, determine what it tells you. If you have a positive number, decide how to save it if you can. If you end up with a negative number, ask yourself questions about what is causing the deficit—where you are spending too much or earning too little. Of course, surprise expenses during some months may cause you to spend more than usual, such as if you have to repair your car, pay equipment fees for a particular course, or have an emergency medical procedure. However, when a negative number comes up for what seems to be a typical month, you may need to adjust your budget over the long term.

Make Decisions About How to Adjust Spending or Earning

Looking at what may cause you to overspend, brainstorm possible solutions that address those causes. Solutions can involve either increasing resources or decreasing spending. To deal with spending, prioritize your expenditures and trim the ones you really don't need to make. Do you eat out too much? Can you live without cable, a beeper, a cellular phone? Be smart. Cut out unaffordable extras. As for resources, investigate ways to take in more money. Taking a part-time job, hunting down scholarships or grants, or increasing hours at a current job may help.

A Sample Budget

Table 10.4 shows a sample budget of an unmarried student living with two other students. It will give you an idea of how to budget (all expenditures are general estimates, based on averages).

To make up the $315 that this student went over budget, he can adjust his spending. He could rent movies or check them out of the library instead of going to the theater. He could socialize with friends at someone's apartment instead of paying high prices and tips at a bar or restaurant. Instead of buying CDs and DVDs, he could borrow them. He could also shop for specials and bargains in the grocery store or go to a warehouse supermarket to stock up on staples at discount prices. He could make his lunch instead of buying it and take public transportation instead of driving.

Not everyone likes the work involved in keeping a budget. While linear, factual, reflective, and verbal learners may take to it more easily, active, holistic, theoretical, and visual learners may resist the structure and detail (see Chapter 3). Visual learners may want to create a budget chart like the one shown in the example or construct a think link that shows the connections between all the month's expenditures. Use images to clarify ideas, such as picturing a bathtub you are filling that is draining at the same time. Use strategies that make budgeting more tangible, such as dumping all of your receipts into a big jar and tallying them at the end of the month. Even if you have to force yourself to do it, you will discover that budgeting can reduce stress and help you take control of your finances and your life.

TABLE 10.4 A student's sample budget.	Part-time salary: $10 an hour, 20 hours a week. $10 \times 20 = \$200$ a week, $\times 4\frac{1}{3}$ weeks (one month) $= \$866$. Student loan from school's financial aid office: $2,000 divided by 12 months $= \$166$. Total income per month: $1,032.

MONTHLY EXPENDITURES	AMOUNT
Tuition ($8000 per year)	$ 667
Public transportation	$ 90
Phone	$ 40
Food	$ 130
Medical insurance	$ 120
Rent (including utilities)	$ 200
Entertainment/miscellaneous	$ 100
Total spending	$ 1347

$1032 (income) - $1347 (spending) = $-315 ($315 over budget)

Savings Strategies

You can save money and still enjoy life. Make your fun less-expensive fun—or save up for a while to splurge on a really special occasion. Here are some suggestions for saving a little bit of money here and there. Small amounts can add up to big savings after a while.

- Rent movies, check them out of the library, or attend bargain movies.
- Borrow movies, CDs, tapes, and books from your library.
- Walk or bike instead of paying for public transportation or driving your own car.
- If you have storage space, buy detergent, paper products, toiletries, and other staples in bulk.
- Keep your possessions neat, clean, and properly maintained—they will last longer.
- Take advantage of weekly supermarket specials and bring coupons when you shop.
- Reuse grocery bags for food storage and garbage instead of buying bags.
- Return bottles and cans for deposits if you live in a state that accepts them.
- Buy display or reconditioned models of appliances or electronics (stereo equipment, TVs, VCRs, DVDs).
- Take your lunch instead of buying it.
- Find a low-rate long distance calling plan, use e-mail, or write letters.
- Save on heat by dressing warmly and using blankets; save on air conditioning by using fans.
- Have pot-luck parties; ask people to bring dinner foods or munchies.

Add your own suggestions here!

You can also maximize savings and minimize spending by using credit cards wisely.

Managing Credit Cards

Most credit comes in the form of a powerful little plastic card. Credit card companies often solicit students on campus or through the mail. When choosing a card, pay attention to the *annual fee* and *interest rates*, the two ways in which a credit card company makes money from you. Some cards have no annual fee; others may charge a flat rate of $10 to $70 per year. Interest rates can be fixed or variable. A variable rate of 12 percent may shoot up to 18 percent when the economy slows down. You might be better off with a mid-range fixed rate that will always stay the same.

Following are some potential effects of using credit.

Positive Effects

Establishing a good credit history. If you use your credit card moderately and pay your bills on time, you will make a positive impression on your **creditors.** Your *credit history* (the record of your credit use, including positive actions such as paying on time and negative actions such as going over your credit limit) and *credit rating* (the score you are given based on your history) can make or break your ability to take out a loan or mortgage. How promptly you make loan payments and pay mortgage and utility bills affects your credit rating as well. Certain companies track your credit history and give you a credit rating. Banks or potential employers will contact these companies to see if you are a good credit risk.

Creditors
People to whom debts are owed, usually money.

Emergencies. Few people carry enough cash to handle unexpected expenses. Your credit card can help you in emergency situations such as when your car needs to be towed.

Record of purchases. Credit card statements give you a monthly record of purchases made, where they were made, and exactly how much was paid. Using your credit card for purchases that you want to track, such as work expenses, can help you keep records for tax purposes.

Negative Effects

Credit can be addictive. If you are not careful, you can wind up thousands of dollars in debt to creditors. The high interest will enlarge your debt; your credit rating may fall, potentially hurting your eligibility for loans and mortgages; and you may lose your credit cards altogether.

REAL WORLD PERSPECTIVE

Brett Cross, *University of Washington*

I am a pre-engineering student at the University of Washington. Recently, I have been receiving a number of credit card applications offering a low interest rate. In fact, I get at least one offer a week. I've been thinking it would be nice to establish credit, but I'm not sure if getting a credit card right now is a good idea. Even though I have a part-time job and have financial aid, it seems like there's never enough to make it to the end of the semester. Should I apply for one of these credit cards? It would be really great to have some extra cash every now and then.

Tim Short, *Washington State Univeristy*

Dealing with financial hardships while in college is a part of life for many people these days. Credit card offers are in abundance for college students, and for good reason. Credit companies know that most college students won't be able to pay off their cards until after they graduate, and that they tend to carry balances and pay interest and hefty fees until they are solvent. Believe me, I know. Throughout my past four years at college, I have acquired several credit cards. On them I have charged things such as books, car repairs, auto insurance, and other personal items. I am still paying interest on these cards monthly and will not be able to pay them off until after I graduate.

My suggestion to you is this: Don't take out a credit card unless you absolutely have to. If you can take out student loans or borrow from your parents, do that instead. Most academic loans have a 6 percent to 8 percent interest rate, which is much lower than the 18 percent to 21 percent that most credit card companies charge. Don't be fooled by offers for a card with a low rate. These invariably expire after one year and then the rate jumps up. If you miss a payment during that year, some companies will raise your rates immediately. Rationalizing that you will pay the card off before that time frame is up is also not a good idea. Unless you are on the verge of graduation, you will probably not have any more cash in a year than you do now. Overall, my advice is this: If you can avoid borrowing from credit card companies, do so! You will be a lot happier in the long run.

Credit spending can be hard to monitor. Paying by credit can seem so easy that you don't realize how much you are spending. When the bill comes at the end of the month, the total can hit you hard.

You are taking out a high-interest loan. Buying on credit is similar to taking out a loan—you are using money with the promise to pay it back. Loan rates, however, especially on fixed-interest loans, are often much lower than the 11 percent to 23 percent on credit card debt. Fifteen percent interest per year on a credit card debt averaging $2000 is approximately $300; 5 percent interest per year on a loan in the same amount is $100.

Bad credit ratings can haunt you. Anytime you are late with a payment, default on a payment, or in any way misuse your card, a record of that occurrence will be entered on your credit history, lowering your credit rating. If a prospective employer or loan officer discovers a low rating, you will seem less trustworthy and may lose the chance at a job or a loan.

Managing Credit Card Debt

There are ways to manage credit card debt so that it doesn't get worse. Stay in control by having only one or two cards and paying bills regularly and on time. Try to pay in full each month. If you can't, at least pay the minimum. Make as much of a dent in the bill as you can.

If you get into trouble, three steps will help you deal with the situation. First, *admit* that you made a mistake, even though you may be embarrassed. Then, *address* the problem immediately and honestly in order to minimize the damages. Call the bank or credit card company to talk to someone about the problem. They may draw up a payment plan that allows you to pay your debt gradually, in amounts that your budget can manage. Creditors would rather accept small payments than nothing at all.

Finally, *prevent* this problem from happening again. Figure out what got you into trouble and take steps to avoid it in the future if you can. Some financial disasters, such as medical emergencies, may be beyond your control. Overspending on luxuries, however, is something you have the power to avoid. Make a habit of balancing your checkbook. Cut up a credit card or two if you have too many. Don't let a high credit limit tempt you to spend. Pay every month, even if you pay only the minimum. If you work to clean up your act, your credit history will gradually clean up as well.

Name   Date

CHAPTER 10 Applications

KEY INTO YOUR LIFE *Opportunities to Apply What You Learn*

EXERCISE 10.1 **Mentors**

First, consider the people you go to with problems and questions, people whom you trust and with whom you share a lot of yourself. Name up to three—don't fill the list unless you can really think of three people you trust.

1. _____

2. _____

3. _____

Evaluate your list. With which of those people do you feel you could have a mentoring relationship? Name up to two; for each, name two steps you can take to invest even further in your relationship.

1. _____

_____

2. _____

_____

EXERCISE 10.2 **Networking**

Make a list of people you know whom you could contact for information, jobs, or advice. Don't limit yourself—include people from categories such as co-workers, student organizations, members of your study group, other fellow students, professors, community organizations, people your parents know, friends of your siblings, people you know from your religious affiliation, anyone you know.

Consider an issue you are facing in your life right now. Which two of these people could you consult on this issue?

1. _____

2. _____

Your Job Priorities

What kind of job could you manage while you're in school? How would you want a job to benefit you? Discuss your requirements in each of the following areas:

Salary/wage level _____

Time of day _____

Hours per week (part time vs. full time) _____

Duties _____

Location _____

Flexibility _____

Affiliation with school or financial aid program _____

What kind of job might fit all or most of your requirements? List two possibilities here.

1. _____

2. _____

Savings Brainstorm

As a class, brainstorm areas that require financial management (such as funding an education, running a household, or putting savings away for the future) and write them on the board. Divide into small groups. Each group should choose one area to discuss (make sure all areas are chosen). In your group, brainstorm strategies that can help with the area you have chosen. Think of savings ideas, ways to control spending, ways to earn more money, and any other methods of relieving financial stress. Agree on a list of possible ideas for your area and share it with the class.

11

Changing with the Future

The end of one path can be the beginning of another. For example, graduation is often referred to as commencement, because the end of your student career is the beginning or renewal of your life as a working citizen. As you come to the end of your work in this course, you have built up a wealth of knowledge. Now you have more power to make decisions about what direction you want your studies and your career to take.

This chapter will explore how to manage the constant change you will encounter in your life and career. Developing flexibility will enable you to adjust goals, make the most of successes, and work through failures. You will consider what is important about giving back to your community and continuing to learn throughout your life. Finally, you will revisit your personal mission, exploring how to revise it as you encounter changes in the future.

In this chapter, you will explore answers to the following questions:

● What is the future of engineering?

● How can you live with change?

● What will help you handle success and failure?

● Why give back to the community and the world?

● Why is college just the beginning of lifelong learning?

● How can you live your mission?

WHAT IS THE FUTURE OF ENGINEERING?

Engineers have brought about so many changes in our lives that in the twenty-first century, the life of the typical American is quite different from that of the typical American at the turn of the twentieth century. Think of just a few of the innovations—computers, television, telephones, electricity, faxes, microwaves, cars, airplanes, the Internet, and many more. As you saw in earlier chapters, these technological advances do not come about without raising concerns and issues. This is why engineering accreditation programs now require that colleges teach their students to consider, while engineering a project, such factors as professional and ethical responsibility, environmental factors, economics, and manufacturability, and to look at problems in a global, societal, and legal context. Because things are changing so rapidly, colleges also endeavor to instill in students an understanding that they must embrace lifelong learning in order to succeed in their careers.

Changes in technology bring with them complex and interesting ethical issues. Let's examine one of them: privacy on the Internet.

Privacy Issues on the Internet

DoubleClick Inc. acquired Abacus Direct Corporation on November 23, 1999. Abacus has an electronic direct mail service that enables U. S. consumers on the Internet to receive advertising messages tailored to their individual interests. A database of personally identifiable information is being collected by Abacus that includes the user's name and address; retail, catalog and online purchase history; and demographic data. The data is matched through use of information provided by the user and the DoubleClick cookie.

The matching of information and the gathering of that information is all facilitated by engineers and computer programmers who have developed the equipment and the software that not only constitute the Internet itself but also the software in the browsers and for the Web sites (including the cookies). Are you, as a consumer, concerned about the availability or release of personal information about you? If you were an employee working with these types of companies, how would you see your role in terms of privacy issues?

HOW CAN YOU LIVE WITH CHANGE?

Change can turn even the most carefully constructed plans upside down. In this section, you will explore some ways to make change a manageable part of your life by accepting the reality of change, maintaining flexibility, and adjusting your goals.

Accept the Reality of Change

As Russian-born author Isaac Asimov once said, "It is change, continuing change, inevitable change, that is the dominant factor in society today. No sensible decision can be made any longer without taking into account not only the world as it is, but the world as it will be."[1] Change is a sure thing. Two significant causes of change on a global level are technology and the economy.

Technological Growth

Today's technology has spurred change. Tasks that people have performed for years are now taken care of by computers in a fraction of the time and for a fraction of the price. Advances in technology come into being daily: Computer companies update programs; new models of cars appear, some with in-dashboard mapping systems using satellites for global positioning; and

THE FAR SIDE © 1983 FARWORKS, INC. All rights reserved.

scientists discover new possibilities in medicine and other areas. People make changes in the workplace, school, and home to keep up with the new systems and products that technology constantly offers. People and cultures are linked around the world through the Internet and World Wide Web.

The dominance of the media, brought on by technological growth, has increased the likelihood of change. A few hundred years ago, no television or magazines or Internet existed to show people what was happening elsewhere in the world. A village could operate in the same way for years with very little change, because there would be little to no contact with anyone from the outside who could introduce new ideas, methods, or plans. Now, the media constantly presents people with new ways of doing things. When people can see the possibilities around them, they are more likely to want to find out whether the grass is truly greener on the other side of the fence.

Economic Dynamics

The unpredictable economy is the second factor in this age of constant change. Businesses have had to cut costs in order to survive, which has affected many people's jobs and careers. Some businesses discovered the speed and cost-effectiveness of computers and used them to replace workers. Some busi-

Success in the Real World

Ilene Busch-Vishniac

Dean, Whiting School of Engineering, Johns Hopkins University

I started my university career as a music student, but switched into physics and mathematics after taking a freshman course entitled "The Physics of Music." This stimulated my interest in acoustics, which continues today. My graduate work in noise control took me into the mechanical engineering department of MIT, and I finally felt as if I had found my home. I continue to work in acoustics, through tackling the problem of designing noise walls to prevent sound from reaching homes and schools, and through designing devices such as microphones and loudspeakers.

I love being an engineer because I spend my time solving technical problems. Since solutions tend to require information from more than one discipline, engineering gives me a chance to work with interesting people, to constantly learn from them, and to feel a real sense of accomplishment when we produce a product. Because I am an academic, I have a wonderful opportunity to discover new information and to impart knowledge to students as well.

I believe that engineering has changed profoundly over the last decade, and it will continue to transition quickly. Once, engineering and technology were the domain only of highly trained professionals. Now, engineering and technology touch everyone's lives on a daily basis. It is difficult to conceive of the home and office absent telephones, fax machines, computers, automatic coffeemakers, electronic thermostats and light switches, and new materials. As a result, activities and products that once were enjoyed only by trained engineers now are available to people with a wide range of technical abilities and interests. This simultaneously has made engineering

more important than ever, and richer for a growing realm of applications. With the rapid growth of electronic commerce and the increasing ability to custom-make biomedical devices to enhance and extend our lives, the future for engineering continues to expand. We are rapidly approaching the point at which technical literacy will be at least as important in assuring one's future as the ability to read.

If I could start my professional career over, this time with full knowledge of how the world would develop until the year 2000, there is very little that I would change. My choices have allowed me to assume a position of leadership at a major academic institution, to assure my future financially, to always have interesting challenges ahead, and to enjoy the richness of life. I simply can't imagine a better career today than engineering.

Downsize
To reduce in size; streamline.

nesses have had to **downsize** and have laid off people to save money. Some businesses have merged with others, and people in duplicate jobs were let go. In other cases, new industries have developed rapidly, requiring highly trained, technologically advanced workers. The economy has also had an effect on personal finances. Many people face money problems at home that force them to make changes in how much they work, how they pursue an education, and how they live.

Maintain Flexibility

The fear of change is as inevitable as change itself. When you become comfortable with something, you tend to want it to stay the way it is, whether it is a relationship, a place you live, a job, a schedule, or the racial/cultural mix of people with whom you interact. Change may seem to have only negative effects, and consistency only positive effects. Think about your life right now. What do you wish would always stay the same? What changes have upset you and thrown you off balance?

You may have encountered any number of changes in your life to date, many of them unexpected. You may have experienced ups and downs in relationships, perhaps marriage or divorce. You may have changed schools, changed jobs, or moved to a new home. You may have shifted your course of study. You may have added to your family or lost family members. Financial shifts may have caused you to change the way you live. All of these changes, whether you perceive them as good or bad, cause a certain level of stress. They also cause a shift in your personal needs, which may lead to changing priorities.

Change Brings Different Needs

Your needs can change from day to day, year to year, and situation to situation. Although you may know about some changes ahead of time, such as when you plan to attend school or move in with a partner, others may take you completely by surprise, such as an illness, or losing a loved one or a job. Even the different times of year bring different needs, such as a need for extra cash around the holidays or a need for additional child care when your children are home for the summer.

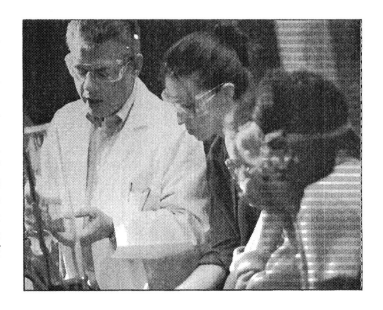

Some changes that shift your needs will occur within a week or even a day. For example, a professor may inform you that you have a quiz or extra assignment at the end of the week, or your supervisor at work may give you an additional goal for the week. Table 11.1 shows how the effects of certain changes can lead to new priorities.

Flexibility versus Inflexibility

When change affects your needs, *flexibility* will help you shift your priorities so that you address those needs. You can react to change with either inflexibility or flexibility, each with its resulting effects.

Inflexibility. Not acknowledging a shift in needs can cause trouble. For example, if you lose your job and continue to spend as much money as you did before, ignoring your need to live more modestly, you can drive yourself into debt and make the situation worse. Or if you continue to spend little time with a partner who has expressed a need for more contact, you may lose your partner or harm the relationship.

TABLE 11.1   Change produces new priorities.

CHANGE	EFFECTS AND CHANGED NEEDS	NEW PRIORITIES
Lost job	Loss of income; need for others in your household to contribute more income	Job hunting; reduction in your spending; additional training or education in order to qualify for a different job
New job	Change in daily/weekly schedule; need for increased contribution of household help from others	Time and energy commitment to new job; maintaining confidence; learning new skills
Started school	Fewer hours for work, family, and personal time; responsibility for classwork; need to plan semesters ahead of time	Careful scheduling; making sure you have time to attend class and study adequately; strategic planning of classes and of career goals
Relationship/marriage	Responsibility toward your partner; merging of your schedules and perhaps your finances and belongings	Time and energy commitment to relationship
Breakup/divorce	Change in responsibility for any children; increased responsibility for your own finances; possibly a need to relocate; increased independence	Making time for yourself; gathering support from friends and family; securing your finances; making sure you have your own income
Bought car	Responsibility for monthly payment; responsibility for upkeep	Regular income so that you can make payments on time; time and money for upkeep
New baby	Increased parenting responsibility; need money to pay for baby or if you had to stop working; need help with other children	Child care; flexible employment; increased commitment from a partner or other supporter
New cultural environment (from new home, job, or school)	Exposure to unfamiliar people and traditions; tendency to keep to yourself	Learning about the culture with which you are now interacting; openness to new relationships

Flexibility. Being flexible means acknowledging the change, examining your different needs, and addressing them in any way you can. As frightening as it can be, being flexible can help you move ahead. Discovering what change brings may help you uncover positive effects that you had no idea were there. For example, a painful breakup or divorce can lead you to discover greater capability and independence. A loss of a job can give you a chance to reevaluate your abilities and look for another job in an area that suits you better. An illness can give you perspective on what you truly value in life. In other words, a crisis can spur opportunity; you may learn that you want to adjust your goals in order to pursue that opportunity.

Sometimes you may need to resist for a while, until you are ready to face an important change. When you do decide you are ready, being flexible will help you cope with the negative effects and benefit from the positive effects.

Adjust Your Goals

Your changing life will often result in the need to adjust goals accordingly. Sometimes goals must change because they weren't appropriate in the first place. Some turn out to be unreachable; some may not pose enough of a challenge; others may be unhealthy for the person who set them or harmful to others.

Step One: Reevaluate

Before making adjustments in response to change, take time to *reevaluate* both your goals and your progress toward them.

Your goals. First, determine whether your goals still fit the person you have become in the past week, or month, or year. Circumstances can change quickly.

Your progress. If you feel you haven't gotten far, determine whether the goal is out of your range or simply requires more stamina than you had anticipated. As you work toward any goal you will experience alternating periods of progress and stagnation. Sticking with a tough goal may be the hardest thing you'll ever do, but the payoff may be worth it. You may want to seek the support and perspective of a friend or counselor as you evaluate your progress.

Step Two: Modify

If after your best efforts it becomes clear that a goal is out of reach, *modifying* your goal may bring success. Perhaps the goal doesn't suit you. For example, you may want to take more classes in an area that interests you, causing you to need five years to graduate instead of four.

Based on your reevaluation, you can modify a goal in two ways:

1. Adjust the existing goal. To adjust a goal, change one or more aspects that define that goal—for example, the time frame, the due date, or the specifics of the expectations. If you find you didn't get a major scholarship or loan that you had expected, you may need to work additional hours at your job. This may cause you to delay your graduation by a semester or a year.

2. Replace it with a different, more compatible goal. If you find that you just can't handle a particular goal, try to find another that makes more sense for you at this time. For example, your goal may have been to graduate without any debt, but you needed to take out a student loan in order to graduate on time. Because you and your circumstances never stop changing, your goals should keep up with those changes.

Being open to adjusting your goals will help you manage both failure and success along the way.

WHAT WILL HELP YOU HANDLE FAILURE AND SUCCESS?

The perfect, trouble-free life is only a myth. The most wonderful, challenging, fulfilling life is full of problems to be solved and difficult decisions to be made. If you want to handle the bumps and bruises without losing your self-esteem, you should prepare to encounter setbacks along with your successes.

> "Risk! Risk anything! Care no more for the opinion of others, for those voices. Do the hardest thing on earth for you. Act for yourself. Face the truth."
>
> KATHERINE MANSFIELD

Dealing with Failure

Things don't always go the way you want them to go. Sometimes you may come up against obstacles that are difficult to overcome. Sometimes you will let yourself down or disappoint others. You may make mistakes or lose your motivation. All people do, no matter who they are or how smart or accomplished they may be. What is important is how you choose to deal with what goes wrong. If you can arrive at reasonable definitions of failure and success, accept failure as part of being human, and examine failure so that you can learn from it, you will have the confidence to pick yourself up and keep improving.

The typical engineering student was at the top of his or her high school class before entering college—the best of the best. Then the first physics or calculus or chemistry test results come back and there is that student's grade—a 28! We have all been through that. Don't let this be a blow to your self-esteem or confidence. You are facing tough competition in engineering school—perhaps for the first time in your life. You may not be the one who ends up on top or at the front of the pack all of the time. Remember, the average grade is a C. And out of all of those top students, someone is going to be at the average.

This doesn't mean that you aren't good enough or that you can't cut it or that you're not smart. It might mean you didn't study enough or that you didn't study the right material for the test. Don't give up! Go see the professor. Go see the TA. Find a tutor. And remember, it doesn't matter if you get straight A's in college—you will get a job when you graduate. What is important is how you react to your experience—this will make all the difference.

Measuring Failure and Success

Most people measure failure by comparing where they are to where they believe they should be. Since individual circumstances vary widely, so do definitions of failure. What you consider a failure may seem like a positive step for someone else. Here are some examples:

- Imagine that your native language is Spanish. You have learned to speak English well, but you still have trouble writing it. Making writing mistakes may seem like failure to you, but to a recent immigrant from the Dominican Republic who knows limited English, your command of the language will seem like a success story.

- If two people apply for internships, one may see failure as receiving some offers but not their first choice, while someone who was turned down may see any offer as a success.

- Having a job that doesn't pay you as much as you want may seem like a failure, but to someone who is having trouble finding any job, your job is a definite success.

Accepting Failure

No one escapes failure, no matter how hard he may try (or how successful he may be at hiding mistakes). The most successful people and organizations have experienced failures and mistakes. America Online miscalculated customer use and offered a flat rate per month, resulting in thousands of customers having trouble logging onto the service. Many an otherwise successful individual has had a problematic relationship, a substance-abuse problem, or a failing grade in a course.

You have choices when deciding how to view a failure or mistake. You can pretend it never happened, blame it on someone or something else, blame yourself, or forgive yourself.

Pretending it didn't happen. Avoiding the pain of dealing with a failure can deny you valuable lessons and could even create more serious problems. Failing your first calculus test, but not admitting that you need help and finding a tutor, may lead to more serious consequences, such as not understanding the basic concepts and doing badly in the class.

Blaming others. Putting the responsibility on someone else stifles opportunities to learn and grow. For example, imagine that an unprepared and inappropriately dressed person interviews for a job and is not hired. If she decides that the interviewer is biased, the interviewee won't learn to improve her preparation or interview strategies. Evaluate causes carefully and try not to assign blame.

Blaming yourself. Getting angry at yourself for failing, or thinking that you aren't smart enough or believing that you should be perfect, can only result in your feeling incapable of success and perhaps becoming afraid to try. Negative self-talk can become self-fulfilling.

Forgiving yourself. This is by far the best way to cope. First, although you should always strive for your best, don't expect perfection of yourself or anyone else. Expect that you will do the best that you can within the circumstances of your life. Just getting through another day as a student, employee, or parent is an important success. Second, forgive yourself when you fail. Your value as a human being does not diminish when you make a mistake. Forgiving yourself will give you more strength to learn from the experience, move on, and try again.

Once you are able to approach failure and mistakes in a productive way, you can explore what you can learn from them.

> "The word impossible is not in my dictionary."
>
> NAPOLEON

Learning from Failure

Learning from your failures and mistakes involves thinking critically through what happened. The first step is to evaluate what happened and decide if it was within your control. It could have had nothing to do with you at all. You could have failed to win a job because someone else with equal qualifications was in line for it ahead of you. A family crisis that disrupted your sleep could have affected your studying, resulting in a failing grade on a test. These are unfortunate circumstances, but they are not failures. On the other hand, something you did or didn't do may have contributed to the failure.

If you decide that you have made a mistake, your next steps are to analyze the causes and effects of what happened, make any improvements that you can, and decide how to change your action or approach in the future.

For example, imagine that after a long night of studying you forgot to appear at your part-time job the next day.

Analyze causes and effects. *Causes:* Your exhaustion and your concern about your test caused you to forget to check on your work schedule. *Effects:* Because you weren't there, a crucial project wasn't completed. Your supervisor, who needed the project, has been adversely affected by your mistake.

Make any possible improvements on the situation. Apologize and see if there is still a chance to finish up your portion of the project that day.

Make changes for the future. You could set a goal to note your work schedule regularly in your date book—maybe in a bright color—and to check it more often. You could also arrange your future study schedule so that you will be less exhausted.

Think about the people you consider exceptionally successful. They did not rise to the top without taking risks and making their share of mistakes. They have built much of their success upon their willingness to recognize and learn from their shortfalls. You too can benefit from staying open to this kind of active, demanding, hard-won education. Learning involves change and growth. Let what you learn from falling short of your goals inspire new and better ideas.

Think Positively About Failure

When you feel you have failed, how can you boost your outlook?

Stay aware of the fact that you are a capable, valuable person. People often react to failure by becoming convinced that they are incapable and incompetent. Fight that tendency by reminding yourself of your successes, focusing your energy on your best abilities, and knowing that you have the strength to try again. Realize that your failure isn't a setback as long as you learn from it and rededicate yourself to excellence. Remember that the energy you might expend on talking down to yourself would be better spent on trying again and moving ahead.

Share your thoughts and disappointment with others. Everybody fails. Trading stories will help you realize you're not alone. People refrain from talking about failures out of embarrassment, often feeling as though no one else could have made as big a mistake as they did. When you open up, though, you may be surprised to hear others exchange stories that rival your own. Be careful not to get caught in a destructive cycle of complaining. Instead, focus on the kind of creative energy that can help you find ways to learn from your failures.

Look on the bright side. At worst, you at least have learned a lesson that will help you avoid similar situations in the future. At best, there may be some positive results of what happened. If your romance flounders, the extra study time you suddenly have may help you boost your grades. If you fail a class, you may discover that you need to hire a tutor or join a study group. What you learn from a failure may, in an unexpected way, bring you around to where you want to be.

Dealing with Success

Success isn't reserved for the wealthy, famous people you see glamorized in magazines and newspapers. Success isn't money or fame, although it can bring such things. Success is being who you want to be and doing what you want to do. Success is within your reach.

Pay attention to the small things when measuring success. You may not feel successful until you reach an important goal you have set for yourself. However, along the way each step is a success. When you are trying to drop a harmful habit, each time you stay on course is a success. When you are juggling work, school, and personal life, just coping with what every new day brings equals success. If you received a C on a test and then earned a B on the next one, your advancement is successful.

Remember that success is a process. If you deny yourself the label of "success" until you reach the top of where you want to be, you will have a much harder time getting there. Just moving ahead toward improvement and growth, however fast or slow the movement, equals success.

Here are some techniques to handle your successes.

First, appreciate yourself. You deserve it. Take time to congratulate yourself for a job well done—whether it be a good grade, an important step in learning a new language, a job offer, a promotion or graduation, or a personal victory over substance abuse. Bask in the glow a bit. Everybody hears about mistakes, but people don't praise themselves (or each other) enough when success happens. Praise can give you a terrific vote of confidence.

Take that confidence on the road. This victory can lead to others. Based on this success, you may be expected to prove to yourself and others that you are capable of growth, of continuing your successes and building upon them. Show yourself and others that the confidence is well founded.

Stay sensitive to others. There could be people around you who may not have been so successful. Remember that you have been in their place, and they in yours, and the positions may change many times over in the future. Enjcy what you have, work to build on it and not to take it for granted, and support others as they need it.

Staying sensitive to others is an important goal always, whether you are feeling successful or less than successful. Giving what you can of your time, energy, and resources to the community and the world is part of being aware of what others need. Your contributions can help to bring success to others.

WHY GIVE BACK TO THE COMMUNITY AND THE WORLD?

Everyday life is demanding. You can become so caught up in the issues of your own life that you neglect to look outside your immediate needs. However, from time to time you may feel that your mission extends beyond your personal life. You have spent time in this course working to improve yourself. Now that you've come so far, why not extend some of that energy and effort to the world outside? With all that you have to offer, you have the power to make positive differences in the lives of others. Every effort you make, no matter how small, improves the world.

Your Imprint on the World

As difficult as your life can sometimes seem, looking outside yourself and into the lives of others can help put everything in perspective. Sometimes you can evaluate your own hardships more reasonably when you look at them in light of what is happening elsewhere in the world. There are always many people in the world in great need. You have something to give to others. Making a lasting difference in the lives of others is something to be proud of.

Your perspective may change after you help build a house for Habitat for Humanity. Your appreciation of those close to you may increase after you spend time with cancer patients at the local hospice. Your perspective on the environment may change after you help clean up litter from stretches of an interstate highway.

If you could eavesdrop on someone *talking about you* to another person, what do you think you would hear? How would you like to hear yourself described? What you do for others makes an imprint that can have far more impact than you may imagine. Giving one person hope, comfort, or help can improve her ability to cope with life's changes. That person in turn may be able to offer help to someone else. As each person makes a contribution, a cycle of positive effects develops. For example, Helen Keller, blind and deaf from the age of two, was educated through the help of her teacher Annie Sullivan, and then spent much of her life lecturing to raise money for the teaching of the blind and deaf. Another example is Betty Ford, who was helped in her struggle with alcoholism and founded the Betty Ford Center to help others with addiction problems.

How can you make a difference? Many schools and companies are realizing the importance of community involvement and have appointed committees to find and organize volunteering opportunities. Make some kind of volunteering activity a priority on your schedule. Work with the student chapter of your professional engineering organization to host math/science/engineering badge days for Scouts. Look for what's available to you or create opportunities on your own. Table 11.2 lists organizations that provide volunteer opportunities; you might also look into more local efforts or private clearinghouses that set up a number of different smaller projects.

		TABLE 11.2
AIDS-related organizations	Kiwanis/Knights of Columbus/ Lions Club/Rotary	Organizations that can use your help.
American Red Cross	Libraries	
Amnesty International	Meals on Wheels	
Audubon Society	Nursing homes	
Battered women shelters	Planned Parenthood	
Big Brothers and Big Sisters	Schools	
Churches, synagogues, temples, and affiliated organizations such as the YMCA/YWCA or YMHA/YWHA	Scouting organizations	
Educational support organizations	Share Our Strength/other food donation organizations	
Environmental awareness/support organizations such as Greenpeace	Shelters and organizations supporting the homeless	
Hospitals	Sierra Club/World Wildlife Fund	
Hot lines		

Volunteerism is also getting a great deal of attention on the national level. The government has made an effort to stress the importance of community service as part of what it means to be a good citizen, and it provides support for that effort through AmeriCorps. AmeriCorps provides financial awards for education in return for community service work. If you work for AmeriCorps, you can use the funds you receive to pay current tuition expenses or repay student loans. You may work either before, during, or after your college education. You can find more information on AmeriCorps by contacting this organization:

The Corporation for National and
Community Service
1201 New York Avenue, NW
Washington, DC 20525
1-800-942-2677

Sometimes it's hard to find time to volunteer when so many responsibilities compete for your attention. One solution is to combine other activities with volunteer work. Get exercise while cleaning litter off the highway or a park or hanging drywall for Habitat for Humanity. Whatever you do, your actions will have a ripple effect, creating a positive impact for those you help and those they encounter in turn. The strength often found in people surviving difficult circumstances can strengthen you as well.

Success in the Real World

Ralph Peterson, P. E.

Chairman and CEO, CH2M Hill

There's no question that the roots of my professional engineering career can be traced to the banks of the Mississippi River where I spent my youth. As is the case of so many people who grew up near the mighty Mississippi, there's simply no escaping the size, power, and dominating influence "the River" casts over your life. The mysteries of this great river have been chronicled in books and song for generations.

In my case the River's mysteries first stirred in me when my family stopped buying fish caught from the River in the late 1950s, because of industrial waste upstream. How human activity could have such an abiding impact on what seemed a nearly infinitely huge river became a compelling mystery to me.

Along the stretch of river in the southeast corner of Missouri where I grew up, we tended to be a pragmatic, problem-solving bunch (not like the day-dreaming clan upriver in Mark Twain's Hannibal). So the notion of applying technology in ways that could improve people's lives held real fascination for me.

In no time, my technical curiosity and a like-minded older brother steered me in the direction of engineering. As I learned more about engineering and chose it as a career path, it all seemed too good to be true. Finding that you could actually make a living by engineering solutions to really interesting problems wasn't so much a career discovery as it was a dream come true. I was hooked, and it couldn't have happened at a more opportune time.

Not long after landing a dream job at CH₂M Hill, I found myself in graduate school at Stanford. That was at the end of the 1960s, precisely at the time when much of the environmental movement that would guide the nation's future was starting to take shape. As fate would have it, I was wrapping up my environmental engineering studies at Stanford when the first Earth Day took place, in 1970. Although I didn't fully appreciate it at the time, that first Earth Day inspired a wave of new environmental legislation that would define the U. S. environmental agenda for the next three decades.

The River's challenge that mystified me in childhood had turned into a lifelong pursuit. Protecting and restoring the water, air, and land resources of the nation gave rise to some of the most interesting engineering problems imaginable, and I had the good fortune to be among those developing solutions to those problems. That was—and still is—pretty heady stuff.

Today, the same technical challenges that first fueled my professional passions continue to energize me. Only now those challenges go far beyond the riverbanks of the Mississippi.

Today those challenges may involve:

- delivering drinking water to people's homes in Egypt
- cleaning up hazardous waste sites in the former Soviet Union
- designing a wastewater treatment system to serve the nation-state of Singapore
- collaborating on a national environmental strategy for the People's Republic of China
- delivering safe, permanent closure of former nuclear weapons plants

In each of these cases (and hundreds more over the course of my career), it's hard to adequately describe the deep sense of satisfaction that comes from delivering technology that profoundly improves people's lives.

Come to think of it, maybe that's the greatest lesson the River had to share: Nurture the lives of everyone you can reach, and keep rolling on.

Valuing Your Environment

Your environment is your home. When you value it, you help to maintain a clean, safe, and healthy place to live. What you do every day has an impact on others around you and on the future. One famous slogan says that if you are not part of the solution, you are part of the problem. Every environmentally aware child, saved bottle, and reused bag is part of the solution. Take responsibility for what you can control—your own habits—and develop sound practices that contribute to the health of the environment.

Strive for sustainable development. Engineers need to be aware of the concept of sustainable development as they work within their communities and industries to develop new products. *Sustainable development* means that the anticipated economic growth and development necessary to maintain expanding communities takes place within the concepts of environmental protection; that environmental protection and economic development are complementary rather than antagonistic processes. Whereas traditional approaches to economic development can lead to congestion, sprawl, pollution, and resource overconsumption, sustainable development is a strategy by which communities seek economic development approaches that also benefit the local environment and quality of life.

Recycle anything that you can. What can be recycled varies with the system set up in your area. You may be able to recycle any combination of plastics, aluminum, glass, newspapers, and magazines. Products that make use of recycled materials are often more expensive, but if they are within your price range, try to reward the manufacturer's dedication by purchasing their products.

Trade and reuse items. Give clothing you don't wear to others who can use it. Organizations like the Salvation Army may pick up used items in your neighborhood on certain days or if you make arrangements with them. Wrap presents in plain newspaper and decorate with markers. Use your imagination—there are many, many items that you can reuse, all around you.

Respect the outdoors. Participate in maintaining a healthy environment. Use products that reduce chemical waste. Pick up after yourself. Through volunteering, voicing your opinion, or making monetary donations, support the maintenance of parks and the preservation of natural, undeveloped land. Be creative. One young woman planned a cleanup of a local lakeside area as the main group activity for the guests at her birthday party (she joined them, of course). Everyone benefits when each person takes responsibility for maintaining the fragile earth.

Remember that valuing yourself is the base for valuing all other things. Improving the earth is difficult unless you value yourself and think you deserve the best living environment possible. Valuing yourself will also help you understand why you deserve to enjoy the benefits of learning throughout your life.

WHY IS COLLEGE JUST THE BEGINNING OF LIFELONG LEARNING?

Although it may sometimes feel more like a burden, being a student is a golden opportunity. As a student, you are able to focus on learning for a period of time, and your school focuses on you in return, helping you gain access to knowledge, resources, and experiences. Take advantage of the academic atmosphere by developing a habit of seeking out new learning opportunities. That habit will encourage you to continue your learning long after you have graduated, even in the face of the pressures of everyday life.

Learning brings change, and change causes growth. As you change and the world changes, new knowledge and ideas continually emerge. Absorb them so that you can propel yourself into the future. Visualize yourself as a student of life who learns something new every single day.

Here are some lifelong learning strategies that can encourage you to continually ask questions and explore new ideas.

Investigate new interests. When information and events catch your attention, take your interest one step further and find out more. If you are fascinated by politics on television, find out if your school has political clubs that you can explore. If a friend of yours starts to take yoga, try out a class with him. If you really like one portion of a particular class, see if there are other classes that focus on that specific topic. Turn the regretful, "I wish I had tried that," into the purposeful, "I'm going to do it."

Read books, newspapers, magazines, and other writings. Reading opens a world of new perspectives. Check out what's on the bestseller list at your bookstore. Ask your friends about books that have changed their lives. Stay on top of current change in your community, your state, your country, and the world by reading newspapers and magazines. A newspaper that has a broad scope, such as *The New York Times* or *Washington Post*, can be an education in itself. Explore religious literature, family letters, and Internet news groups and Web pages. Keep something with you to read for those moments when you have nothing to do.

Spend time with interesting people. When you meet someone new who inspires you and makes you think, keep in touch. Have a potluck dinner party and invite one person or couple from each corner of your life—your family, your work, your school, a club to which you belong, your neighborhood. Sometimes, meet for reasons beyond just being social. Start a hiking group or an investing group. Get to know people of different cultures and perspectives. Learn something new from each other.

Pursue improvement in your studies and in your career. When at school, take classes outside of your major if you have time. After graduation, continue your education both in your field and in the realm of general knowledge. Stay on top of ideas, developments, structural changes, and new technology in your field by seeking out **continuing education** courses. Sign up for career-related seminars. Take single courses at a local college or

Continuing education
Courses that students can take without having to be part of a degree program.

community learning center. Some companies offer additional on-the-job training or will pay for their employees to take courses that will improve their knowledge and skills. If your company doesn't, you may want to set a small part of your income aside as a "learning budget." When you apply for jobs, you may want to ask about what kind of training or education the company offers or supports.

Nurture a spiritual life. You can find spirituality in many places. You don't have to regularly attend a house of worship to be spiritual, although that may be an important part of your spiritual life. "A spiritual life of some kind is absolutely necessary for psychological 'health,'" says psychologist and author Thomas Moore in his book *The Care of the Soul.* "We live in a time of deep division, in which mind is separated from body and spirituality is at odds with materialism."[2] The words *soul* and *spirituality* hold different meaning for each individual. Decide what they mean to you. Whether you discover them in music, organized religion, friendship, nature, cooking, sports, or anything else, making them a priority in your life will help you find a greater sense of balance and meaning.

Experience what others create. Art is "an adventure of the mind" (Eugene Ionesco, playwright); "a means of knowing the world" (Angela Carter, author); something that "does not reproduce the visible; rather, it makes visible" (Paul Klee, painter); "a lie that makes us realize truth" (Pablo Picasso, painter); a revealer of "our most secret self" (Jean-Luc Godard, filmmaker). Through art you can discover new ideas and shed new light on old ones. Explore all kinds of art and focus on any forms that hold your interest. Seek out whatever moves you—music, visual arts, theater, photography, dance, domestic arts, performance art, film and television, poetry, prose, and more.

Make your own creations. Bring out the creative artist in yourself. Take a class in drawing, in pottery, or in quilting. Learn to play an instrument. Write poems for your favorite people or stories to read to your kids. Invent a recipe. Design and build a set of shelves for your home. Create a memoir of your life. You are a creative being. Express yourself, and learn more about yourself, through art.

Lifelong learning is the master key that unlocks every door you will encounter on your journey. If you keep it firmly in your hand, you will discover worlds of knowledge—and a place for yourself within them.

HOW CAN YOU LIVE YOUR MISSION?

As you learn and change, so may your life's mission. Whatever changes occur, your continued learning will give you a greater sense of security in your choices. Your mission will change as you learn and develop. It will continue to reflect your goals, values, and strengths if you live with integrity, roll with the changes that come your way, continue to observe the role models in your life, and work to achieve your personal best in all that you do.

Success in the Real World

Richard Weingardt, P.E.

CEO and Chairman, Richard Weingardt Consultants, Inc.

Excitement reigned whenever engineers came to my dad's construction site. They would check on the project's progress and answer questions concerning whatever building or bridge my dad, a general contractor, was constructing at the time. He had a lot of respect for engineers and, because I greatly admired my father, engineers became my heroes at an early age.

Later, a couple of summers before I entered high school, my family went on a vacation in Colorado's Rocky Mountains. We stopped along the way to see the famous Royal Gorge Suspension Bridge, majestically spanning the gorge a half mile above the sheer rock cliffs of the Arkansas River Canyon. When my father told me structural engineers were responsible for its design, I knew what my life's career would be—I was hooked. Luckily, math and science were both strong subjects for me in school.

I have never regretted that choice. Becoming a structural engineer has allowed me to fulfill a lifelong dream. I now design great structures, see them built, and point to them with the sense of pride that comes with being responsible for creating something significant and useful. That, in essence, is what engineering is all about—building, improving, and contributing to making everyone's standard of life better.

When you look at important manmade improvements on this planet, you can see that they would not be possible without the input of engineers. Throughout history, this has been the case. The Seven Wonders of the Ancient World, for example, are structural engineering feats. Indeed, the history

of engineering is the history of civilization. As engineering skills and techniques advance, so does the progress of society.

Increasingly, the world becomes more technologically complex. Major public decisions will need meaningful input from those with a solid knowledge of engineering and technology. Because of this, large numbers of engineering leaders will be needed, not just in the engineering industry, but in the public arena and communities as well. These demands require that tomorrow's engineers develop both their technical and people skills to the highest level possible.

In a perfect world, it would be wonderful if engineers could be community leaders and top engineers at the same time. This is not always the case. An

engineer's years in college are so short, it is impossible to fulfill all the technical course work needed and still adequately study art, history, literature, and the humanities—those subjects that broaden a person's education.

If engineers truly want to affect the world around them and help set public direction, they must commit to lifelong learning—taking courses and attending seminars to stay on the leading edge of the field, while at the same time developing their interpersonal and communication skills.

Because we live in a global marketplace—developed and developing countries both depending on their engineering base—the demand for engineers and engineering leaders will continue to remain high, now and into the future.

Live with Integrity

You've spent time exploring who you are, how you learn, and what you value. **Integrity** is about being true to that picture you have drawn of yourself while also considering the needs of others. Living with integrity will bring you great personal and professional rewards.

Honesty and sincerity are at the heart of integrity. Many of the decisions you make and act upon in your life are based on your underlying sense of what is "the right thing to do." Having integrity puts that sense into day-to-day action.

> **Integrity**
> Adherence to a code of moral values; incorruptibility, honesty.

The Marks of Integrity

A person of integrity lives by the following principles:

1. Honest representation of yourself and your thoughts. For example, you tell your partner when you are hurt over something that he or she did or didn't do.

2. Sincerity in word and action. You do what you say you will do. For example, you tell a co-worker who has to leave early that you will finish a project, and you follow through by completing the work.

3. Consideration of the needs of others. When making decisions, you take both your needs and the needs of others into account. You also avoid hurting others for the sake of your personal goals. For instance, you take into account the needs of all members of your study group when scheduling meetings so that everyone can attend.

The Benefits of Integrity

When you act with integrity, you earn trust and respect from yourself and from others. If people can trust you to be honest, to be sincere in what you say and do, and to consider the needs of others, they will be more likely to encourage you, support your goals, and reward your hard work. Integrity is a must for workplace success. To earn promotions, it helps to show that you have integrity in a variety of situations.

Think of situations in which a decision made with integrity has had a positive effect. Have you ever confessed to a professor that your paper is late without a good excuse, only to find that despite your mistake you have earned the professor's respect? Have extra efforts in the workplace ever helped you gain a promotion or a raise? Have your kindnesses toward a friend or spouse moved the relationship to a deeper level? When you decide to act with integrity, you can improve your life and the lives of others.

Most important, living with integrity helps you believe in yourself and in your ability to make good choices. A person of integrity isn't a perfect person, but one who makes the effort to live according to values and principles, continually striving to learn from mistakes and to improve. Take responsibility for making the right moves, and you will follow your mission with strength and conviction.

> "And life is what we make it, always has been, always will be."
>
> GRANDMA MOSES

Roll with the Changes

Think again about yourself. How has your idea of where you want to be changed since you first opened this book? How has your self-image changed? What have you learned about your values, your goals, and your styles of communication and learning? Consider how your educational, professional, and personal goals have changed. As you continue to grow and develop, keep adjusting your goals to your changes and discoveries.

Stephen Covey says in *The Seven Habits of Highly Effective People*, "Change—real change—comes from the inside out. It doesn't come from hacking at the leaves of attitude and behavior with quick fix personality ethic techniques. It comes from striking at the root—the fabric of our thought, the fundamental essential **paradigms** which give definition to our character and create the lens through which we see the world."[3]

Paradigm
An especially clear pattern or typical example.

Examining yourself deeply in that way is a real risk. Most of all, it demands courage and strength of will. Questioning your established beliefs and facing the unknown are much more difficult than staying with how things are. When you have the courage to face the consequences of trying something unfamiliar, admitting failure, or challenging what you thought you knew, you open yourself to growth and learning opportunities. You can make your way through changes you never anticipated if you make the effort to live your mission—in whatever forms it takes as it changes—each day, each week, each month, and for years to come.

Learn from Role Models

People often derive the highest level of motivation and inspiration from learning how others have struggled through the ups and downs of life and achieved their goals. Somehow, seeing how someone else went through difficult situations can give you hope for your own struggles. The positive effects of being true to one's self become more real when an actual person has earned them.

Role model
A person whose behavior in a particular role is imitated by others.

Learning about the lives of people who have achieved their own version of success can teach you what you can do in your own life. Bessie and Sadie Delany, sisters and accomplished African-American women born in the late 1800s, are two valuable **role models.** They took risks, becoming professionals in dentistry and teaching at a time when women and minorities were often denied both respect and opportunity. They worked hard to fight racial division and prejudice and taught others what they learned. They believed in their intelligence, beauty, and ability to give, and lived without regrets. Says Sadie in their *Book of Everyday Wisdom*, "If there's anything I've learned in all these years, it's that life is too good to waste a day. It's up to you to make it sweet."[4]

Engineers as Leaders

Our society faces many significant technological issues as we move into the twenty-first century. Unfortunately, not many of our elected officials—at the city, state, or federal level—are individuals with a technical background. How can we expect well-meaning people who are not technically literate to make significant decisions related to the Internet, transportation, pollution, and development without input from engineers?

We challenge you to think about how you can become involved in professional or community issues. Exercise 11.3 at the end of this chapter helps you think about how you can begin to examine leadership options within the professional and technical organizations on campus. We would argue that engineers are quite capable as leaders and that the local, state, and federal government will make better decisions if engineers are involved. When you are thinking of your long-range plan, don't forget this area of community involvement.

Aim for Your Personal Best

Your personal best is simply the best that you can do, in any situation. It may not be the best you have ever done. It may include mistakes, for nothing significant is ever accomplished without making mistakes and taking risks. It may shift from situation to situation. As long as you aim to do your best, though, you are inviting growth and success.

Aim for your personal best in everything you do. As a lifelong learner, you will always have a new direction in which to grow and a new challenge to face. Seek constant improvement in your personal, educational, and professional life, knowing that you are capable of that improvement. Enjoy the richness of life by living each day to the fullest, developing your talents and potential into the achievement of your most valued goals.

ENDNOTES

1. Isaac Asimov, "My Own View," in *The Encyclopedia of Science Fiction*, ed. Robert Holdstock (1978).

2. Thomas Moore, *The Care of the Soul* (New York: Harper Perennial, 1992), xi–xx.

3. Stephen Covey, *The Seven Habits of Highly Effective People* (New York: Simon & Schuster, 1989), 70–144, 309–318.

4. Sarah Delany and Elizabeth Delany with Amy Hill Hearth, *Book of Everyday Wisdom* (New York: Kodansha International, 1994), 123.

CHAPTER 11 Applications

KEY INTO YOUR LIFE   *Opportunities to Apply What You Learn*

EXERCISE 11.1   Looking at Change, Failure, and Success

Life can go by so fast that you don't take time to evaluate what changes have taken place, what failures you could learn from, and what successes you have experienced. Take a moment now and answer the following questions for yourself.

What are the three biggest changes that have occurred in your life this year?

1. _____
2. _____
3. _____

Choose one that you feel you handled well. What shifts in priorities or goals did you make?

_____
_____
_____
_____

Choose one that you could have handled better. What happened? What do you think you should have done?

_____
_____
_____
_____

Now name a personal experience, occurring this year, that you would consider a failure. What happened?

_____
_____

How did you handle it—did you ignore it, blame it on someone else, or admit and explore it?

_____

_____

_____

What did you learn from experiencing this failure?

_____

_____

_____

Finally, describe a recent success of which you are the most proud.

_____

_____

_____

How did this success give you confidence in other areas of your life?

_____

_____

_____

Volunteering

EXERCISE 11.2

Research volunteering opportunities in your community that would integrate with your engineering studies. What are the organizations? What are their needs? List three possibilities for which you have an interest or a passion.

1. _____

2. _____

3. _____

Of these three, choose one that you feel you will have the time and ability to try next semester. Name your choice here and tell why you selected it.

_____

_____

_____

_____

Research the suggestion you have chosen. Describe the activity. What is the time commitment? Is there any special training involved? Is this an activity you would do as part of a group or on your own?

_____

_____

_____

_____

_____

_____

_____

_____

EXERCISE | **11.3** | **Engineers as Leaders**

Determine which technical or professional organization is on campus for your engineering major. Find out when the group meets and start attending the meetings. Determine which committee chair or officer positions are available now, are expected to open in the next semester, or will be available next academic year. Decide which one you are interested in and develop a plan for becoming active as a leader in this organization.

Types of Engineers

APPENDIX

Many different types of engineers and engineering exist. This appendix presents a brief overview of the various types of engineering. Many of the fields of engineering are interrelated and grew out of a few basic types of engineering (chemical, civil, electrical, and mechanical). Trees developed by the College of Engineering at Villanova are provided to show those relationships.

Aerospace (or aeronautical or astronautical) engineers design, develop, and implement new and existing technologies in airplanes, space vehicles, and helicopters. These engineers are also involved in control and guidance systems, information systems, and instruments used for navigation of aircraft. Areas of specialty for aerospace/aeronautical/astronautical engineers include aerodynamics, manufacture, acoustics, rocket technology, computational fluid dynamics, and thermodynamics. An engineer in this field can even end up as an astronaut or as the Secretary of the Air Force.

Agricultural engineers become involved in every aspect of food production, including processing, storage, handling, and distribution. An important aspect of the agricultural engineer's job is to maintain or improve the environmental quality of the agro-ecosystem. Agricultural engineers might work in areas including the genetic manipulation of plants and animals, development of environmentally friendly pesticides, or the production of enzymes for food processing, as well as such traditional areas as design of tractors, barns, drainage systems, harvesters, and processing units. (See Figure A.1.)

Architectural engineers work with architects on buildings and focus on safety, costs, constructability, and sound construction methods. They work on building systems including illumination and heating, ventilation, and air conditioning. (See Figure A.2.)

Biomedical engineers design, test, and analyze equipment and materials used in treating medical conditions. Such equipment and materials include artificial joints and body parts, surgical tools, scanning equipment, and breathing and heart monitors. (See Figures A.1, A.2, and A.3.)

Ceramic engineers work with processes that convert nonmetallic minerals, clay, or silicates to ceramic products, such as the tiles used to deflect heat on the space shuttle. (See Figure A.1.)

Chemical engineers plan, design, and operate facilities that take ideas from scientists and translate them into large-scale commercial plants to meet the needs of society. Chemical engineers are employed in many industries including chemical (including synthetic rubber and fiber), petrochemical, food-processing (including breweries and distilleries), forestry, and pharmaceutical. (See Figure A.1.)

Civil engineers plan, design, and construct buildings, dams, airports, water and wastewater treatment and distribution systems, mass transit systems including roads and bridges, and drainage systems. (See Figure A.2.)

Computer engineers design, construct, and operate computer hardware and software systems. Knowledge of electrical engineering and computer science is generally required for computer engineers. (See Figure A.3.)

Construction engineers plan and build buildings and other facilities in coordination with engineers from many other disciplines. They are very concerned with the cost of the facilities being built, the timely provision of the needed materials, and the safety of the project. (See Figure A.2.)

Electrical/electronic engineers are involved with the production and delivery of electricity, telecommunications, cable, electronics, control systems, and digital systems. Some electrical engineers may be involved in biomedical engineering and digital signal processing. (See Figure A.3.)

Engineering management concentrates on preparing engineers for management positions early in their careers through a focus on such areas as research and development, operations and logistics, and quality and process. Courses emphasize broad-based management skills, analytical tools, and practical methods.

Engineering physicists are involved in applying mathematical and physical concepts and developments to many engineering fields.

Environmental engineers design products and systems to solve environmental problems, particularly cleaning up (or keeping clean) the air, water, and land (including cleaning up oil spills in the ocean). (See Figures A.1, A.2, and A.4.)

Geological engineers become involved in aspects of discovering and recovering minerals from the earth. (See Figure A.2.)

Geotechnical engineers understand the properties of soils and use this knowledge to establish soil bearing capacities to support structures such as dams, foundations of structures, and harbors. (See Figure A.2.)

Industrial engineers determine the most effective ways for an organization to use its resources—people, money, and time—to make a product. Industrial engineers are generally concerned about such issues as reliability, optimum performance, cost efficiency, quality control, plant design, and management of human resources.

Manufacturing engineers are involved in all aspects of manufacturing products, from the design of equipment processes and products, to the management of manufacturing facilities. Their concerns include the manufacturing operation itself, quality management, on-time delivery, capacity, and cost. (See Figure A.4.)

Marine or ocean engineers design harbors, underwater machines, and offshore drilling platforms. They specifically take into account the additional factors that must be considered in designing and manufacturing for the ocean environment, including wave motion, currents, temperature variations, and chemical and biological factors. (See Figures A.2 and A.4.)

Materials engineers develop new materials (polymers, ceramics, composites, and electronic materials) to meet the needs of products that must withstand conditions such as high pressures or high temperatures. Such materials include alloys for auto engines, airplanes, and spacecraft. (See Figures A.1 and A.4.)

Mechanical engineers design, test, and analyze machines, structures, and devices including cars, pumps, heating, ventilation and cooling systems, combustion systems, and sports equipment (such as bicycles and skis). Mechanical engineers get involved in a wide variety of areas including manufacturing; metallurgy and materials; machine design; systems engineering; plant design; construction, and operation; environmental engineering; and power and energy. (See Figure A.4.)

Metallurgical engineers focus on metals with regard to mining location, ore refining, and part fabrication. (See Figure A.4.)

Mining engineers design and plan mining operations such as for coal, gold, bauxite, and copper. Mining engineers have areas of expertise ranging from estimating ore reserves, geostatistics, geology, and underground and surface mine design, to the design of mining equipment, rock and soil mechanics, and mineral processing. One mining engineer, Herbert Hoover, became President of the United States. (See Figure A.4.)

Nuclear engineers design, develop, and implement projects relating to the nuclear industry, from nuclear power plants for the electric power industry to nautical propulsion systems for the U.S. Navy. Nuclear engineers are involved in the handling of nuclear fuels used in the commercial and military sectors and the handling of radioactive materials used in hospitals, clinics, laboratories, and military facilities. Jimmy Carter, a nuclear engineer, became President of the United States. (See Figures A.1 and A.4.)

Petroleum engineers are involved in ensuring the discovery, recovery, processing, and delivery of oil and gas. (See Figures A.1 and A.4.)

Software engineers develop programs to operate computers and microprocessors. (See Figure A.3.)

Structural engineers plan and design bridges, towers, stadiums, drilling platforms, and high-rise buildings. Their job is to ensure the structure is safe, stable, effective, and economical. (See Figure A.2.)

Surveying engineers learn to apply and expand the principles of land surveying to ensure that projects are located where they are supposed to be. Today, surveying includes up-to-date technology such as satellites, aerial and terrestrial photogrammetry, and computers.

Systems engineers use logic, mathematics, and science as well as an understanding of human and institutional needs, wants, and limitations to design, develop, implement, and control complex large-scale groups of resources and processes to achieve a common objective. (See Figure A.4.)

BIO-ENGINEERING

Body Implants
Kidney Machines
Artificial Body Organs
Synthetic Protein
Enzyme Catalysis

CRYOGENICS

Freeze Drying
Liquid Hydrogen
Oxygen and Nitrogen
Liquid Natural Gas
Food Preservation

PLASTICS, POLYMERS & FIBERS

Nylon   Vinyls
Polyethylene   Polyester
Polypropylene   Polyacrylate
Phenolics   Polystyrene

GRADUATE STUDIES

Law
Engineering
Business Administration
Public Service
Medicine

AGRICULTURAL CHEMICAL MANUFACTURE

Fertilizers
Plant Hormones
Herbicides-Fungicides
Insecticides

ADVANCED & ELECTRONIC MATERIALS

FUELS & ENERGY

Ceramics
Vapor Deposition
Composites

INDUSTRIAL CHEMICAL MANUFACTURE

Solar Cells
Coal Gasification
Nuclear Isotopes
Synthetic Lubricants
Synthetic Natural Gas
Petroleum Refining
Liquid Natural Gas

Acids
Organics
Alkalis
Salts

ENVIRONMENTAL PROTECTION

Water Reuse
Sewage Treatment
Stack-Gas Scrubbers
Industrial Waste Treatment
Recycling Processes
Catalytic Mufflers

PETRO-CHEMICAL MANUFACTURE

PHARMACEUTICALS & DRUGS

Styrene
Ketones
Acetic Acid
Ethers-Esters
Alcohols-Antifreeze
Vinyl Chloride
Propylene
Ethylene

BIOTECHNOLOGY

Mycins   Vitamins
Germicides   Penicillins
Vaccines   Sulfas

Production
Genetic Manufacturing
Purification

DESIGN
RESEARCH AND DEVELOPMENT
PRODUCTION/CONSTRUCTION/OPERATIONS
TECHNICAL SERVICES
MARKETING/SALES
MANAGEMENT

This tree was developed by the College of Engineering at Villanova University in order to demonstrate some career opportunities available to chemical engineers. The sign on the tree notes general functions of the chemical engineer, while the branches provide some specific examples of those functional areas. The lists located by each branch refer to direct outcomes of the examples; they may be products, projects, or applications.

FIGURE A.2

The Civil Engineering Tree.

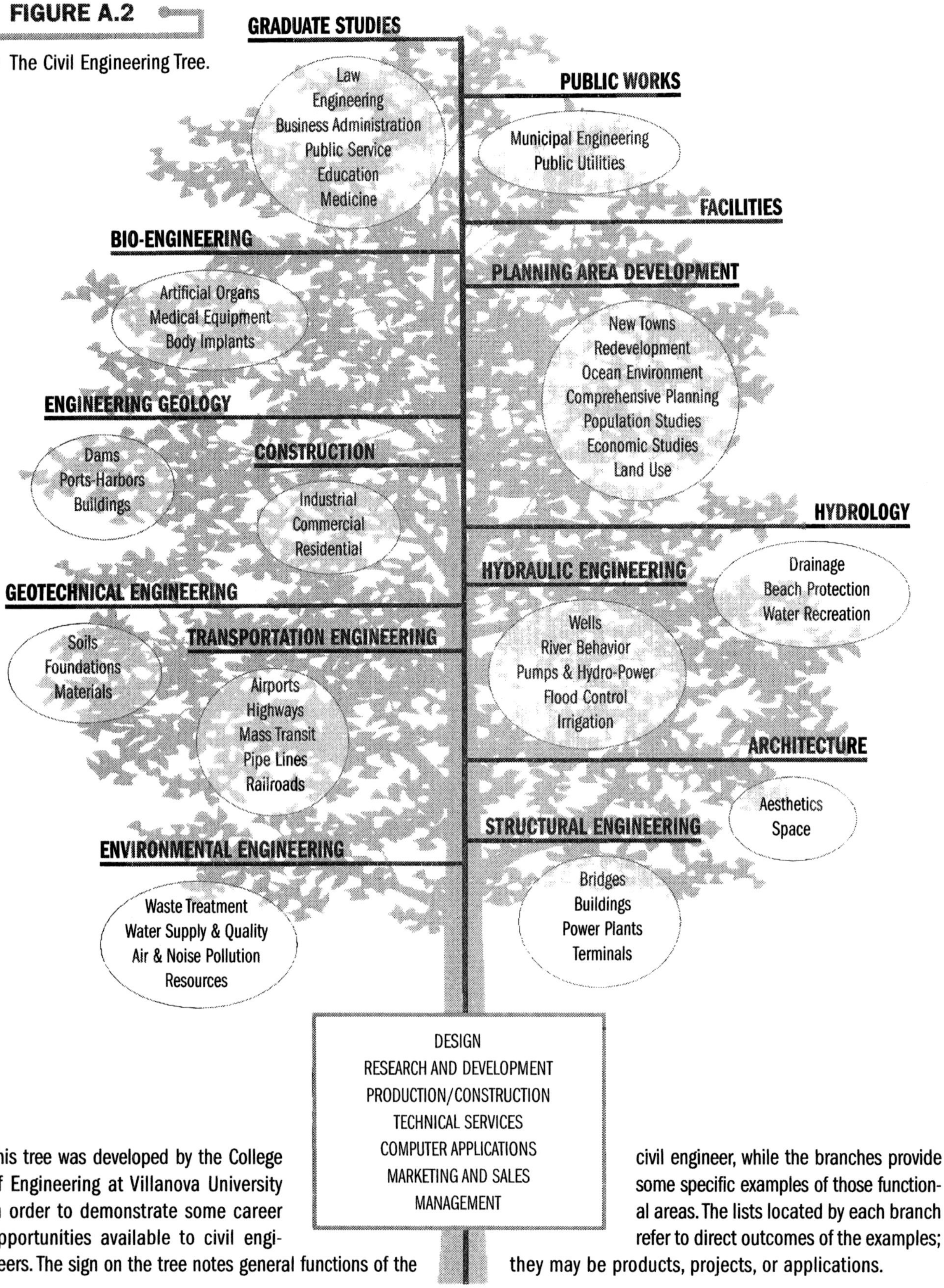

GRADUATE STUDIES

Law
Engineering
Business Administration
Public Service
Education
Medicine

PUBLIC WORKS

Municipal Engineering
Public Utilities

FACILITIES

BIO-ENGINEERING

Artificial Organs
Medical Equipment
Body Implants

PLANNING AREA DEVELOPMENT

New Towns
Redevelopment
Ocean Environment
Comprehensive Planning
Population Studies
Economic Studies
Land Use

ENGINEERING GEOLOGY

Dams
Ports-Harbors
Buildings

CONSTRUCTION

Industrial
Commercial
Residential

HYDROLOGY

Drainage
Beach Protection
Water Recreation

GEOTECHNICAL ENGINEERING

Soils
Foundations
Materials

TRANSPORTATION ENGINEERING

Airports
Highways
Mass Transit
Pipe Lines
Railroads

HYDRAULIC ENGINEERING

Wells
River Behavior
Pumps & Hydro-Power
Flood Control
Irrigation

ARCHITECTURE

Aesthetics
Space

ENVIRONMENTAL ENGINEERING

Waste Treatment
Water Supply & Quality
Air & Noise Pollution
Resources

STRUCTURAL ENGINEERING

Bridges
Buildings
Power Plants
Terminals

DESIGN
RESEARCH AND DEVELOPMENT
PRODUCTION/CONSTRUCTION
TECHNICAL SERVICES
COMPUTER APPLICATIONS
MARKETING AND SALES
MANAGEMENT

This tree was developed by the College of Engineering at Villanova University in order to demonstrate some career opportunities available to civil engineers. The sign on the tree notes general functions of the civil engineer, while the branches provide some specific examples of those functional areas. The lists located by each branch refer to direct outcomes of the examples; they may be products, projects, or applications.

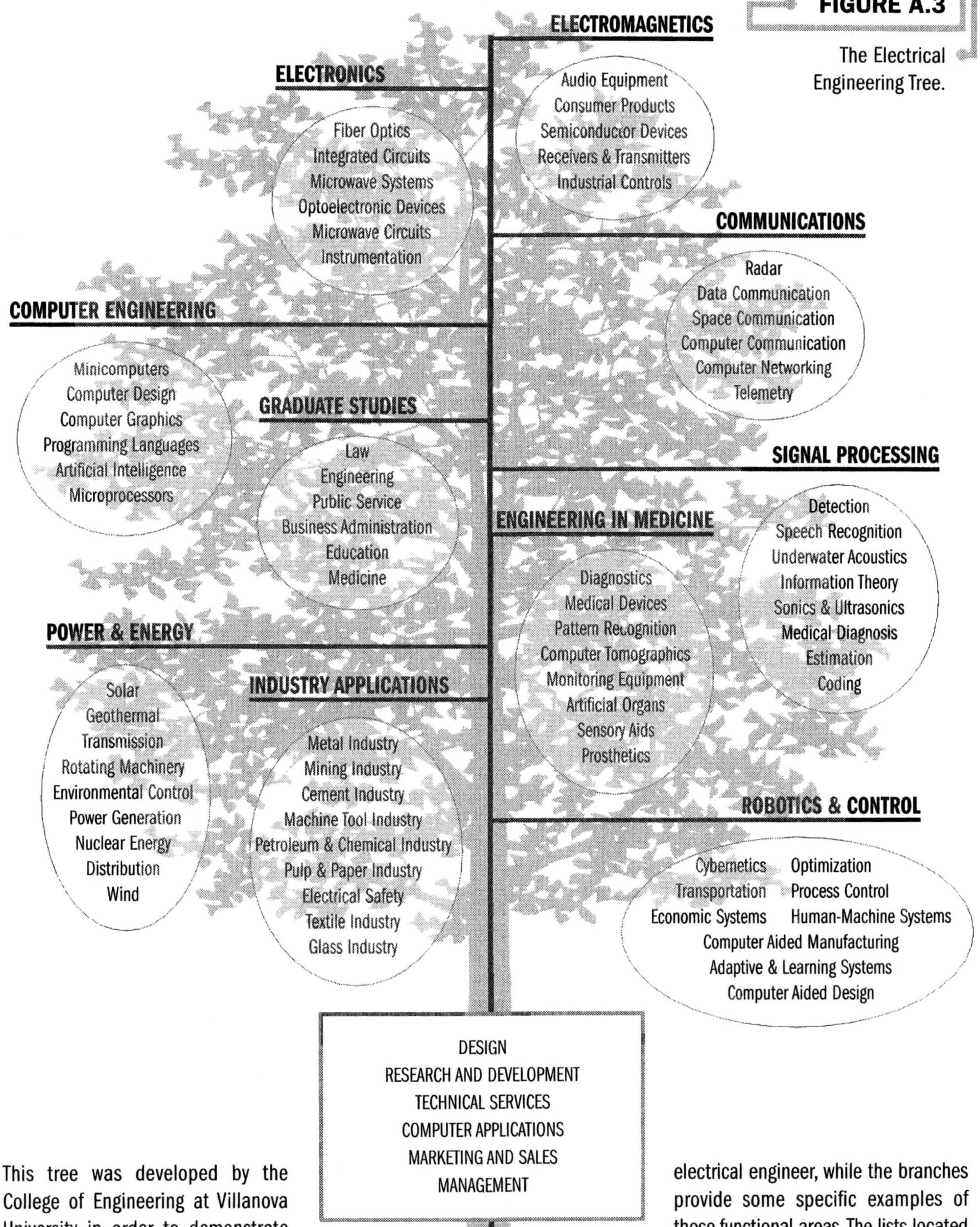

FIGURE A.3

The Electrical Engineering Tree.

ELECTROMAGNETICS

Audio Equipment
Consumer Products
Semiconductor Devices
Receivers & Transmitters
Industrial Controls

ELECTRONICS

Fiber Optics
Integrated Circuits
Microwave Systems
Optoelectronic Devices
Microwave Circuits
Instrumentation

COMMUNICATIONS

Radar
Data Communication
Space Communication
Computer Communication
Computer Networking
Telemetry

COMPUTER ENGINEERING

Minicomputers
Computer Design
Computer Graphics
Programming Languages
Artificial Intelligence
Microprocessors

GRADUATE STUDIES

Law
Engineering
Public Service
Business Administration
Education
Medicine

SIGNAL PROCESSING

Detection
Speech Recognition
Underwater Acoustics
Information Theory
Sonics & Ultrasonics
Medical Diagnosis
Estimation
Coding

ENGINEERING IN MEDICINE

Diagnostics
Medical Devices
Pattern Recognition
Computer Tomographics
Monitoring Equipment
Artificial Organs
Sensory Aids
Prosthetics

POWER & ENERGY

Solar
Geothermal
Transmission
Rotating Machinery
Environmental Control
Power Generation
Nuclear Energy
Distribution
Wind

INDUSTRY APPLICATIONS

Metal Industry
Mining Industry
Cement Industry
Machine Tool Industry
Petroleum & Chemical Industry
Pulp & Paper Industry
Electrical Safety
Textile Industry
Glass Industry

ROBOTICS & CONTROL

Cybernetics   Optimization
Transportation   Process Control
Economic Systems   Human-Machine Systems
Computer Aided Manufacturing
Adaptive & Learning Systems
Computer Aided Design

DESIGN
RESEARCH AND DEVELOPMENT
TECHNICAL SERVICES
COMPUTER APPLICATIONS
MARKETING AND SALES
MANAGEMENT

This tree was developed by the College of Engineering at Villanova University in order to demonstrate some career opportunities available to electrical engineers. The sign on the tree notes general functions of the electrical engineer, while the branches provide some specific examples of those functional areas. The lists located by each branch refer to direct outcomes of the examples; they may be products, projects, or applications.

FIGURE A.4

The Mechanical Engineering Tree.

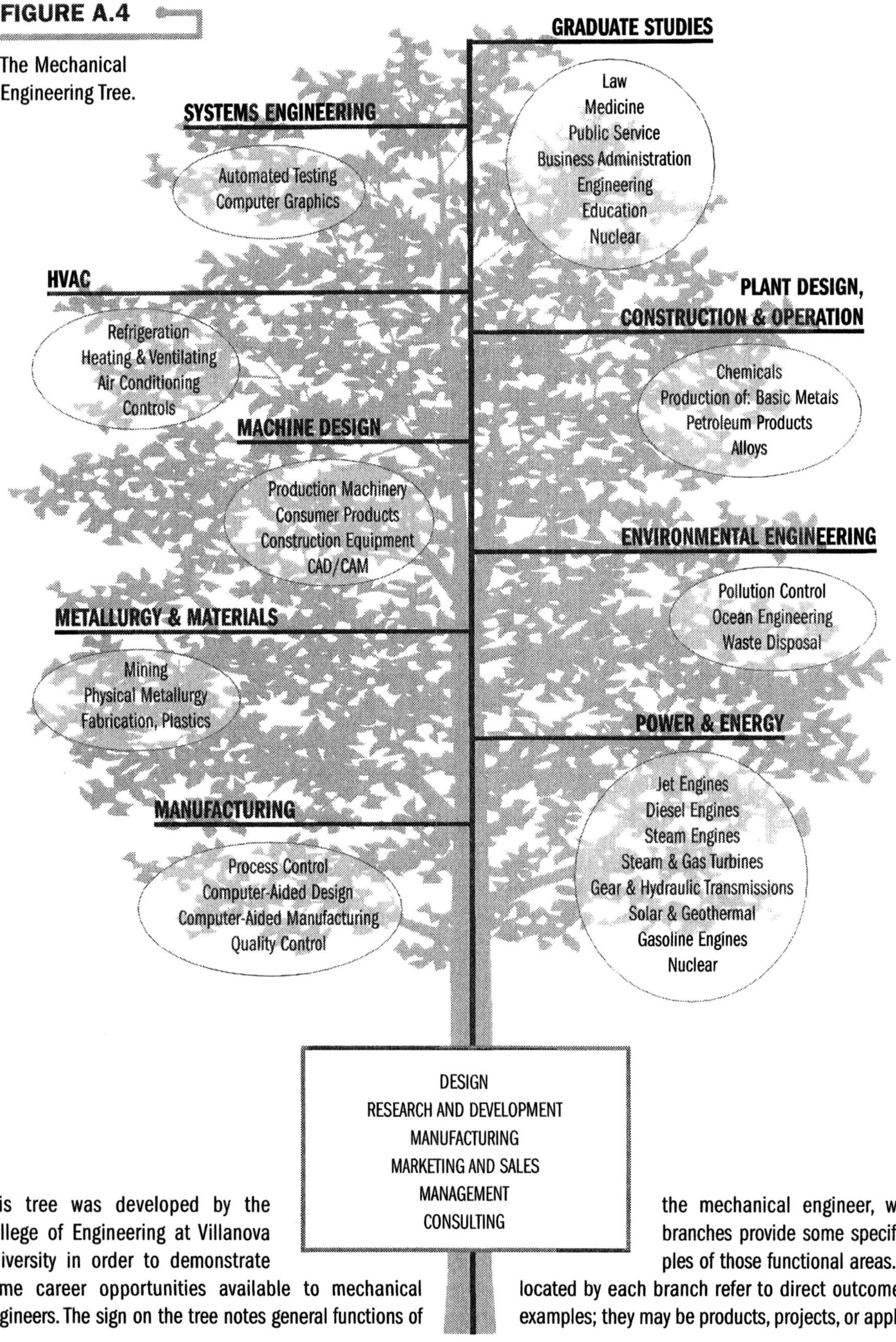

GRADUATE STUDIES

Law
Medicine
Public Service
Business Administration
Engineering
Education
Nuclear

SYSTEMS ENGINEERING

Automated Testing
Computer Graphics

HVAC

Refrigeration
Heating & Ventilating
Air Conditioning
Controls

PLANT DESIGN, CONSTRUCTION & OPERATION

Chemicals
Production of: Basic Metals
Petroleum Products
Alloys

MACHINE DESIGN

Production Machinery
Consumer Products
Construction Equipment
CAD/CAM

ENVIRONMENTAL ENGINEERING

Pollution Control
Ocean Engineering
Waste Disposal

METALLURGY & MATERIALS

Mining
Physical Metallurgy
Fabrication, Plastics

POWER & ENERGY

Jet Engines
Diesel Engines
Steam Engines
Steam & Gas Turbines
Gear & Hydraulic Transmissions
Solar & Geothermal
Gasoline Engines
Nuclear

MANUFACTURING

Process Control
Computer-Aided Design
Computer-Aided Manufacturing
Quality Control

DESIGN
RESEARCH AND DEVELOPMENT
MANUFACTURING
MARKETING AND SALES
MANAGEMENT
CONSULTING

This tree was developed by the College of Engineering at Villanova University in order to demonstrate some career opportunities available to mechanical engineers. The sign on the tree notes general functions of the mechanical engineer, while the branches provide some specific examples of those functional areas. The lists located by each branch refer to direct outcomes of the examples; they may be products, projects, or applications.

B
APPENDIX

Web Resources

INTERNET RESEARCH TOOLS

The Internet contains many tools that speed the search for information and resources. Research tools called "search directories" and "search engines" are extremely helpful.

Search Directories

Search directories are essentially descriptive subject indexes of Web sites. They also have searching options. When you connect to a search directory's page, you will find a query box for entering keywords. The search engine at these sites searches only for keyword matches in the directory's databases. Directories are excellent places to begin your research.

Search Engines

Search engines are different from search directories in that they search World Wide Web sites, Usenet newsgroups, and other Internet resources to find matches to your descriptor keywords. Many search engines also rank the results according to a degree of relevancy. Most search engines provide options for advanced searching to refine your search.

Basic Guidelines for Internet Research

Search directories and search engines are marvelous tools to help you find information on the Internet. Search directories are often the best places to begin a search, as they frequently yield more relevant returns on a topic than does a search engine, which may produce a high proportion of irrelevant information.

Search engines can be frustrating to use and may not prove to be the best Internet resources to begin with, often providing thousands of links on your keyword search. Although these search tools have advanced options for refining and limiting a search, researchers may find that locating the desired information is not easy and that search results frequently provide a high percentage of irrelevant and useless information. For example, using a search engine for a search with the keywords *business management* returned 500,000 occurrences (hits) of the words *business* and *management*. Many of the occurrences of these words were in job listings or companies that were advertising their services. This is why search directories are frequently an excellent resource to begin with when starting your research. The search directory may lead you to the gold mine of electronic resources you are searching for.

When researching information on the Internet it is essential that you use several search tools. The basic approach to finding information involves the following steps:

1. Use search directories such as Yahoo (http://www.yahoo.com), Excite (http://www.excite.com), Galaxy (http://galaxy.einet.net/galaxy.html), Magellan (http://magellan.mckinley.com), or Infoseek (http://guide. infoseek.com) to search for the information under a related topic or category. Explore the links that seem relevant to your topic, and make bookmarks of the ones you would like to investigate further. Look for one site that has a large collection of links on your topic. This is the resource gold mine you are looking for.

2. Use search engines to further research your topic by determining one or more descriptive words (keywords) for the subject. Enter your keywords into the search dialog box.

3. Determine how specific you want your search to be. Do you want it to be broad or narrow? Use available options to refine or limit your search. Some search engines permit the use of *Boolean operators* (phrases or words such as "and," "or," and "not" that restrict a search). Others provide help for refining searches, and some have pull-down menus or selections to be checked for options.

4. Submit your query.

5. Review your list of hits (references to Web pages or documents that match your search).

6. Adjust your search based on the information returned. Did you receive too much information and need to narrow your search? Did you receive too little or no information and need to broaden your keywords?

7. Use several search directories and search engines for your research. No one search tool will provide a complete resource list.

USING INTERNET SOURCES FOR RESEARCH

Internet resources provide a valuable source for finding information that you can use for class presentations, papers, research, dissertations, and theses. However, the Internet should never be your sole source of information but rather another resource that you use to find information on a topic. The Internet can be a valuable resource for accessing

- information collections and databases,
- government documents,
- exhibitions,
- research papers,
- publications,
- news,
- on-line educational events, and
- the latest and most current information on a topic, and for
- communicating with experts on your topic.

In this section you will learn

- how to evaluate Internet information sources, and
- how to reference Internet sources.

Evaluating Internet Information

Unlike scholarly publications, there is no editorial board for most Internet information. With an estimate of between 20 and 50 million pages of data created from a variety of sources—individuals, business, corporations, non-profit organizations, schools, special interest causes, or illicit (if not illegal) sources—it is not surprising that not all the information is accurate, unbiased, reputable, scientifically valid, or up to date. It is therefore essential that you understand how to evaluate information you research on the Net.

How strict you are with your evaluation will depend on what you are using the information for. For example, if you are writing a factual report, dissertation, thesis, or paper that others will rely on for accurate content, it will be essential that you are judicious in choosing what information will be reported from the Net.

The first thing you must do when using Internet sources for your studies is to determine which resources to use. The following guidelines will assist you with evaluating which sources to use.

- Information Source. Where does the information come from—an individual, organization, educational institution, or other source? One way to determine the source of the information quickly is to look at the URL—the Internet site address. The first address protocol often will tell you the source of the information, the name of the institution, and the domain. For example, an address such as **http://gort.ucsd.edu** provides the name of the institution—University of California, San Diego—and the edu ending indicates an educational institution. An educational institution has a good chance of being a reputable source. Other address endings that are highly likely to be reputable are *gov* for government or *mil* for military. Naturally, you will want to evaluate the information further. Just because the information is from an educational institution, government, or military source you cannot be sure that the content is factual and reliable.

Check to see if the document resides in an individual's personal Internet account or is part of the organization's official Internet site. You can often determine this by looking at the URL address pathway.

Is the organization that publishes this document recognized in the field you are studying? Is the organization qualified as an expert in this topic?

- Authorship. Closely related to the information source is the reputation of the data and the reliability of its source. Although the information may be from an educational institution, who wrote and compiled the data—a professor, student, or other source? Information on an educational institution Web site may be compiled by a student or graduate student who is not as yet an authority on the subject and may enter written errors or present incorrect data without realizing it. The content may not have been reviewed for accuracy and reliability.

  Who is the author? Does the author have credentials as an expert on the topic? Consider educational background, experience, and other published writings. Have you encountered the author's name in your reading or bibliographies?

  Does the Internet document provide information on the author such as institutional affiliation, position, and experience and credentials? If none of this is provided, is there an e-mail address or a mailing address where you can request biographical information? Correspond with the author to obtain more information about the source of the content.

- Accuracy. Is the data accurate? Check to see if there is a reference for the information. Where does the information come from—a published research paper or report, historical document, or news publication? Or is it a personal viewpoint? Does the document include a bibliography? Does the author acknowledge related knowledge sources?

  Although information may be written from a personal point of view, don't necessarily invalidate it. Bias is to be expected, especially if one is a participant in an event. If the writing seems biased, look for inconsistencies or incorrect thinking. Does the author acknowledge that his treatment of the subject is controversial? Are there political or ideological biases? Can you separate fact from opinion? Do any statements seem exaggerated or overly simplified? Has the author omitted any important details? Is the writer qualified as an authority?

  One example of inaccuracy in Web writing is the use of the words *endangered species* when referring to animals that may in fact be only threatened or vulnerable. Many authors use the words *endangered species* loosely. To cross-check this information, you must use a reliable source such as the Convention on International Trade and Endangered Species (CITES) and the International Union for the Conservation of Nature (IUCN). These international organizations keep the working lists of species categorized as either extinct, endangered, threatened, vulnerable, indeterminate, or out of danger.

- Verifiable. Can the data be verified? Does it appear to be well researched? Does the author make generalizations without proof or validation? Always be thinking, "Show me why or how." In some instances you may need to ask if the data has statistical validity (is supported by statistical testing). Watch for errors or omissions.

When numbers or statistical information are reported, it is critical that the data be cross-checked with a reliable publication source. For example, some Web factual data contain errors caused by carelessness in copying and transposing numbers from a print version to a Web site. Reporting that 17,000 acres of rain forest are destroyed daily when the correct number is 700 acres is an inexcusable error in sloppy copy.

- Consistency of data. Are the data consistent or does it reflect contradictions with other information on the topic? Are definitions used consistently throughout?

  For example, in our rain forest research we found reputable Web sites such as the Public Broadcasting System (PBS) or the Rain Forest Action Network. These are excellent on-line references for cross-checking the consistency of data.

- Quality. Is the text error free? Is it well organized and grammatically correct? Check for the misspelling of names or carelessness and lack of attention to details in other areas. Information that contains careless errors probably should not be relied on.

  Is the tone scholarly, technical, factual, authoritative, or personal?

- Currency. Is the information current and up to date? Does the document include a publication date or a date of copyright? Does it appear to be appropriate and relevant for today? Information that was reported in 1985 is probably not valid today. Look for the most current information unless currency is not an issue.

Bonus guidelines—other important suggestions:

- Question everything you read. Learn to be critical and skeptical.
- Never use Internet information as your sole source of knowledge. Information found on the Internet should complement information from traditional research resources.
- "When in doubt, leave it out."

Tip

If you don't know where to find a reliable source to cross-check your information, talk with a resource librarian, teacher, or professor. These individuals can be excellent resources for finding publications to verify your data. You can also call a reputable organization.

Referencing Electronic Media

As with any published reference, the goal of an electronic reference is to credit the author and to enable the reader to find the material. The International Standards Organization (ISO) continues to modify a uniform system of citing electronic documents. The following guidelines and examples have been compiled from *The American Psychological Association (APA) Publication Manual*, *MLA-Style*, and *The Chicago Manual of Style*.

- Be consistent in your references to on-line documentation or information.

- Capitalization follows the "accepted practice for the language or script in which the information is given."
- Use your discretion for the choice of punctuation used to separate elements and in the use of variations in typeface or underscoring to distinguish or highlight elements.
- If a print form is available and the same as the electronic form, referencing of the print form is preferred.

Include the following in your reference:

- The author's name if it is available or important for identification.
- The most recent date of publication or a modification date if document undergoes revision.
- The date you accessed the document on the Internet.
- Title of the document, file, or World Wide Web site.
- The protocol: Telnet, Gopher, FTP, World Wide Web.
- The Internet address or retrieval path for accessing the information, including the file name, directory, and pathway. Do not end a path statement with a period, because it is not part of the Internet address and may hinder retrieval if used.
- Subscription information, if the information is available via a listserv mailing list.

Format for Referencing On-Line Information—APA Style

Author, I. (date of work). <u>Title of full work</u> [online]. Available: Specify protocol and path (date document was accessed).

Author, I., & Author, I. (date). <u>Title of full work</u> [online]. Specify protocol and path (date document was accessed).

NOTE

The examples provided in this section use APA style. Although the type of information required for referencing is similar, the format for the references varies among the APA, MLA, and Chicago styles. Check with your professor to see which style to use. Refer to the style manual for the reference format.

Examples of References

World Wide Web

The World Wide Web provides many types of information you may want to reference: text, images, video, or sound. To reference these information sources, provide the following:

- Author's name (if known)
- Date of Web site information (if known or different from date you accessed)

- Title of the page or article
- Any additional information such as version or edition
- The URL for the page you are referencing
- Date you accessed this page

Gopher

When referencing Gopher sites, include the following information.

- Author's name (if known)
- Date of publication
- Title of the page, article, or file
- Any additional information such as version or edition
- The URL for the page you are referencing and the pathway to this information
- Date you accessed this page

File Transfer Protocol

When referencing documents that you have accessed through FTP, include the following:

- Author's name (if known)
- Date of publication (if available)
- Title of the document, article, or file
- The address for the FTP site you used along with the pathway to this information
- Date you accessed this site

Telnet

When referencing telnet sites, include the following:

- Author's name (if known)
- Date of publication (if available)
- Title of the work or the name of the telnet site
- The address for the telnet site
- Directions for accessing the publication when connected
- Date you accessed this site

E-Mail, Listserv Mailing Lists, and Usenet Newsgroups

Information from e-mail, listservs, and newsgroups is both timely and personal, often representing an individual's point of view. This information must also be referenced. Do not reference personal e-mail. E-mail references will mainly come from listservs and newsgroups. To reference these information sources, provide the following:

- Author's name (if known)
- Date of the e-mail message, listserv message, or Usenet posting
- Subject of the message or posting
- Name of the listserv or newsgroup
- Address of the listserv or newsgroup
- Information on how to find the group's archives if available
- Date accessed

NOTE

For more information on referencing Internet resources visit the following Web site:

MLA Reference at

    http://www.columbia.edu/cu/cup/cgos/idx_basic.html

An excellent online resource, "Beyond the MLA Handbook: Documenting Electronic Sources on the Internet," can be found at

    http://english.ttu.edu/kairos/1.2/inbox/mla_archive.html

"Online! A Reference Guide to Using Internet Sources" offers detailed advice for citing on-line sources.

    http://www.bedfordstmartins.com/online/

For more information on utilizing the Internet for research and services, please refer to *Student Resource Guide to the Internet: Student Success Online* by Cynthia Leshin © 1998 by Prentice Hall, Inc., ISBN 0-13-621079-1).

The material in this appendix has been adapted from *Researching Information and Student Resources on the Internet* by Cynthia Leshin.

Index